250 BEST
Cakes &
Pies

250 BEST
Cakes &
Pies

Esther Brody

Robert
ROSE

For complete cataloguing information, see page 185.

Disclaimer
The recipes in this book have been carefully tested by our kitchen and our tasters. To the best of our knowledge, they are safe and nutritious for ordinary use and users. For those people with food or other allergies, or who have special food requirements or health issues, please read the suggested contents of each recipe carefully and determine whether or not they may create a problem for you. All recipes are used at the risk of the consumer.

We cannot be responsible for any hazards, loss or damage that may occur as a result of any recipe use.

For those with special needs, allergies, requirements or health problems, in the event of any doubt, please contact your medical adviser prior to the use of any recipe.

Design & Production: PageWave Graphics Inc.
Editor: Sue Sumeraj
Test Kitchen/Recipe Editor: Jennifer MacKenzie
Photography: Mark T. Shapiro
Food Stylist: Kate Bush
Prop Stylist: Charlene Erricson
Index: Sue Sumeraj
Colour Scans: Colour Technologies

The publisher and author wish to express their appreciation to the following supplier of props used in the food photography:

TABLE WARE AND LINENS
The Kitchen and Glass Place
840 Yonge Street
Toronto, Ontario M4W 2H1
Tel: (416) 927-9925

Cover Image: Mom's Sour Cream Chocolate Layer Cake (page 58)

We acknowledge the financial support of the Government of Canada through the Book Publishing Industry Development Program (BPIDP) for our publishing activities.

Published by Robert Rose Inc.
120 Eglinton Avenue East, Suite 800, Toronto, Canada M4P 1E2
Tel: (416) 322-6552   Fax: (416) 322-6936

Printed in Canada
1 2 3 4 5 6 7 GP 09 08 07 06 05 04 03

To my son, Leonard, who has worked
so hard for me to be able to write and publish
all of my cookbooks and to my daughter, Lisa,
a wonderful cook in her own right.

To my granddaughter, Natalie Arielle, now
four years old, who continues to light up my life
with her unconditional love, her beautiful head
of Shirley Temple curls and her heartfelt sense
of caring ("Are you okay, Baba," "Don't worry,
Baba, I will help you"), and who has given me
so many endearing names, from Baba, to
Babala, to Bub, to Bubby,
all of which I cherish.

To my friends, who have given me so much
encouragement over the years.

To my sister Betty Shapiro and her family;
to my niece, Shauna Jackson and her family:
David, Drew and Brandon (P.J. and Scruffy);
and to my twin sister, Cecille Shtabsky,
and her family.

In memory of my mom and dad, Mary and
Louis Goldstein, who were wonderful parents.

And in memory of my dear friend, Arlene
Kushner, who was gone so suddenly but is
not forgotten, and who constantly encouraged
me through my book-writing years.

Contents

PART ONE

Cakes

Introduction to Cakes

The first cooking experience children, especially little girls, want to learn and help with is baking a cake. To me, it seemed like such a huge accomplishment compared to baking cookies. I can recall listening to grown-ups discussing recipes, and it seemed like a woman's reputation as a good cook depended a great deal on the success of her cakes. Cakes have always given a festive atmosphere to special occasions or milestones such as weddings, birthdays, holidays, banquets, showers, picnics and numerous others.

Everyone loves cakes, and success has always relied on being able to bake attractive, fluffy, delicate and, of course, delicious cakes. Cake baking is considered a culinary art and a great creative achievement, and women take pride in their baking. Every year there are county fairs and exhibitions, the main event of which is sampling and judging champion cake and pie bakers, and their old family favorites, handed down from generation to generation, and newly created recipes.

It is so tempting and so much easier to grab a readily available cake mix, add one or two other ingredients, and end up with a pretty decent tasting, authentic cake that looks like it was "made from scratch." A mix is so versatile: it can be transformed into layer cakes, cupcakes, loaves, upside-down cakes and so on. But a cake you have baked yourself, from scratch, gives you a wonderful feeling of pride and accomplishment. And doing it the old-fashioned way has become much easier because of new types of pans, utensils, methods and ingredients such as soups, mayonnaise, puddings and other "secret" ingredients.

In the 1800s, cakes were a small mass of dough baked on a turning spit or hot stone and made from crushed grains, moistened and formed into round, flat shapes or patties. They were considered to be small breads. Over the years, cakes came to be considered a dessert, "a mixture of flour, eggs, sugar, milk, etc., baked and often covered with icing," but other round, flat discs of food — pancakes, tea cake biscuits — are still called cakes.

When I first became interested in baking cakes, I was amazed at how many different recipes there are. Just some of the cake names familiar to us are wedding cakes, tortes, layer cakes, jelly rolls, coffee cakes, cheesecakes, chocolate cakes, loaf cakes, cupcakes, pound cakes, angel food cakes, sponge cakes, chiffon cakes, spice cakes and gingerbread cakes. But there are basically three types of cakes:

* cakes made with shortening, fat or oil, such as butter cakes
* lighter cakes such as angel and sponge cakes, called "shortened" or "foam" cakes, made without shortening
* a combination of the first two, using butter or oil and egg yolks. These cakes, such as chiffon cakes, combine the richness of butter cakes and the lightness of angel cakes. Also cakes in which the only fat is from egg yolks or whole eggs, such as sponge cakes.

You can take any basic cake, add whatever flavorings you like, bake it in any of numerous shapes of pans, add any type of filling and spread any flavor of icing or other decorations, and presto — you have a popular, beautiful cake!

Then there are the fancier specialty cakes, which include:

* Genoise cake: a firm, sturdy, foam-style cake
* Boston cream pie: not really a pie but a sponge-type cake with lots of creamy filling and a chocolate glaze over top (this has always been my favorite!)
* Baked Alaska: a sponge-type cake with ice cream and stiffly beaten egg whites, browned in the oven
* King cake: a round, braided cinnamon coffee roll with colored icings and a coin, bean or small figurine inside, made especially for Mardi Gras
* Charlotte Russe cake: sponge cake ladyfingers, lining a mold pan, with custard filling
* Sally Lunn cake: a bread-like cake
* Lady Baltimore cake: a rich white cake iced with a fluffy frosting full of nuts and raisins — a favorite for weddings

* Fruitcakes: made with nuts, raisins, dried or candied fruits, fruitcakes are also popular for weddings and holidays
* Très leches cake: a three-milk cake, sweet, dense and moist
* Red velvet (devil) cake: a bright red chocolate cake, made using red food coloring, and usually iced with a thick white icing
* Linzer torte: considered the oldest known cake, it contains fruit or jam filling
* Sachertorte: a chocolate sponge 3-layer cake, with apricot jam filling
* Black Forest cake: a chocolate cake with cream and sour cherries
* Babka: a round yeast-dough cake with raisins or currants, flavored with rum or wine

I have included many of these familiar and less familiar cake recipes to help widen your experiences in cake baking. Happy baking!

Tips for Successful Cake Baking

1. Always read your recipe over carefully before commencing.
2. Preheat your oven according to recipe instructions.
3. Set out the pan you will be using, and all ingredients and utensils.
4. Remove shortening, butter or margarine from the refrigerator to soften 1 hour before baking, unless your recipe calls for cold or chilled.
5. If you will be using egg whites, allow them to come to room temperature for 5 to 10 minutes before beating. Always use large eggs for baking unless otherwise indicated.
6. Use the flour indicated in the recipe. Do not substitute. If the recipe does not indicate a specific kind of flour, use all-purpose flour.
7. Measure ingredients accurately, using the necessary measuring cup or spoons.
8. To prepare your baking pan, coat generously with shortening (unless otherwise specified) and dust lightly with flour. For chocolate cakes, I sometimes dust lightly with cocoa powder. Pans for foam cakes are never greased.
9. Mix ingredients according to the instructions in the recipe. Pans should be filled about ¾ full, as cakes will rise during baking. Spread batter evenly to sides and fill corners. Tap the filled pan lightly on the counter to get rid of any air bubbles that may have formed.
10. Place pan in the center of the oven, so that it is not touching the sides, and bake for the time stated in the recipe. For best results, bake one cake at a time. Cake is done when the top is lightly browned and the sides shrink away a little from the pan, or when you press lightly in the center of the cake and it springs back. I usually insert a toothpick in the center — if it comes out clean and dry, the cake is done.
11. When you remove pan from oven, place it on a wire rack to cool for about 10 minutes. Then take a knife and loosen the cake around the edges. Invert pan over a plate or on the rack to cool completely.
12. If frosting is desired, wait until the cake is completely cooled or it will become soggy. Brush off any loose pieces or crumbs. Spoon about half of the frosting onto the top of the cake and, with a knife, start swirling over top. Then work toward the sides and cover them with a swirling motion. You can also get a good effect by frosting the sides *before* the top.
13. Decorate to suit your taste, or the occasion, using colored icings, fruits, nuts, chocolate curls, and so on.

Cake Troubleshooting

Here are some of the problems you may encounter and possible causes.

Cake falls
* too much liquid, sugar, leavening agents or butter or shortening
* over-beating of egg whites, if used in recipe
* not enough flour
* oven not hot enough and/or baking time too short

Cake expands over top of pan
* pan may be too small; check recipe again for the proper size
* too much batter for the size of the pan; only fill pan from half to ¾ full, depending on the type of cake
* too much shortening, sugar or leavening agent

Cake texture is coarse and dense
* not enough creaming of shortening or butter with sugar; the mixture should be smooth and creamy
* over-beating of batter after flour mixture is added

* all-purpose flour used instead of cake flour
* oven temperature too low; try raising it by 25°F (10°C) and note the results

Cake is too dry
* the most common reasons for this problem are over-baking or not having enough fat, sugar or liquid in the batter
* too much leavening agent or flour in the batter
* over-beating egg whites until they are too stiff
* substituting cocoa for chocolate without adding more fat
* baking time is too long, and/or the oven is too hot

Cake is heavy
* not enough sugar or leavening agent
* over-mixing and baking temperature too high
* too much liquid, fat or egg

Cracks or bumps on top of cake
* too much flour or sugar and not enough liquid
* oven too hot
* over-mixing batter or spreading batter unevenly

Cake rises higher on one side
* pan slightly warped or batter spread unevenly in the pan
* pan set too close to another pan or the side of the oven
* oven temperature uneven or oven rack not level

Cake sticks to pan
* pan not greased properly
* cake left in pan too long

Cake burns on bottom
* uneven heat distribution in the oven; the back of the oven is often slightly hotter than the front, so rotate the pan halfway through baking to achieve a more even heat distribution
* oven too hot
* pan too close to the side of the oven

Cake has a sticky, too moist crust
* not baking long enough
* too much sugar; check amount in your recipe and be sure to measure correctly

Cake is soggy, heavy or has streaks at the bottom
* too much leavening agent or sugar in the batter, and it has not been mixed thoroughly until completely blended
* butter or shortening too soft
* an excess of liquid or eggs underbeaten
* oven not hot enough and/or baking time too short

Cake crumbles when sliced
* too much fat, sugar or leavening agent in the batter
* ingredients not measured accurately
* oven temperature too low and/or insufficient baking time
* cake removed from pan before completely cooled

Crust is too pale in color
* not enough batter to fill pan properly
* oven not hot enough
* not enough sugar, fat or leavening agent
* too much flour
* baking pan may be too large

Classic Cakes

Old-fashioned Chocolate Cake

Serves 12 to 16		
2¾ cups	all-purpose flour	675 mL
2 tsp	baking soda	10 mL
½ tsp	baking powder	2 mL
½ tsp	salt	2 mL
2 cups	boiling water	500 mL
1 cup	unsweetened cocoa powder, sifted	250 mL
1 cup	butter or margarine, softened	250 mL
2½ cups	granulated sugar	625 mL
1½ tsp	vanilla	7 mL
4	eggs	4

CHOCOLATE FROSTING

1 cup	butter or margarine	250 mL
1 cup	semi-sweet chocolate pieces or chips	250 mL
½ cup	light (5%) cream	125 mL
2½ cups	confectioner's (icing) sugar	625 mL

Preheat oven to 350°F (180°C)

10-inch (4 L) tube pan, greased and dusted with cocoa powder

1. In a medium bowl, sift together flour, baking soda, baking powder and salt.

2. In another bowl, whisk together boiling water and cocoa until smooth. Let cool to room temperature.

3. In a large mixer bowl, beat butter, sugar, vanilla and eggs on high speed. Beat in flour mixture alternately with cocoa mixture, making 3 additions of flour and 2 of cocoa, on low speed until well blended. Do not over-beat.

4. Pour into prepared baking pan and tap pan lightly on counter to get rid of any air bubbles that may have formed.

5. Bake in preheated oven for 60 to 70 minutes, or until a toothpick inserted in the center comes out clean and dry. Cool in pan on wire rack for 10 minutes. Loosen around edges of cake with a spatula or knife, then invert onto wire rack or plate to cool completely.

6. *Prepare Chocolate Frosting:* In a medium saucepan, over low heat, combine butter, chocolate and cream, stirring until smooth. Remove from heat and add confectioner's sugar. Transfer to a small bowl, place bowl over ice and whisk until frosting is of the right consistency for spreading. Frost sides and top of cake, swirling with a knife or spatula to decorate.

TIP: When your recipe calls for sifting, put the ingredients to be sifted in the mixing bowl and stir them with a whisk. It does an equally good job.

Dutch Chocolate Mayo Cake

Serves 12 to 16		
2 cups	all-purpose flour	500 mL
¾ cup	unsweetened cocoa powder, sifted	175 mL
1¼ tsp	baking soda	6 mL
¼ tsp	baking powder	1 mL
3	eggs	3
1½ cups	granulated sugar	375 mL
1 tsp	vanilla	5 mL
1 cup	real mayonnaise	250 mL
1¼ cups	water	300 mL

NOTE: If desired, frost with your favorite frosting or dust with confectioner's sugar.

Preheat oven to 350°F (180°C)

13- by 9-inch (3 L) metal baking pan, greased and floured

1. In a bowl, combine flour, cocoa powder, baking soda and baking powder.
2. In a large mixer bowl, on high speed, beat eggs, sugar and vanilla. Add mayonnaise and beat, on low speed, until well combined. Beat in flour mixture alternately with water, making 3 additions of flour and 2 of water, beating only until well blended.
3. Spoon into prepared baking pan. Bake in preheated oven for 35 to 40 minutes, or until cake springs back when touched lightly with fingertip. Cool in pan on wire rack for 10 minutes, then remove to wire rack to cool completely.

Easy Chocolate Caramel Pecan Cake

Serves 12 to 16		
¼ cup	evaporated milk	50 mL
½ cup	butter or margarine	125 mL
60	vanilla caramels	60
1	package (about 18.25 oz/515 g) chocolate cake mix	1
1 cup	chopped pecans or walnuts	250 mL
1 cup	chocolate chips (optional)	250 mL

NOTE: Frost with a chocolate frosting, if desired.

Preheat oven according to cake mix instructions

13- by 9-inch (3 L) metal baking pan, greased

1. Prepare the filling: In a small saucepan, over low heat, melt milk, butter and caramels, stirring until smooth. Set aside.
2. In a large mixer bowl, prepare cake mix as directed on the package. Pour half of the batter into the prepared baking pan and bake in preheated oven for 15 minutes.
3. Remove from oven and pour the caramel mixture over top of cake, spreading evenly. Sprinkle pecans over the caramel and then the chocolate chips, if using, over top of the nuts.
4. Pour remaining half of batter over top, spreading evenly. Bake at 350°F (180°C) for another 25 to 35 minutes, or until a toothpick inserted in the center comes out clean and dry. Cool in pan on a wire rack.

TIP: Bake any type of cake mix, cut it into small or large squares, and serve hot with a caramel sauce. To make this sauce, combine a jar of caramel ice cream topping and ⅓ cup (75 mL) of milk over low heat.

German Chocolate Cake

Serves 10 to 12		
4 oz	sweet baking chocolate	125 g
½ cup	water	125 mL
1½ cups	all-purpose flour	375 mL
¾ tsp	baking soda	4 mL
¼ tsp	salt	1 mL
¾ cup	butter, margarine or shortening, softened	175 mL
1 cup	granulated sugar	250 mL
1 tsp	vanilla	5 mL
3	eggs	3
¾ cup	buttermilk or sour cream	175 mL

PECAN FROSTING

1	egg	1
⅔ cup	evaporated milk	150 mL
⅔ cup	granulated sugar	150 mL
¼ cup	butter or margarine	50 mL
1⅓ cups	flaked coconut (sweetened or unsweetened)	325 mL
½ cup	chopped pecans	125 mL

Preheat oven to 350°F (180°C)

Two 9-inch (23 cm) round metal cake pans, greased and lightly dusted with cocoa powder

1. In a small saucepan, over low heat, stir chocolate and water until chocolate has melted. Set aside to cool.

2. In a bowl, combine flour, baking soda and salt.

3. In a large mixer bowl, on medium speed, cream butter until smooth. Add sugar and beat until light and fluffy. Beat in vanilla and eggs, on low speed, until blended, and then beat on medium for about 2 minutes more. Stir in chocolate mixture. Beat in flour mixture alternately with the buttermilk, making 3 additions of flour and 2 of buttermilk, on low speed until well blended.

4. Pour batter evenly into prepared pans. Bake in preheated oven for 35 to 40 minutes, or until a toothpick inserted in the center comes out clean and dry. Cool in pans on wire racks for 10 minutes and then remove and cool completely on wire racks.

5. *Prepare Pecan Frosting:* In a saucepan, over medium heat, lightly beat the egg. Add the milk, sugar and butter, stirring until thickened and bubbly, about 10 minutes. Remove from heat and add coconut and pecans. Cover and cool completely before frosting cake. Place one cake layer on serving plate. Spread about ⅓ of the frosting evenly over top and top with the second cake. Frost sides and top with remaining frosting.

TIP: If you have a lot of leftover frosting, use it up making sandwich cookies from plain ones.

Chocolate Chunk
Banana Snackin' Cake

Serves 6 to 8

1½ cups	all-purpose flour	375 mL
¾ tsp	baking soda	4 mL
3 oz	semi-sweet baking chocolate, chopped	90 g
½ cup	granulated sugar	125 mL
½ cup	butter or margarine, softened	125 mL
1 tsp	vanilla	5 mL
2	eggs	2
¼ cup	sour cream	50 mL
1 cup	mashed ripe bananas (about 4 medium)	250 mL

NOTE: Frost with your favorite chocolate or mocha frosting, if desired.

Preheat oven to 350°F (180°C)

8-inch (2 L) square metal baking pan, buttered

1. In a bowl, combine flour, baking soda and chocolate.

2. In a large mixer bowl, cream sugar and butter until smooth. Beat in vanilla and eggs, one at a time, beating until light and fluffy. Add sour cream, beating to blend well. Stir in flour mixture alternately with the mashed bananas, making 3 additions of flour and 2 of bananas, just until moistened and thoroughly combined.

3. Spoon into prepared baking pan. Bake in preheated oven for 30 to 35 minutes, or until a toothpick inserted in the center comes out clean and dry. Cool in pan on a wire rack.

TIP: If you have a lot of overripe bananas, don't throw them away. Save them by peeling, slicing and pureeing them in the blender with a few drops of lemon juice to prevent browning. Freeze in zippered freezer bags and keep handy for future recipes.

Turnover Chocolate Pecan Cake

Serves 12 to 16		
1¾ cups	sifted cake flour	425 mL
2 tsp	baking powder	10 mL
Pinch	salt	Pinch
¼ cup	firmly packed light brown sugar	50 mL
⅔ cup	butter or margarine, softened, divided	150 mL
¼ cup	whipping (35%) cream	50 mL
⅔ cup	light corn syrup	150 mL
1 cup	chopped pecans	250 mL
1⅓ cups	granulated sugar	325 mL
2	eggs, separated	2
1 tsp	vanilla	5 mL
3 oz	unsweetened chocolate, melted	90 g
1 cup	milk	250 mL

Preheat oven to 350°F (180°C)

10-inch (3 L) Bundt pan, buttered and dusted with cocoa powder

1. In a medium bowl, combine flour, baking powder and salt.

2. In a small saucepan, mix together brown sugar and ¼ cup (50 mL) of the butter, stirring over low heat until bubbly. Add cream and corn syrup, stirring constantly to boiling. Remove from heat and stir in pecans. Spoon into prepared baking pan and set aside.

3. In a large mixer bowl, cream remaining butter and granulated sugar until smooth. Beat in egg yolks, vanilla and chocolate, beating on medium speed until thoroughly blended. Stir in flour mixture alternately with milk, making 3 additions of flour and 2 of milk, until well blended.

4. In small mixer bowl with clean beaters, beat egg whites on high speed until stiff peaks form. Fold into the batter gently until well blended.

5. Pour batter over nut mixture in pan. Bake in preheated oven for 45 to 50 minutes, or until a toothpick inserted in the center comes out clean and dry.

6. Place pan on wire rack and loosen around the edges of the cake with a knife or spatula. Place a serving plate over top of pan and invert, gently shaking to remove the cake. Remove pan. If any of the nut mixture is still clinging to the pan, scrape back onto cake with a rubber spatula. Leave on plate to cool completely before serving.

> **TIP:** To substitute all-purpose flour for cake flour in a recipe, remove 2 tbsp (25 mL) of flour from every cup of all-purpose flour, and add 2 tbsp (25 mL) cornstarch.

Devil's Food Cupcakes

Makes 18 cupcakes		
2¼ cups	sifted cake flour	550 mL
1 tsp	baking powder	5 mL
1 tsp	baking soda	5 mL
1 tsp	salt	5 mL
⅔ cup	butter or margarine, softened	150 mL
2 cups	granulated sugar	500 mL
1¼ cups	milk	300 mL
3	eggs	3
1 tsp	red food coloring	5mL
3 oz	unsweetened chocolate, melted	90 g

Preheat oven to 400°F (200°C)

18 muffin cups, lined with paper baking cups

1. In a medium bowl, sift together flour, baking powder, baking soda and salt.
2. In a large mixer bowl, cream butter and sugar until smooth. Beat in flour mixture on low speed. Add milk, eggs and food coloring and beat on medium speed until well blended. Stir in melted chocolate and beat for another 2 to 3 minutes until thoroughly combined.
3. Spoon into muffin cups, filling ¾ full. Bake in preheated oven for 18 to 20 minutes, or until a toothpick inserted in the center of a cupcake comes out clean and dry.
4. Cool in muffin cups for 5 minutes, then remove from muffin cups and cool completely on a wire rack. Decorate as desired.

> **TIP:** To make cupcakes and muffins uniform in size, use a ¼ cup (50 mL) measuring cup to fill each muffin cup, making each cup ¾ full.

Carrot Spice Cake

Serves 12 to 16		
1½ cups	all-purpose flour	375 mL
1 cup	whole wheat flour	250 mL
4 tsp	baking powder	20 mL
2 tsp	baking soda	10 mL
1 tsp	ground cinnamon	5 mL
½ tsp	ground nutmeg	2 mL
¼ tsp	ground cloves	1 mL
1 cup	butter or margarine, melted	250 mL
2	eggs, lightly beaten	2
1 cup	liquid honey	250 mL
1 cup	vegetable oil	250 mL
½ cup	lemon juice	125 mL
2 cups	grated carrots (about 4 medium)	500 mL
½ cup	chopped nuts (optional)	125 mL
	Cream Cheese Frosting (see recipe, page 19)	
	Chopped nuts (optional)	

Preheat oven to 350°F (180°C)

13- by 9-inch (3 L) metal baking pan, lightly greased

1. In a large bowl, combine all-purpose and whole wheat flours, baking powder, baking soda, cinnamon, nutmeg and cloves.
2. In a medium bowl, whisk together butter, eggs, honey, oil and lemon juice. Add this mixture to the flour mixture and mix until thoroughly combined. Stir in grated carrots and then chopped nuts, if using, and mix well.
3. Spoon into prepared baking pan, spreading evenly, and bake in preheated oven for 50 to 60 minutes, or until toothpick inserted in the center comes out clean and dry Cool completely in pan on wire rack.
4. Frost with Cream Cheese Frosting and sprinkle more chopped nuts over top, if using.

> **TIP:** To prevent the cake from sliding on the plate while you are carrying it, drizzle a bit of frosting in a circle where the cake will rest on the plate before transferring the cake from the pan. This will hold the cake in place.

Carrot Streusel Crumb Cake

Serves 6 to 8		
2 cups	all-purpose flour	500 mL
2 tsp	baking powder	10 mL
1/2 tsp	baking soda	2 mL
1/2 tsp	salt	2 mL
1/2 tsp	ground cinnamon	2 mL
1/2 tsp	ground nutmeg	2 mL
1/4 tsp	ground cloves	1 mL
1/4 tsp	ground ginger	1 mL
1/2 cup	butter or shortening, softened	125 mL
1 1/2 cups	firmly packed brown sugar	375 mL
3/4 cup	mashed cooked carrots (about 2 medium)	175 mL
3/4 cup	milk, divided	175 mL
2	eggs	2

STREUSEL CRUMB TOPPING

1/3 cup	lightly packed brown sugar	75 mL
3 tbsp	all-purpose flour	45 mL
1 tsp	ground cinnamon	5 mL
1/3 cup	chopped nuts (pecans or walnuts)	75 mL
3 tbsp	butter or margarine, melted	45 mL

Preheat oven to 350°F (180°C)

9-inch (2.5 L) square metal baking pan, greased and floured

1. *Prepare Streusel Crumb Topping:* In a small bowl, mix together brown sugar, flour, cinnamon and nuts until combined. Stir in melted butter to form a crumbly mixture. Set aside.

2. In another bowl, combine flour, baking powder, baking soda, salt and spices.

3. In a large mixer bowl, on medium speed, cream butter and brown sugar until smooth. Beat in carrots and 1/2 cup (125 mL) of the milk and continue beating for 2 to 3 minutes. Add eggs and the remaining 1/4 cup (50 mL) of milk and beat for 2 minutes until well blended.

3. Stir in flour mixture and beat for 2 minutes until mixed thoroughly. Spoon into prepared baking pan.

4. Sprinkle topping over batter evenly. Bake in preheated oven for 45 to 50 minutes, or until toothpick inserted in center comes out clean and dry. Cool completely in pan on wire rack.

> **TIP:** An easy way to measure shortening is to fill a 2-cup (500 mL) liquid measuring cup with 1 cup (250 mL) of cold water. Add the shortening — for 1/2 cup (125 mL) of shortening, the water level will rise to 1 1/2 cups (375 mL).

Pineapple Carrot Cake

Serves 12 to 16		
2 cups	all-purpose flour	500 mL
1 tbsp	ground cinnamon	15 mL
2 tsp	baking soda	10 mL
1 tsp	ground cloves	5 mL
½ tsp	salt	2 mL
3	eggs	3
1½ cups	vegetable oil	375 mL
1¾ cups	granulated sugar	425 mL
2 cups	grated carrots (about 4 medium)	500 mL
1 cup	chopped walnuts	250 mL
1	can (8 oz/250 g) crushed pineapple, drained	1
¾ cup	shredded coconut (sweetened or unsweetened), toasted (optional)	175 mL

CREAM CHEESE FROSTING

6 oz	cream cheese, softened	175 g
½ cup	butter or margarine, softened	125 mL
2 tsp	vanilla	10 mL
4½ cups	confectioner's (icing) sugar, sifted	1.125 L

Preheat oven to 350°F (180°C)

10-inch (4 L) tube pan, greased and floured

1. In a medium bowl, sift together flour, cinnamon, baking soda, cloves and salt.

2. In a large mixer bowl, combine eggs, oil and sugar and beat on medium speed until well blended. Add flour mixture and mix until well combined. Stir in carrots, walnuts and pineapple and mix until well blended.

3. Pour into prepared cake pan, smoothing top. Bake in preheated oven for 1 hour, or until a toothpick inserted in the center comes out clean and dry. Cool in pan on a wire rack for 10 minutes, then remove from pan to cool completely on wire rack.

4. *Prepare Cream Cheese Frosting:* In a small mixer bowl, cream together cream cheese, butter and vanilla, beating on medium speed until light and fluffy. Gradually add half of the confectioner's sugar, beating well. Beat in the remainder of the confectioner's sugar gradually, until you reach the right spreading consistency.

5. If desired, split cake into two layers. Spread about ⅓ of the frosting on the bottom layer and top with top layer. Cover complete cake, top and sides with the cream cheese frosting. If you do not split the cake, cover completely with frosting. Either way, you can sprinkle coconut over top and sides, if desired.

TIP: Frosting spreads easier and frosted cakes are easier to cut when you dip your knife in cold water.

Chocolate Walnut Carrot Cupcakes

Makes 18 cupcakes		
2 cups	all-purpose flour	500 mL
2 cups	granulated sugar	500 mL
1/3 cup	unsweetened cocoa powder, sifted	75 mL
1 tsp	baking powder	5 mL
1 tsp	baking soda	5 mL
1 tsp	ground cinnamon	5 mL
4	eggs	4
1 cup	vegetable oil	250 mL
3 cups	finely grated carrots (about 6 medium)	750 mL
3/4 cup	chopped walnuts	175 mL

NOTE: Frost with your favorite frosting, if desired, and sprinkle some chopped nuts over top.

Preheat oven to 350°F (180°C)

18 muffin cups, lined with paper baking cups

1. In a large mixer bowl, combine flour, sugar, cocoa powder, baking powder, baking soda and cinnamon.

2. In another bowl, whisk eggs and oil. Stir in carrots and walnuts and mix well. Add to flour mixture and beat on medium speed until thoroughly combined.

3. Spoon into prepared muffin cups until 3/4 full. Bake in preheated oven for 18 to 20 minutes, or until toothpick inserted in center of a cupcake comes out clean and dry. Remove from muffin cups and cool on wire rack until completely cooled.

TIP: To make a delicious instant frosting for cupcakes, top each one with a marshmallow about 2 minutes before taking them out of the oven. The marshmallows will melt onto the cupcakes and become frosting. Then decorate as you wish with sprinkles, shaved chocolate, etc.

Turnover Apple Cake

Serves 6 to 8		
2 cups	prepared biscuit mix	500 mL
2 tbsp	granulated sugar	25 mL
1 tsp	ground cinnamon	5 mL
1/4 tsp	ground nutmeg	1 mL
1	egg	1
2/3 cup	milk	150 mL
TOPPING		
1/2 cup	granulated sugar	125 mL
1 tsp	ground cinnamon	5 mL
4	Granny Smith apples, peeled and thinly sliced	4

NOTE: If desired, top with ice cream or a dollop of whipped cream.

Preheat oven to 400°F (200°C)

9-inch (23 cm) round or 9-inch (2.5 L) square metal baking pan, well-buttered

1. *Prepare topping:* In a medium bowl, toss sugar, cinnamon and apples, mixing well to coat. Spoon into prepared baking pan.

2. In a large mixer bowl, combine biscuit mix, sugar, cinnamon, nutmeg, egg and milk. Beat on low speed until blended, then on medium speed until thoroughly blended. Pour over top of apple mixture, spreading evenly.

3. Bake in preheated oven for 25 to 30 minutes, or until a toothpick inserted in the center comes out clean and dry. Cool in pan on wire rack for 5 to 10 minutes, then invert onto a serving plate and cool completely, or serve slightly warm.

Easy Apple Pie Dump Cake

Serves 12 to 16		
1	can (20 oz/590 mL) apple pie filling	1
½ tsp	ground cinnamon	2 mL
1	package (about 18.25 oz/515 g) yellow or white cake mix	1
½ cup	butter or margarine, melted	125 mL
	Ice cream or whipped cream	

Preheat oven to 400°F (200°C)

13- by 9-inch (3 L) metal baking pan, lightly greased

1. In a medium bowl, mix together apple pie filling and cinnamon. Pour into prepared baking pan.
2. Spread dry cake mix over top. Pour the melted butter evenly over the cake mix.
3. Bake in preheated oven for 40 to 45 minutes, or until golden brown. Serve warm with ice cream or whipped cream.

VARIATIONS

Pumpkin Dump Cake: Use a yellow cake mix. Omit apple pie filling and cinnamon and replace with 1 can (20 oz/590 mL) pumpkin pie filling. Stir 1 cup (250 mL) chopped nuts into the pumpkin filling.

Cherry Pineapple Dump Cake: Use a yellow cake mix. Omit apple pie filling and cinnamon. Use ½ can (10 oz/300 mL) cherry pie filling and ½ can (10 oz/300 mL) crushed pineapple, undrained.

Blueberry Dump Cake: Use a yellow cake mix. Omit apple pie filling and cinnamon. Use 1 can (20 oz/380 mL) blueberry pie filling.

Coconut Apricot Cake

Serves 6 to 8		
1 cup	all-purpose flour	250 mL
¾ cup	granulated sugar	175 mL
1¼ tsp	baking powder	6 mL
Pinch	salt	Pinch
6 tbsp	butter or margarine	90 mL
⅔ cup	packed brown sugar	150 mL
1 tbsp	light corn syrup	15 mL
1¼ cups	flaked coconut (sweetened or unsweetened)	300 ml
1¼ cups	canned apricot halves, drained	300 mL
¼ cup	shortening, softened	50 mL
1	egg	1
½ cup	milk	125 mL
½ tsp	vanilla	2 mL

NOTE: If desired, serve warm with whipped cream or ice cream.

Preheat oven to 375°F (190°C)

8-inch (20 cm) round or 8-inch (2 L) square metal baking pan, ungreased

1. In a large mixer bowl, sift together flour, granulated sugar, baking powder and salt.
2. In a small saucepan, melt butter over low heat. Remove from heat and stir in brown sugar, coconut and corn syrup. Pat evenly onto bottom and sides of baking pan.
3. Place apricot halves, cut side up, over top of coconut mixture.
4. To the flour mixture, add shortening, egg, milk and vanilla, beating on low speed until blended. Beat for another 2 to 3 minutes on medium speed. Spoon over the apricots.
5. Bake in preheated oven for 45 to 50 minutes, or until golden. Cool in pan on wire rack for 2 to 3 minutes and invert onto a serving plate.

Blueberry Streusel Cake

	Serves 8 to 10	
2 cups	all-purpose flour	500 mL
1 tsp	baking powder	5 mL
¼ tsp	baking soda	1 mL
Pinch	salt	Pinch
¼ cup	butter or margarine, softened	50 mL
1 cup	granulated sugar	250 mL
	Grated zest of 1 lemon	
1 tsp	vanilla	5 mL
2	eggs	2
1 cup	sour cream	250 mL
1 cup	fresh blueberries, washed and dried (or frozen, thawed and drained)	250 mL

STREUSEL TOPPING

⅓ cup	all-purpose flour	75 mL
¼ cup	packed brown sugar	50 mL
1 tsp	ground cinnamon	5 mL
3 tbsp	butter or margarine, softened	45 mL

Preheat oven to 350°F (180°C)

9-inch (23 cm) round metal baking pan or springform pan, greased and floured

1. *Prepare Streusel Topping:* In a small bowl, mix together flour, brown sugar and cinnamon. Cut in butter with a fork, or by hand, until mixture is crumbly. Set aside.

2. In a medium bowl, sift together flour, baking powder, baking soda and salt.

3. In a large mixer bowl, cream butter and sugar until smooth. Add lemon zest and vanilla. Beat in eggs, on medium speed, until light and fluffy. Beat in flour mixture alternately with sour cream, making 3 additions of flour and 2 of sour cream, on low speed until well blended. Pour into prepared baking pan. Sprinkle blueberries over top of batter. Sprinkle streusel topping evenly over blueberries.

4. Bake in preheated oven for 60 minutes, or until a toothpick inserted in the center comes out clean and dry. Cool in pan on a wire rack for 10 minutes, then remove onto a plate or wire rack to cool completely. This cake is delicious served warm or cold.

Date (Matrimony) Cake

	Serves 12 to 16	
2 cups	quick-cooking rolled oats	500 mL
1 cup	firmly packed brown sugar	250 mL
1 cup	all-purpose flour, sifted	250 mL
1 tsp	baking soda	5 mL
½ tsp	salt	2 mL
1 cup	butter or margarine, softened	250 mL
DATE FILLING		
1 cup	chopped dates	250 mL
1 cup	boiling water	250 mL
½ cup	firmly packed brown sugar	125 mL

Preheat oven to 400°F (200°C)
13- by 9-inch (3 L) metal baking pan, greased

1. *Prepare Date Filling:* In a medium saucepan, over medium heat, combine dates, boiling water and brown sugar, stirring until mixture becomes thick, about 5 to 6 minutes. Set aside to cool.

2. In a large bowl, combine oats, brown sugar, flour, baking soda and salt. Cut in butter with two knives, a pastry blender or your fingers, until mixture resembles coarse crumbs. Spread a little over half of the oat mixture into the prepared baking pan, packing down firmly with your hand.

3. Spoon filling, by teaspoonfuls, carefully over the oat layer in pan. Top with the remaining oat mixture and pat lightly with your hand.

4. Bake in preheated oven for 25 to 30 minutes, or until golden brown. Cool completely in pan on wire rack.

Orange Ripple Cake

	Serves 8 to 10	
2 cups	all-purpose flour	500 mL
2½ tsp	baking powder	12 mL
¼ tsp	baking soda	1 mL
Pinch	salt	Pinch
1 cup	granulated sugar	250 mL
½ cup	butter or margarine, softened	125 mL
2	eggs, beaten	2
½ cup	chopped nuts	125 mL
1 tbsp	grated orange zest	15 mL
1 cup	sour cream	250 mL
RIPPLE MIXTURE		
½ cup	granulated sugar	125 mL
2 tbsp	unsweetened cocoa powder, sifted	25 mL
2 tsp	ground cinnamon	10 mL

NOTE: If desired, frost with your favorite chocolate frosting after removing cake from the pan.

Preheat oven to 375°F (190°C)
9-inch (2.5 L) square or 9-inch (23 cm) round metal baking pan, greased

1. *Prepare Ripple Mixture:* In a small bowl, combine sugar, cocoa powder and cinnamon, mixing until well combined. Set aside.

2. In another bowl, sift together flour, baking powder, baking soda and salt.

3. In a large mixer bowl, cream sugar and butter until smooth. Beat in eggs until light and fluffy. Stir in nuts and orange zest, and mix well. Stir in flour mixture alternately with sour cream, making 3 additions of flour and 2 of sour cream, on low speed, mixing until well blended.

4. Spread half of the batter into the prepared baking pan. Sprinkle ripple mixture over batter. Top with remaining batter, spreading evenly. Bake in preheated oven for 40 to 45 minutes, or until a toothpick inserted in the center comes out clean and dry. Cool in pan on a wire rack for 10 minutes. Remove from pan and cool completely on wire rack.

Sour Cream Peach Kuchen

Serves 8 to 10		
2 cups	all-purpose flour	500 mL
2 tsp	baking powder	10 mL
½ tsp	baking soda	2 mL
½ tsp	salt	2 mL
1 cup	granulated sugar	250 mL
½ cup	butter or margarine, softened	125 mL
1 tsp	vanilla	5 mL
3	eggs	3
1⅓ cups	sour cream	325 mL
1	can (28 oz/796 mL) sliced peaches, drained	1

NUT TOPPING

1 tbsp	all-purpose flour	15 mL
⅓ cup	brown sugar	75 mL
½ tsp	ground cinnamon	2 mL
⅓ cup	chopped pecans	75 mL
1 tbsp	butter or margarine, melted	15 mL

Preheat oven to 350°F (180°C)

10-inch (25 cm) springform pan or 10-inch (4 L) tube pan, greased

1. *Prepare Nut Topping:* In a small bowl, combine flour, brown sugar, cinnamon, pecans and butter. Set aside.

2. In a medium bowl, sift together flour, baking powder, baking soda and salt.

3. In a large mixer bowl, cream sugar, butter and vanilla until smooth. Beat in eggs, one at a time, beating well until light and fluffy. Stir in flour mixture alternately with sour cream, making 3 additions of flour and 2 of sour cream, on low speed until well blended.

4. Pour into prepared baking pan, spreading evenly. Bake in preheated oven for 40 minutes.

5. Arrange peach slices on top in a circular, or pinwheel, pattern. Sprinkle nut topping over top. Bake for 15 to 20 minutes more, or until golden. Cool slightly in pan on a wire rack and serve warm, or cool completely.

Spiced Pear Gingerbread Cake

Serves 8 to 10		
3 cups	all-purpose flour	750 mL
1 tbsp	ground ginger	15 mL
½ tsp	ground cinnamon	2 mL
¼ tsp	salt	1 mL
¼ tsp	ground cloves	1 mL
2 tsp	baking soda	10 mL
1 cup	boiling water	250 mL
1 cup	butter or margarine, softened	250 mL
½ cup	firmly packed brown sugar	125 mL
1	egg	1
1 cup	fancy molasses	250 mL
2 tbsp	packed brown sugar	25 mL
1	can (14 oz/398 mL) pear halves, drained and cut into quarters (or 2 large pears, peeled and sliced)	1

Preheat oven to 350°F (180°C)

9-inch (23 cm) round or 9-inch (2.5 L) square metal baking pan, greased

1. In a medium bowl, sift together flour, ginger, cinnamon, salt and cloves.

2. In another bowl, dissolve the baking soda in the boiling water and set aside.

3. In a large mixer bowl, cream butter and ½ cup (125 mL) brown sugar until smooth. Beat in egg until mixture is light and fluffy. Stir in molasses and blend well. Stir in flour mixture alternately with baking soda mixture, making 3 additions of flour and 2 of baking soda, until well blended. Pour into prepared baking pan. Sprinkle with 2 tbsp (25 mL) brown sugar and arrange pear slices over top.

4. Bake in preheated oven for 60 to 65 minutes, or until a toothpick inserted in the center comes out clean and dry. Cool in pan on wire rack for 10 minutes, then remove onto wire rack and cool slightly. Best when served warm.

TIP: To soften brown sugar that has become hard, put a slice of soft bread in the package and close the bag tightly. The sugar will be soft again in a few hours.

Pineapple Upside-down Cake

Serves 8 to 10

2 tbsp	butter or margarine	25 mL
1/3 cup	firmly packed brown sugar	75 mL
1 tbsp	water	15 mL
1	can (14 oz/398 mL) pineapple slices, drained	1
4	maraschino cherries, cut in half	4
1 1/3 cups	all-purpose flour	325 mL
2/3 cup	granulated sugar	150 mL
2 tsp	baking powder	10 mL
1	egg	1
2/3 cup	milk	150 mL
1/4 cup	butter or margarine, softened	50 mL
1 tsp	vanilla	5 mL

NOTE: You can also cut the pineapple slices in half and place a halved cherry in the center of each.

Preheat oven to 350°F (180°C)
9-inch (23 cm) round metal baking pan

1. Put the 2 tbsp (25 mL) butter in baking pan, and put the pan in the oven while preheating to melt the butter. Remove from oven and stir in the brown sugar and water.

2. Arrange pineapple slices over top and place a halved cherry, cut side down, in the center of each slice.

3. In a medium bowl, mix together flour, sugar and baking powder.

4. In a large mixer bowl, combine egg, milk, butter and vanilla, beating on low speed until blended. Beat in flour mixture on medium speed for 2 to 3 minutes, until thoroughly combined. Spoon into baking pan over the fruit, spreading evenly.

5. Bake in preheated oven for 30 to 35 minutes, or until a toothpick inserted in the center comes out clean and dry. Cool in pan on wire rack for 5 to 10 minutes, loosen around the sides with a knife and then invert onto a serving plate. Best when served slightly warm.

TIP: Use any reserved pineapple juice to sprinkle over sliced apples or bananas to prevent discoloring without adding a strong flavor.

Streusel Sugar Plum Cake

Serves 8 to 10		
1½ cups	all-purpose flour	375 mL
1 tsp	baking powder	5 mL
⅔ cup	granulated sugar	150 mL
¼ cup	butter or margarine, softened	50 mL
2	eggs, separated	2
½ cup	milk	125 mL
2 cups	canned plums, drained and halved (or fresh plums)	500 mL

STREUSEL TOPPING

½ cup	brown sugar	125 mL
1 tbsp	all-purpose flour	15 mL
2 tsp	ground cinnamon	10 mL
2 tbsp	butter or margarine, melted	25 mL

GLAZE (OPTIONAL)

1	jar (4 oz/114 mL) strained plum baby food (or plum-apple)	1
1 cup	confectioner's (icing) sugar	250 mL
2 tbsp	milk	25 mL

Preheat oven to 350°F (180°C)
9-inch (23 cm) springform pan, greased

1. *Prepare Streusel Topping:* In a small bowl, mix together brown sugar, flour and cinnamon. Add melted butter and mix well until crumbly.

2. In a medium bowl, mix together flour and baking powder.

3. In a large mixer bowl, cream sugar and butter until smooth. Add egg yolks and beat on medium speed until light and fluffy. Beat in flour mixture alternately with milk, making 3 additions of flour and 2 of milk, on low speed until well blended.

4. In a small mixer bowl with clean beaters, on high speed, beat egg whites until stiff peaks form. Fold into the batter, gently, until well combined. Spoon into prepared baking pan. Arrange plum halves on top, cut side down. Sprinkle streusel topping evenly over top of plums. Bake in preheated oven for 45 to 50 minutes, or until top is golden brown. Cool completely in pan on a wire rack.

5. *If desired, prepare glaze:* In a small bowl, combine plum baby food, confectioner's sugar and milk, and mix well until smooth and of the right consistency for spreading. Drizzle over cooled cake.

TIP: When your baking seems to brown too quickly on top and is not completely done in the center, place a pan of water on the rack above it. On the contrary, if the bottom browns too quickly, place a pan of water on the rack underneath.

Lemon-Glazed Pumpkin Cake

Serves 12 to 16		
2 cups	all-purpose flour	500 mL
2 tsp	baking powder	10 mL
2 tsp	baking soda	10 mL
2 tsp	ground cinnamon	10 mL
1 tsp	ground nutmeg	5 mL
1 tsp	pumpkin pie spice	5 mL
½ tsp	salt	2 mL
4	eggs	4
2 cups	granulated sugar	500 mL
1 cup	vegetable oil	250 mL
2 cups	canned pumpkin purée (not pie filling)	500 mL

LEMON GLAZE

1½ cups	confectioner's (icing) sugar	375 mL
1 tsp	grated lemon zest	5 mL
2 to 3 tbsp	lemon juice	25 to 45 mL

> **NOTE:** If desired, you could add ½ cup (125 mL) raisins and/or ½ cup (125 mL) chopped nuts to the batter before baking.

Preheat oven to 350°F (180°C)
10-inch (4 L) tube pan, greased

1. In a medium bowl, sift together flour, baking powder, baking soda, cinnamon, nutmeg, pumpkin pie spice and salt.

2. In a large mixer bowl, cream eggs and sugar until smooth and fluffy. Add oil and pumpkin and beat on medium speed until well blended.

3. Add flour mixture to the creamed mixture, beating until thoroughly combined. Do not over-beat. Spoon into prepared baking pan.

4. Bake in preheated oven for 45 to 55 minutes, or until a toothpick inserted in the center comes out clean and dry. Cool in pan on wire rack for 10 minutes. Loosen around edges of cake with a knife or spatula and invert onto wire rack to cool completely.

5. *Prepare Lemon Glaze:* In a small bowl, combine confectioner's sugar, zest and enough lemon juice for a glazing consistency. Mix together to blend. Drizzle over cooled cake.

> **TIP:** To get more juice from a lemon, pop it into the microwave and cook on high for 15 seconds, then cool before squeezing. You can also roll the lemon back and forth on the countertop until slightly softened.

Strawberry Cream Shortcake

	Serves 12 to 16	
1	package (3 oz/90 g) strawberry gelatin powder	1
1	package (16 oz/475 g) frozen sweetened sliced strawberries, thawed, or 2 cups (500 mL) fresh strawberries, washed and sliced	1
1 cup	miniature white marshmallows	250 mL
2¼ cups	all-purpose flour	550 mL
1 tbsp	baking powder	15 mL
¼ tsp	salt	1 mL
1½ cups	granulated sugar	375 mL
½ cup	shortening, softened	125 mL
3	eggs	3
1 tsp	vanilla	5 mL
1 cup	milk	250 mL
	Whipped cream	
	Fresh strawberries	

Preheat oven to 350°F (180°C)

13- by 9-inch (3 L) metal baking pan, greased

1. In a small bowl, combine gelatin and strawberries. Set aside.
2. Sprinkle the marshmallows into prepared baking pan, spreading evenly.
3. In a bowl, mix together flour, baking powder and salt.
4. In a large mixer bowl, cream sugar and shortening until smooth. Beat in eggs, one at a time, until light and fluffy. Add vanilla. Beat in flour mixture alternately with milk on low speed, making 3 additions of flour and 2 of milk, until well blended. Pour batter over the marshmallows in pan. Spoon strawberry mixture over top of batter.
6. Bake in preheated oven for 45 to 50 minutes, or until a toothpick inserted into the center comes out clean and dry. Cool on a wire rack. To serve, top each slice with a dollop of whipped cream and a whole, fresh strawberry.

Special Holiday Fruitcake

Makes 7 or 8 small cakes

2½ cups	(approx.) all-purpose flour, divided	625 mL
2 tsp	salt	10 mL
2 tsp	ground allspice	10 mL
2 tsp	ground cinnamon	10 mL
1 tsp	ground cloves	5 mL
1 tsp	baking powder	5 mL
4	eggs	4
1½ cups	packed brown sugar	375 mL
1 cup	vegetable oil	250 mL
1½ cups	chopped nuts	375 mL
1 cup	chopped candied pineapple	250 mL
1 cup	whole candied cherries	250 mL
1 cup	raisins	250 mL
1 cup	chopped dates or figs	250 mL
½ cup	candied orange peel	125 mL
½ cup	flaked coconut (sweetened or unsweetened)	125 mL
1 cup	orange juice	250 mL
	Red wine or brandy	

Preheat oven to 300°F (150°C)

Seven or eight 12-oz (375 mL) cans, greased and floured

1. In a medium bowl, sift together 2 cups (500 mL) of the flour, salt, allspice, cinnamon, cloves and baking powder and mix well.

2. In another bowl, combine nuts, pineapple, cherries, raisins, dates, orange peel and coconut. Spoon in enough flour to dredge the fruit, about ½ cup (125 mL), or more as required.

3. In a large mixer bowl, combine eggs, brown sugar and oil, and beat on medium speed until well blended. Stir in flour mixture alternately with orange juice, making 3 additions of flour and 2 of juice, until well combined. Fold in the dredged fruit mixture until well incorporated into the batter.

4. Spoon into the prepared cans, filling ¾ full, and bake in preheated oven for 90 minutes, or until a toothpick inserted in center comes out clean and dry. Cool completely in the cans on a rack, then remove from cans. Wrap each cake in a cloth soaked with wine. Then wrap each in tin foil. Store in a cool place for 2 to 3 weeks. Re-moisten the cloths once or twice during this time. To serve, chill for easier slicing, then cut into slices.

TIP: To prevent fruit from rising to the top of a cake, dredge it in flour before adding to the batter.

Crusted Lemon Poppy Seed Cake

Serves 12 to 16		
¼ cup	fine dry bread crumbs	50 mL
2¼ cups	sifted cake flour	550 mL
½ cup	poppy seeds	125 mL
1 tsp	baking powder	5 mL
½ tsp	salt	2 mL
3	eggs	3
1½ cups	granulated sugar	375 mL
¾ cup	butter or margarine, softened	175 mL
1 tbsp	grated lemon zest	15 mL
2 tbsp	lemon juice	25 mL
⅔ cup	milk	150 mL

Preheat oven to 350°F (180°C)
10-inch (3 L) Bundt pan, well-greased

1. Dust greased pan evenly with the dry bread crumbs. When cake is baked and removed from pan, this will form a lovely brown crust.

2. In a medium bowl, combine flour, poppy seeds, baking powder and salt.

3. In a large mixer bowl, combine eggs, sugar and butter, and beat on high speed for 3 to 5 minutes, until well beaten and smooth. Slowly beat in lemon juice and lemon zest. Beat in flour mixture alternately with milk, making 3 additions of flour and 2 of milk, on low speed just until blended.

4. Pour into prepared baking pan. Bake in preheated oven for 50 to 55 minutes, or until a toothpick inserted in center comes out clean and dry. Cool in pan on wire rack for about 10 minutes and then loosen cake around the edges with a knife or spatula and invert onto wire rack to cool completely.

VARIATION

Glazed Lemon Poppy Seed Cake: Omit the bread crumbs and just grease the baking pan. To make a lemon glaze, mix together in a small saucepan, over low heat, ½ cup (125 mL) granulated sugar, ⅓ cup (75 mL) fresh lemon juice and 1 tbsp (15 mL) water. Heat until sugar is dissolved. When cool, drizzle over top of cake.

> **TIP:** If you have rust marks on your Bundt pans (or other baking pans) that just won't come off, pour some cola into them and soak overnight. The pans should be free of rust the next morning.

Lemon Blueberry Cake

Serves 12 to 16		
3 cups	all-purpose flour	750 mL
2 tsp	baking powder	10 mL
1/2 tsp	salt	2 mL
3/4 cup	butter, margarine or shortening, softened	175 mL
2 cups	granulated sugar	500 mL
4	eggs	4
1 tsp	vanilla	5 mL
1 tsp	grated lemon zest	5 mL
1 tsp	lemon juice	5 mL
1 cup	milk	250 mL
1 1/2 cups	fresh blueberries (or thawed, drained frozen blueberries	375 mL

Preheat oven to 350°F (180°C)

13- by 9-inch (3 L) metal baking pan, greased and floured

1. In a medium bowl, combine flour, baking powder and salt.

2. In a large mixer bowl, on medium speed, cream butter and sugar until smooth. Add eggs, one at a time, beating until light and fluffy. Beat in vanilla, lemon juice and lemon zest until blended. Beat in flour mixture alternately with milk, making 3 additions of flour and 2 of milk, on low speed until well combined.

3. Fold in blueberries and spoon into prepared baking pan. Bake in preheated oven for 50 to 60 minutes, or until toothpick inserted in the center comes out clean and dry. Cool completely in pan on wire rack.

Lemon Cupcakes

Makes 18 cupcakes		
2 3/4 cups	cake flour	675 mL
1 1/2 cups	granulated sugar	375 mL
2 1/2 tsp	baking powder	12 mL
1/2 tsp	salt	2 mL
4	eggs	4
3/4 cup	buttermilk	175 mL
2 tbsp	lemon juice	25 mL
2 tbsp	grated lemon zest	25 mL
1 cup	butter or margarine, softened	250 mL

NOTE: If desired, frost with your favorite frosting or drizzle with a lemon glaze.

Preheat oven to 350°F (180°C)

18 muffin cups, lined with paper baking cups

1. In a medium bowl, combine flour, sugar, baking powder and salt.

2. In a large mixer bowl, on medium speed, beat together eggs, buttermilk, lemon juice and lemon zest until well combined. Add half of flour mixture and the butter to the egg mixture, and beat on low speed until well blended. Add remaining flour mixture and beat until well blended.

3. Spoon into muffin tins until 3/4 full. Bake in preheated oven for 18 to 20 minutes, or until a toothpick inserted in the center of a cupcake comes out clean and dry. Cool completely on wire rack.

Orange Ripple Cake *(page 23)* ➤

Easy Coconut Snowball Cake

	Serves 12 to 16	
1	package (about 18.25 oz/515 g) yellow cake mix	1

FILLING

2 cups	granulated sugar	500 mL
2 cups	sour cream	500 mL
¼ cup	orange juice (optional)	50 mL
1½ cups	flaked coconut (sweetened or unsweetened)	375 mL
1	carton (8 oz/250 mL) whipped topping	1
1	can (10 oz/284 mL) mandarin orange segments, drained	1

Preheat oven according to cake mix instructions
Two 9-inch (2.5 L) square metal baking pans, greased and floured

1. In a large bowl, prepare cake mix according to package directions. Pour batter into the two prepared baking pans and bake as directed on the package. Cool in pans for 10 minutes, then remove onto wire racks to cool completely.

2. *Prepare filling:* In a medium bowl, mix together sugar and sour cream, and orange juice, if desired, until well blended. Add coconut and mix well. The mixture will be soft. Set aside 1 cup (250 mL) of this filling.

3. Split each cake layer horizontally. Place one layer on a plate and spread about ⅓ of the filling over top. Top with another cake layer and ⅓ of the filling. Repeat with the third layer and top with the fourth layer.

4. Fold the reserved 1 cup (250 mL) of filling into the whipped topping and frost top and sides of cake. Decorate with mandarin orange segments.

White Sheet Cake

	Serves 16 to 20	
4 cups	all-purpose flour	1 L
4 tsp	baking powder	20 mL
½ tsp	salt	2 mL
¾ cup	butter, margarine or shortening, softened	175 mL
2 cups	granulated sugar	500 mL
6	egg whites	6
¾ cup	water	175 mL
¾ cup	milk	175 mL
½ tsp	vanilla	2 mL
½ tsp	almond extract (optional)	2 mL

NOTE: These sheet cakes can be cut into 2-inch squares to serve, or made fancy by using cookie cutters to make individual shapes. They can be frosted or left plain. Decorate as desired.

Preheat oven to 375°F (190°C)
17- by 11- by 1-inch (45 by 29 by 2.5 cm) rimmed baking sheet, greased, and bottom lined with parchment paper

1. In a medium bowl, sift together flour, baking powder and salt.

2. In a large mixer bowl, cream butter until smooth. Gradually add in sugar, beating until light and fluffy. Add egg whites, one at a time, beating well after each addition. Stir in vanilla and almond extract, if desired. Stir in flour mixture alternately with water and milk, making 3 additions of flour and 1 each of water and milk, until mixture is smooth. Pour into prepared baking pan, smoothing top.

3. Bake in preheated oven for 30 to 35 minutes, or until cake top springs back when touched lightly with fingertip. Cool in pan on a wire rack.

VARIATIONS

Lemon Sheet Cake: Omit almond extract and replace with 2 tsp (10 mL) lemon extract.

Chocolate Sheet Cake: Add ½ cup (125 mL) unsweetened cocoa powder, sifted, to the dry ingredients before baking.

◀ Apple Crumb Coffee Cake *(page 43)*

Graham Streusel Cake

3	eggs, separated	3
1⅔ cups	graham wafers, finely crushed (about 20 whole wafers)	400 mL
¼ cup	all-purpose flour	50 mL
1½ tsp	baking powder	7 mL
¼ tsp	salt	1 mL
½ cup	butter, margarine or shortening, softened	125 mL
1 cup	granulated sugar	250 mL
½ tsp	vanilla	2 mL
¾ cup	milk	175 mL
½ cup	chopped nuts (optional)	125 mL

STREUSEL TOPPING

2 cups	graham wafer crumbs (about 25 whole wafers)	500 mL
¾ cup	firmly packed brown sugar	175 mL
¾ cup	butter or margarine, melted	175 mL
1½ tsp	ground cinnamon	7 mL

Preheat oven to 350°F (180°C)

13- by 9-inch (3 L) metal baking pan, greased and floured

1. Set aside egg whites in a small bowl to come to room temperature.

2. *Prepare Streusel Topping:* In a small bowl, mix together graham crumbs, brown sugar, melted butter and cinnamon until well combined.

3. In a medium bowl, combine graham wafer crumbs, flour, baking powder and salt.

4. In a large mixer bowl, cream butter until smooth. Gradually add sugar and vanilla, and beat on medium speed until blended. Beat in egg yolks until light and fluffy. Beat in flour mixture alternately with milk, making 3 additions of flour and 2 of milk, on low speed until mixed. Stir in nuts, if desired.

5. In a small mixer bowl with clean beaters, on high speed, beat egg whites until stiff peaks form. Gently fold into the batter until thoroughly blended. Spoon into prepared baking pan, spreading evenly. Sprinkle streusel topping evenly over batter.

6. Bake in preheated oven for 45 to 50 minutes, or until a toothpick inserted in the center comes out clean and dry. Cool in pan on wire rack for 10 minutes, then remove to wire rack to cool completely.

Mom's War Cake

Serves 8 to 10		
2 cups	water	500 mL
2 cups	granulated sugar (or 1 cup (250 mL) granulated and 1 cup (250 mL) packed brown sugar)	500 mL
1 cup	raisins	250 mL
⅔ cup	lard or shortening	150 mL
2 tsp	ground cinnamon	10 mL
1 tsp	ground cloves	5 mL
½ tsp	ground nutmeg	2 mL
½ tsp	salt	2 mL
⅓ cup	cold water or coffee	75 mL
2 tsp	baking soda	10 mL
4 cups	all-purpose flour	1 L
1 tsp	baking powder	5 mL
1 cup	chopped nuts (optional)	250 mL

NOTE: If you wish to have an icing for this cake, warm 2 tbsp (25 mL) evaporated milk in a small saucepan, add ½ to ¾ tsp (2 to 4 mL) lemon extract and 1 cup (250 mL) confectioner's (icing) sugar and mix until the right consistency for spreading. Spread over top of cake when both cake and icing are cooled.

This cake was developed during the First and Second World Wars, when supplies were rationed; it is therefore made without milk, eggs or butter.

Preheat oven to 350°F (180°C)

9-inch (2.5 L) square metal baking pan, greased and floured

1. In a large saucepan, bring to a boil the 2 cups (500 mL) of water, sugar, raisins, lard, cinnamon, cloves, nutmeg and salt. Boil for about 5 minutes, or until the lard is smooth and melted. Set aside to cool.

2. In a small bowl, mix together cold water and baking soda and add to the mixture in the saucepan.

3. Mix in flour and baking powder until blended. Add chopped nuts, if desired, and mix well. Spoon into prepared baking pan, spreading evenly.

4. Bake in preheated oven for 30 minutes, or until a toothpick inserted in the center comes out clean and dry. Cool in pan on wire rack for 10 minutes, then remove from pan to cool completely on wire rack.

TIP: To keep a cake fresh for several days longer, place an apple cut in half in the cake box.

Poppy Seed Bundt Cake

	Serves 12 to 16	
¾ cup	milk	175 mL
½ cup	poppy seeds	125 mL
2 cups	all-purpose flour	500 mL
2 tsp	baking powder	10 mL
Pinch	salt	Pinch
¾ cup	butter or margarine, softened	175 mL
1½ cups	granulated sugar	375 mL
5	eggs, separated	5
	Confectioner's (icing) sugar	

Preheat oven to 350°F (180°C)

10-inch (3 L) Bundt pan, greased and floured

1. In a small bowl, soak poppy seeds in milk and let stand for 1 hour, or overnight.

2. In a medium bowl, combine flour, baking powder and salt.

3. In a large mixer bowl, cream butter and sugar until smooth. Beat in egg yolks, one at a time, on medium speed until light and fluffy. Add poppy seed mixture and mix until well blended. Beat in flour mixture on low speed until well blended.

4. In a small mixer bowl with clean beaters, on high speed, beat egg whites until stiff peaks form. Gently fold into batter, blending thoroughly. Spoon into prepared baking pan.

5. Bake in preheated oven for 50 to 60 minutes, or until a toothpick inserted in the center comes out clean and dry. Cool in pan on wire rack for 20 to 30 minutes. Remove from pan and cool completely on wire rack. Sift icing sugar over top, or decorate as desired.

Raisin Spice Cake

	Serves 12 to 16	
2 cups	all-purpose flour	500 mL
2 tsp	ground cinnamon	10 mL
2 tsp	ground allspice	10 mL
1 tsp	baking soda	5 mL
½ tsp	ground nutmeg	2 mL
½ tsp	ground cloves	2 mL
¼ tsp	salt	1 mL
½ cup	butter or margarine, softened	125 mL
2 cups	firmly packed brown sugar	500 mL
3	eggs	3
1 cup	sour cream or buttermilk	250 mL
¾ cup	raisins	175 mL
	Cream Cheese Frosting (see recipe, page 19) or other favorite frosting	

Preheat oven to 350°F (180°C)

13- by 9-inch (3L) metal baking pan, greased and floured

1. In a medium bowl, sift together flour, cinnamon, allspice, baking soda, nutmeg, cloves and salt.

2. In a large mixer bowl, cream butter and brown sugar until light and fluffy. Add eggs, one at a time, beating well on medium speed after each addition. Beat in flour mixture alternately with sour cream, making 3 additions of flour and 2 of sour cream, on low speed until well combined. Stir in raisins. Mix well.

3. Pour into prepared baking pan, spreading evenly. Bake in preheated oven for 45 to 50 minutes, or until a toothpick inserted in the center comes out clean and dry. Cool in pan on wire rack for 10 minutes. Remove from pan and cool completely on wire rack.

4. Frost with Cream Cheese Frosting or another favorite.

> **TIP:** To rehydrate dried-out raisins, steam them over hot water for a few minutes.

Pound Cakes, Coffee Cakes and Loaf Cakes

Traditional Pound Cake

Serves 12 to 16		
1½ cups	butter, softened	375 mL
4 cups	confectioner's (icing) sugar, sifted	1 L
1 tsp	vanilla	5 mL
6	eggs	6
2¾ cups	cake flour, sifted	675 mL
	Confectioner's (icing) sugar (optional)	

NOTE: To make an authentic, rich pound cake, always use butter instead of margarine.

Preheat oven to 325°F (160°C)
10-inch (3 L) Bundt pan, greased and floured

1. In a large mixer bowl, cream butter until smooth. Slowly add confectioner's sugar, beating well after each addition, and then add vanilla, beating until light and fluffy.
2. Add eggs, one at a time, beating well after each addition, until blended.
3. Stir in cake flour gradually until thoroughly blended, but do not over-mix.
4. Pour into prepared baking pan and tap pan lightly on the table or counter to get rid of any air bubbles that may have formed.
5. Bake in preheated oven for 80 minutes, or until a toothpick inserted in the center comes out clean and dry. Cool in pan on a wire rack for 5 to 10 minutes, loosen cake from the edges with a spatula or knife, invert, and cool completely on a rack. Sprinkle with more confectioner's sugar over top, if desired.

VARIATIONS

Cinnamon Nut Pound Cake: Before baking, add 1 tsp (5 mL) ground cinnamon, ¼ tsp (1 mL) ground nutmeg and ½ cup (125 mL) finely chopped nuts to the batter, mixing well.

Pound Cake Kabobs: Cut a pound cake into 1½-inch (4 cm) cubes. Spear each on a fork and dip in melted currant jelly or in sweetened condensed milk. Then roll in flaked coconut to cover. Thread on skewers and toast over very hot coals, turning often.

Marble Pound Cake

Serves 8 to 10

2¼ cups	cake flour, sifted	550 mL
1 tsp	baking powder	5 mL
1 tsp	salt	5 mL
¾ cup	butter or margarine, softened (preferably butter)	175 mL
1¼ cups	granulated sugar	300 mL
½ cup	milk	125 mL
1 tsp	grated lemon zest	5 mL
1 tbsp	lemon juice	15 mL
3	eggs	3
	Confectioner's (icing) sugar (optional)	

MARBLING

1 oz	unsweetened chocolate, melted	30 g
1 tbsp	granulated sugar	15 mL
2 tbsp	boiling water	25 mL

Preheat oven to 325°F (160°C)

9-inch (2.5 L) square metal baking pan, or 9- by 5-inch (1.5 L) metal loaf pan, greased and floured

1. In a medium bowl, combine flour, baking powder and salt.
2. In a large mixer bowl, cream butter and sugar on medium speed, beating until light and fluffy. Add milk, lemon zest and juice, and continue beating for 2 to 3 minutes, until blended. Add eggs, one at a time, beating well after each addition, until well blended.
3. Gradually add flour mixture to creamed mixture, beating on low speed for about 2 to 3 minutes, until smooth. Transfer half of the batter into a separate bowl.
4. *Prepare Marbling:* In a small bowl, mix together melted chocolate, sugar and boiling water. Stir the chocolate mixture into one bowl of the batter and mix well.
5. Spoon into prepared baking pan by alternating spoonfuls of light and dark batter, making a checkerboard effect. With a knife or narrow spatula, gently stir through the batter, making a marbling effect.
6. Bake in preheated oven for about 75 minutes, or until a toothpick inserted in the center comes out clean and dry. Cool in pan on a wire rack for 10 minutes, remove from pan and cool completely on wire rack. Sift confectioner's sugar over top, if desired.

VARIATION

Chocolate Swirl Pound Cake: Do not mix marbling ingredients into half of the batter. Instead spoon half of the batter into the prepared pan, spoon chocolate mixture over top, spreading evenly, and top with remaining half batter. Bake as above.

> **TIP:** Cut a pound cake into slices, arrange in a circle around edge of serving plate, and place scoops of chocolate, strawberry and vanilla ice cream in the center so that everyone can pick their favorite flavor to top their slice of cake.

Cranberry Pound Cake

Serves 12 to16		
3 cups	all-purpose flour	750 mL
1 tsp	baking powder	5 mL
Pinch	salt	Pinch
5	eggs	5
1¼ cups	butter or margarine, softened	300 mL
2½ cups	granulated sugar	625 mL
1 tsp	almond extract or vanilla	5 mL
1 cup	evaporated milk	250 mL
2 cups	chopped fresh cranberries (or frozen, thawed)	500 mL
	Confectioner's (icing) sugar (optional)	

Preheat oven to 350°F (180°C)

10-inch (3L) Bundt pan, greased and floured

1. In a medium bowl, mix together flour, baking powder and salt.
2. In a large mixer bowl, cream butter and sugar until smooth. Beat in eggs, one at a time, beating on medium speed after each addition. Add almond extract and beat until light and fluffy.
3. Stir in flour mixture alternately with milk, making 3 additions of flour and 2 of milk, mixing gently until blended. Gently fold in cranberries until all ingredients are well combined. Pour into prepared baking pan.
4. Bake in preheated oven for 75 minutes, or until a toothpick inserted in the center comes out clean and dry. Cool in pan on a wire rack for 10 minutes, then remove and cool completely on a wire rack. Sprinkle confectioner's sugar over top, if desired.

Pumpkin Pound Cake

Serves 16 to 20		
3 cups	all-purpose flour	750 mL
½ tsp	salt	2 mL
½ tsp	baking powder	2 mL
1 tsp	ground cinnamon	5 mL
¼ tsp	ground cloves	1 mL
½ tsp	ground ginger	2 mL
1½ cups	butter or margarine, softened	375 mL
2½ cups	granulated sugar	625 mL
1 tsp	vanilla	5 mL
6	eggs	6
1 cup	canned or cooked pumpkin purée (not pie filling)	250 mL

Preheat oven to 350°F (180°C)

Two 9- by 5-inch (2 L) metal loaf pans, greased and floured

1. In a medium bowl, combine flour, salt, baking powder, cinnamon, cloves and ginger.
2. In a large mixer bowl, cream butter, sugar and vanilla on medium speed until smooth. Beat in eggs, one at a time, beating after each addition, until well blended.
3. Beat in flour mixture alternately with pumpkin, making 3 additions of flour and 2 of pumpkin, on low speed, beating only until well combined. Spoon into the two prepared baking pans, dividing evenly.
4. Bake in preheated oven for 60 to 70 minutes, or until a toothpick inserted in the center comes out clean and dry. Cool in pans on a wire rack for 10 minutes and then remove to wire racks to cool completely.

TIP: For a special treat, and to use up leftover pound cake slices, melt about ¼ cup (50 mL) of butter in a skillet and fry slices on each side to brown. Place slices on a plate and top each slice with a spoonful of strawberry jam and a dollop of whipped topping.

Chocolate-Glazed Pound Cake

Serves 12 to 16		
3 cups	all-purpose flour	750 mL
Pinch	salt	Pinch
1 tsp	baking powder	5 mL
½ cup	sifted unsweetened cocoa powder	125 mL
2⅔ cups	granulated sugar	650 mL
1¼ cups	butter, softened	300 mL
5	eggs	5
1 tsp	vanilla	5 mL
1 cup	evaporated milk	250 mL
GLAZE		
2 tbsp	butter or margarine	25 mL
½ cup	semi-sweet chocolate chips	125 mL
1¼ cups	confectioner's (icing) sugar	300 mL
½ tsp	vanilla	2 mL
3 to 4 tbsp	milk	45 to 50 mL

NOTE: You could omit glaze and dust top of cake with confectioner's sugar.

Preheat oven to 350°F (180°C)

10-inch (3 L) Bundt or 10-inch (4 L) tube baking pan, greased and floured

1. In a medium bowl, combine flour, salt, baking powder and cocoa.

2. In a large mixer bowl, cream sugar and butter on medium speed until smooth. Beat in eggs, one at a time, beating after each addition. Add vanilla and beat until well blended.

3. Stir in flour mixture alternately with the milk, making 3 additions of flour and 2 of milk, mixing after each addition until well combined. Spoon into prepared baking pan.

4. Bake in preheated oven for 70 to 75 minutes, or until a toothpick inserted in the center comes out clean and dry. Cool in pan on a wire rack for 10 minutes, then loosen edges of cake with a narrow spatula or knife and invert onto wire rack or plate to cool completely.

5. *Prepare glaze:* Melt butter and chocolate chips in a small saucepan over low heat. Remove from heat and add confectioner's sugar, vanilla and 3 tbsp (45 mL) milk. Whisk until blended and smooth, adding more milk as necessary to make a drizzling consistency. Drizzle over cooled cake.

VARIATION

Chocolate Chip Pound Cake: Omit cocoa and fold 2 cups (500 mL) of semi-sweet chocolate chips into the batter, until well combined. Bake as above. Dust top with confectioner's sugar when cooled, if desired.

Easy Banana Pound Cake

1	package (about 18.25 oz/515 g) yellow cake mix	1
½ cup	water	125 mL
⅓ cup	vegetable oil	75 mL
4	eggs	4
1	package (4-serving size) instant vanilla pudding mix	1
½ tsp	ground cinnamon	2 mL
½ tsp	ground nutmeg	2 mL
1½ cups	mashed ripe bananas (4 to 5 medium)	375 mL
	Confectioner's (icing) sugar (optional)	

Preheat oven to 350°F (180°C)

10-inch (3 L) Bundt pan, greased and floured

1. In a large mixer bowl, combine cake mix, water, oil and eggs. Mix together on medium speed until blended.
2. Stir in pudding mix, cinnamon and nutmeg. Add mashed bananas and mix well until thoroughly blended. Pour into prepared baking pan, smoothing top.
3. Bake in preheated oven for 55 to 60 minutes, or until a toothpick inserted in the center comes out clean and dry. Cool in pan on a wire rack for 20 to 25 minutes, and then remove to cool completely on wire rack. Dust with confectioner's sugar, if desired.

Raspberry Ice Cream Pound Cake

2¾ cups	cake flour, sifted	675 mL
2 tsp	baking powder	10 mL
¼ tsp	salt	1 mL
1 cup	granulated sugar	250 mL
1 cup	butter or margarine, softened	250 mL
1½ tsp	vanilla	7 mL
3	eggs	3
⅔ cup	milk	150 mL
2 cups	vanilla ice cream	500 mL
	Raspberry jam	

Preheat oven to 325°F (160°C)

9- by 5-inch (1.5 L) metal loaf pan, greased

1. In a medium bowl, sift together flour, baking powder and salt.
2. In a large mixer bowl, cream sugar and butter on medium speed until smooth. Beat in vanilla, and then eggs, one at a time, until well blended.
3. Stir in flour mixture alternately with milk, making 3 additions of flour and 2 of milk, on low speed, mixing well until thoroughly combined. Spoon into prepared baking pan.
4. Bake in preheated oven for 70 to 75 minutes, or until a toothpick inserted in the center comes out clean and dry. Cool on wire rack. Meanwhile, soften ice cream in refrigerator just until soft enough to spread.
5. Slice cake into 3 layers. Place first layer on a freezer-safe plate and spread jam evenly and thickly on top. Cover with second layer of cake and spread ice cream over top. Top with the remaining layer and spread jam thickly and evenly over top. Freeze until firm, and then slice and serve.

Apple Crumb Coffee Cake

Serves 12 to 16

3¼ cups	all-purpose flour	800 mL
1½ tsp	baking powder	7 mL
¾ tsp	baking soda	4 mL
¾ cup	butter or margarine, softened	175 mL
1¼ cups	granulated sugar	300 mL
3	eggs	3
2 tsp	vanilla	10 mL
2 cups	plain low-fat yogurt	500 mL
2	apples (such as Golden Delicious), peeled, cored and chopped	2

CRUMB TOPPING

1¼ cups	firmly packed brown sugar	300 mL
¾ cup	all-purpose flour	175 mL
½ cup	cold butter or margarine, cut into small chunks	125 mL
2 tsp	ground cinnamon	10 mL
1 cup	chopped nuts (optional)	250 mL

Preheat oven to 350°F (180°C)

10-inch (3 L) Bundt pan, greased and floured

1. *Prepare Crumb Topping:* In a medium bowl, combine brown sugar, flour, butter and cinnamon. Use a pastry blender or fork to mix until mixture is coarse and crumbly and the butter is well incorporated. Stir in the nuts, if using, and mix well. Set aside.

2. In another bowl, combine flour, baking powder and baking soda.

3. In a large mixer bowl, cream butter and sugar on medium speed until smooth and fluffy. Beat in eggs, one at a time, beating well after each addition. Add vanilla and yogurt and beat on low speed until blended. Beat in flour mixture, beating on low speed until well blended.

4. Spoon half of the batter into the prepared baking pan. Sprinkle evenly with ¼ cup (50 mL) of the crumb topping, then the apples, and then ½ cup (125 mL) of the crumb topping. Spoon on the remaining batter and top with the remaining crumb topping.

5. Bake in preheated oven for 55 to 60 minutes, or until a toothpick inserted in the center comes out clean and dry. Cool in pan on a wire rack for 10 minutes. Put a large plate over top and carefully invert. Remove pan. Place another plate on top of cake and invert so that crumb topping is facing up. Cool completely.

Babka

Serves 16 to 20		
1 cup	warm milk	250 mL
1	envelope (1/4 oz/7 g) active dry yeast or 1 cake (1 oz/30 g) compressed yeast	1
3/4 cup	granulated sugar, divided	175 mL
1/4 tsp	salt	1 mL
3 3/4 cups	all-purpose flour, divided	925 mL
1/2 cup	butter, softened	125 mL
3	eggs, well beaten	3
1 tbsp	grated lemon zest	15 mL
1/2 cup	raisins	125 mL
1/4 cup	butter, melted	50 mL

STREUSEL TOPPING

1/2 cup	firmly packed brown sugar	125 mL
1/2 cup	chopped nuts	125 mL
1/4 cup	all-purpose flour	50 mL
3 tbsp	butter, melted	45 mL
1 1/2 tsp	ground cinnamon	7 mL

A yeast-batter coffee cake

Two 8-inch (2 L) square metal baking pans, well greased

1. In a small bowl, sprinkle yeast (or mash, if using compressed yeast) over 1/4 cup (50 mL) of the warm milk. If using dry yeast, let stand for 10 minutes, or until foamy. Then add the remaining milk, 1 tsp (5 mL) of the sugar and 1 cup (250 mL) of the flour. Beat well and let rise until the mixture is at least 1 1/2 times the original size and is spongy, about 30 minutes.

2. In a large mixer bowl, cream the softened butter and remaining sugar on medium speed until smooth. Beat in the eggs and the yeast mixture, beating until thoroughly blended.

3. Add lemon zest, raisins and the remaining flour, beating on low speed. Mix well until batter is smooth and thick. Cover and let rise in a warm draft-free place until doubled in size, about 1 1/2 hours.

4. When dough is doubled, stir to deflate bubbles. Divide batter in half and place each half in the prepared baking pans, pressing out to edges with a moistened spatula. Cover and let rise again until doubled in size, about 1 hour.

5. Preheat oven to 375°F (190°C).

6. *Prepare Streusel Topping:* In another bowl, mix together brown sugar, chopped nuts, flour, melted butter and cinnamon until mixture resembles coarse crumbs. Brush dough with melted butter, if desired. Sprinkle streusel topping over top.

7. Bake in preheated oven for 45 to 50 minutes, or until lightly browned. Cool completely in pans on wire racks.

Banana Chip Coffee Cake

Serves 12 to 16		
3 cups	all-purpose flour	750 mL
2 tsp	baking powder	10 mL
2 tsp	baking soda	10 mL
2	eggs	2
1¾ cups	granulated sugar	425 mL
1 cup	butter or margarine, softened	250 mL
1 tsp	vanilla	5 mL
2 cups	mashed ripe bananas (about 6 medium)	500 mL
1 cup	sour cream	250 mL

TOPPING

½ cup	firmly packed brown sugar	125 mL
1½ tsp	ground cinnamon	7 mL
1 cup	semi-sweet chocolate chips	250 mL

Preheat oven to 350°F (180°C)

13- by 9-inch (3 L) metal baking pan, greased

1. *Prepare topping:* In a small bowl, combine brown sugar and cinnamon and mix well to blend.

2. In a medium bowl, sift together flour, baking powder and baking soda.

3. In a large mixer bowl, beat eggs, sugar and butter on medium speed until smooth. Add vanilla and bananas. Mix until smooth and well blended.

4. Stir in flour mixture alternately with sour cream, making 3 additions of flour and 2 of sour cream, mixing until well incorporated.

5. Spoon half of the batter into the prepared baking pan. Sprinkle half of the topping mixture over batter and then half of the chocolate chips. Spoon on remaining batter. Sprinkle on remaining topping mixture, and then top with the remaining chocolate chips.

6. Bake in preheated oven for 50 to 55 minutes, or until a toothpick inserted in the center comes out clean and dry. Cool completely in pan on a wire rack before removing to a serving plate.

TIP: If your cake falls but still tastes great, cut it into squares and serve with a sauce, or dip squares in melted chocolate for instant petits fours.

Blueberry Streusel Coffee Cake

Serves 8 to 10		
2 cups	all-purpose flour	500 mL
1 tsp	baking powder	5 mL
1 tsp	baking soda	5 mL
¼ tsp	salt	1 mL
¾ cup	granulated sugar	175 mL
¾ cup	butter or margarine, softened	175 mL
1	egg	1
1 tsp	vanilla	5 mL
1 cup	sour cream or buttermilk	250 mL
2 cups	blueberries, fresh (or well-drained, thawed frozen blueberries)	500 mL

STREUSEL TOPPING

½ cup	lightly packed brown sugar	125 mL
2 tbsp	butter or margarine, melted	25 mL
1 tbsp	all-purpose flour	15 mL
2 tsp	ground cinnamon	10 mL

Preheat oven to 350°F (180°C)

9-inch (23 cm) springform pan, greased

1. *Prepare Streusel Topping:* In a small bowl, mix together brown sugar, melted butter, flour and cinnamon until blended and crumbly.

2. In a medium bowl, combine flour, baking powder, baking soda and salt.

3. In a large mixer bowl, cream sugar and butter on medium speed until smooth. Add egg, vanilla and sour cream and beat on low speed until well blended. Beat in flour mixture on low speed until well blended.

4. Pour about ⅔ of the batter into the prepared baking pan, spreading evenly. Top with blueberries. Spoon remaining batter evenly over blueberry filling. Sprinkle streusel topping over top.

5. Bake in preheated oven for 60 to 70 minutes, or until a toothpick inserted in the center comes out clean and dry. Cool completely in pan on wire rack before removing cake.

Chocolate Swirl Coffee Cake

Serves 6 to 8		
2 cups	prepared biscuit mix	500 mL
¼ cup	granulated sugar	50 mL
1	egg	1
⅔ cup	milk	150 mL
2 tbsp	butter or margarine, melted	25 mL
½ cup	semi-sweet chocolate pieces or chips, melted	125 mL

Preheat oven to 400°F (200°C)

8- or 9-inch (20 or 23 cm) round metal baking pan, greased

1. In a large mixer bowl, combine biscuit mix, sugar, egg, milk and butter. Beat on medium speed until thoroughly combined.

2. Pour into prepared baking pan, smoothing top. Spoon the melted chocolate over top and cut through the batter several times with a knife for a swirl or marbled effect.

3. Bake in preheated oven for 20 to 25 minutes, or until a toothpick inserted in the center comes out clean and dry. Cool completely in pan on a wire rack.

VARIATION

Cherry Swirl Coffee Cake: Omit chocolate and replace with 1 can (19 oz/540 mL) cherry pie filling. If desired, top with a streusel topping (see above) and sprinkle ¼ cup (50 mL) sliced almonds over top.

Glazed Lemon Coffee Cake

Serves 12 to 16		
1¾ cups	cake flour	425 mL
2 tsp	baking powder	10 mL
1 tsp	baking soda	5 mL
1 cup	evaporated milk	250 mL
1 tsp	grated lemon zest	5 mL
2 tbsp	lemon juice	25 mL
½ cup	butter or margarine, softened	125 mL
1 cup	granulated sugar	250 mL
2	eggs, well beaten	2

SUGAR-CINNAMON MIXTURE

½ cup	lightly packed brown sugar	125 mL
1 tbsp	ground cinnamon	15 mL

LEMON GLAZE

1¾ cups	confectioner's (icing) sugar, sifted	425 mL
2 tbsp	lemon juice	25 mL

Preheat oven to 350°F (180°C)

10-inch (4 L) tube pan, greased and floured

1. *Prepare Sugar-Cinnamon Mixture:* In a small bowl, mix together brown sugar and cinnamon. Set aside.

2. In a medium bowl, sift together flour and baking powder.

3. In another bowl, combine baking soda, milk and lemon juice. Mix well.

4. In a large mixer bowl, cream butter and sugar on medium speed until light and fluffy. Add eggs and lemon zest, beating on low until blended. Beat in flour mixture alternately with the milk mixture, making 3 additions of flour and 2 of milk, on low speed, beating until well combined.

5. Pour half of the batter into prepared baking pan. Sprinkle half of the sugar-cinnamon mixture over top. Spoon on remaining batter and sprinkle remaining sugar-cinnamon over top.

6. Bake in preheated oven for 45 to 50 minutes, or until a toothpick inserted in the center comes out clean and dry. Cool in pan on a wire rack for 10 minutes, and then remove from pan to cool completely on wire rack.

7. *Prepare Lemon Glaze:* In a small bowl, mix together confectioner's sugar and lemon juice until the right consistency for drizzling. Spread over top of cooled cake and drizzle over the edges.

> **TIP:** When greasing a baking pan, if the shortening is cold and not spreading easily, turn your baking pan upside down and hold it under the hot water tap for just a few seconds. When the pan feels warm, the shortening will spread easily.

Raspberry Cream Coffee Cake

¾ cup	cold butter or margarine	175 mL
2¼ cups	all-purpose flour	550 mL
½ cup	granulated sugar	125 mL
½ tsp	baking powder	2 mL
½ tsp	baking soda	2 mL
¾ cup	sour cream	175 mL
1	egg	1
1 tsp	grated lemon zest	5 mL
½ cup	raspberry jam	125 mL

CREAM CHEESE FILLING

8 oz	cream cheese, softened	250 g
1	egg	1
⅓ cup	granulated sugar	75 mL

Preheat oven to 350°F (180°C)

9-inch (23 cm) springform pan, greased

1. In a large bowl, combine butter, flour and sugar, cutting in the butter with 2 knives or a pastry blender until mixture resembles coarse crumbs. Take 1 cup (250 mL) of this crumb mixture and set aside.

2. Stir baking powder and baking soda into the remaining crumb mixture.

3. In a small bowl, whisk together sour cream, egg and zest. Add to the crumb mixture and mix just until moistened and blended. Spoon into prepared baking pan, spreading over bottom and part way up the sides.

4. *Prepare Cream Cheese Filling:* In a small mixer bowl, combine cream cheese, egg and sugar on medium speed and beat until well blended. Pour over the batter in the pan. Spoon jam carefully over the filling. Sprinkle the reserved crumb mixture over top.

5. Bake in preheated oven for 45 to 50 minutes, or until cake is golden brown and filling is firmly set. Cool completely in pan on wire rack.

Strawberry Rhubarb Coffee Cake

	Serves 12 to 16	
3 cups	all-purpose flour	750 mL
1 cup	granulated sugar	250 mL
1 tsp	baking powder	5 mL
1 tsp	baking soda	5 mL
1 tsp	salt	5 mL
1 cup	butter or margarine, softened	250 mL
1 cup	buttermilk	250 mL
1 tsp	vanilla	5 mL
2	eggs, slightly beaten	2

FILLING

3 cups	small chunks fresh rhubarb	750 mL
1	package (10 oz/300 g) frozen unsweetened strawberries	1
2 tbsp	lemon juice	25 mL
1 cup	granulated sugar	250 mL
1/3 cup	cornstarch	75 mL

TOPPING

3/4 cup	granulated sugar	175 mL
1/2 cup	all-purpose flour	125 mL
1/4 cup	butter or margarine, softened	50 mL

Preheat oven to 350°F (180°C)

13- by 9-inch (3 L) metal baking pan, greased

1. *Prepare filling:* Combine rhubarb and strawberries in a saucepan over low heat and cook covered for 5 to 6 minutes, until thoroughly heated. Add lemon juice and mix well. Mix together sugar and cornstarch and stir into mixture. Cook until thick, about 5 minutes, and set aside to cool to room temperature, about 10 to 15 minutes.

2. *Prepare topping:* In a small bowl, combine sugar and flour. Cut in butter to make fine crumbs. Set aside.

3. In a large bowl, combine flour, sugar, baking powder, baking soda and salt. Cut in butter with 2 knives or a pastry blender until mixture resembles fine crumbs.

4. In another bowl, whisk buttermilk, vanilla and eggs until well combined. Stir into flour mixture just until moistened and thoroughly blended.

5. Spoon half of the batter into prepared baking pan. Spoon filling over top of batter in pan. Top with remaining batter. Swirl through with a knife or spoon. Sprinkle topping evenly over batter.

6. Bake in preheated oven for 40 to 45 minutes, or until top becomes golden brown. Cool completely in pan on wire rack.

Banana Nut Loaf

	Serves 8 to 10	
2 cups	all-purpose flour	500 mL
¾ cup	granulated sugar	175 mL
1 tsp	baking powder	5 mL
½ tsp	baking soda	2 mL
¼ tsp	salt	1 mL
2	eggs	2
1 tsp	vanilla	5 mL
¼ cup	buttermilk	50 mL
¼ cup	butter or margarine, melted and cooled	50 mL
1½ cups	mashed ripe bananas (about 4 to 5 medium)	375 mL
¾ cup	chopped nuts	175 mL

NOTE: If desired, replace nuts with ¾ cup (175 mL) chocolate chips, or use both nuts and chocolate chips (½ cup/125 mL each).

Preheat oven to 350°F (180°C)
9- by 5-inch (1.5 L) metal loaf pan, greased

1. In a medium bowl, combine flour, sugar, baking powder, baking soda and salt.
2. In a large bowl, whisk together eggs, vanilla, buttermilk and butter until well blended.
3. Gradually stir in flour mixture. Stir in mashed bananas and mix until just moistened and blended. Do not over-mix. Fold in chopped nuts and mix well. Pour into prepared baking pan, spreading evenly.
4. Bake in preheated oven for 50 to 60 minutes, or until a toothpick inserted in the center comes out clean and dry. Cool in pan on a wire rack for 10 minutes. Loosen around edges of cake with a knife or spatula. Remove onto wire rack to cool completely.

Lemon Tea Loaf

	Serves 8 to 10	
1½ cups	all-purpose flour	375 mL
1 tsp	baking powder	5 mL
Pinch	salt	Pinch
1 tbsp	grated lemon zest	15 mL
½ cup	butter or margarine, softened	125 mL
1 cup	granulated sugar	250 mL
2	eggs	2
½ cup	milk	125 mL

LEMON SYRUP

1¾ cup	confectioner's (icing) sugar, sifted	425 mL
2 tbsp	lemon juice	25 mL

Preheat oven to 350°F (180°C)
9- by 5-inch (1.5 L) metal loaf pan, greased and floured

1. In a medium bowl, combine flour, baking powder, salt and lemon zest.
2. In a large mixer bowl, cream butter and sugar on medium speed until smooth. Beat in eggs, one at a time, beating until blended and light and fluffy.
3. Stir in flour mixture alternately with milk, making 3 additions of flour and 2 of milk, until thoroughly combined. Pour into prepared baking pan.
4. Bake in preheated oven for 45 to 50 minutes, or until a toothpick inserted in the center comes out clean and dry. Let cool in pan on a wire rack for 10 minutes and then remove to a wire rack.
5. *Prepare Lemon Syrup:* In a small bowl, mix together sugar and lemon juice. Cool slightly.
6. Pierce the top of the loaf all over with a fork, and drizzle lemon syrup over top. Cool loaf completely before serving.

Glazed Chocolate Pumpkin Loaf

Serves 16 to 20

3⅓ cups	all-purpose flour	825 mL
3 cups	granulated sugar	750 mL
2 tsp	baking soda	10 mL
1 tsp	salt	5 mL
1 tsp	ground cinnamon	5 mL
1 tsp	ground nutmeg	5 mL
4	eggs, lightly beaten	4
1 cup	vegetable oil	250 mL
⅔ cup	water	150 mL
2 cups	canned or cooked pumpkin purée (not pie filling)	500 mL
½ cup	chopped nuts	125 mL
4 oz	semi-sweet chocolate, melted and cooled	125 g

ICING SUGAR GLAZE

1½ cups	confectioner's (icing) sugar, sifted	375 mL
4 to 6 tsp	cold water	20 to 30 mL
1 oz	semi-sweet chocolate, melted and cooled	30 g
2 to 4 tsp	hot water	10 to 20 mL

NOTE: Cooled, unglazed loaf can be wrapped (sliced or unsliced) and frozen for up to 1 month. Thaw (wrapped) in refrigerator overnight. Glaze before serving.

Preheat oven to 350°F (180°C)

Two 9- by 5-inch (1.5 L) metal loaf pans, greased and floured

1. In a large bowl, combine flour, baking soda, salt, sugar, cinnamon and nutmeg, and mix together thoroughly.

2. In a medium bowl, whisk together eggs, oil, water and pumpkin until well blended. Pour into the flour mixture, mixing just until well blended. Fold in nuts.

3. Transfer 2 cups (500 mL) of batter to a small bowl, add the melted chocolate and mix well.

4. Spoon ½ of the remaining plain batter into the two prepared baking pans, ¼ in each. Spoon chocolate batter over top, ½ in each pan. Spoon remaining plain batter, ½ in each pan, over the chocolate batter.

5. Bake in preheated oven for 60 to 65 minutes, or until a toothpick inserted in the center comes out clean and dry. Cool in pans on a wire rack for 10 minutes, and then remove onto wire rack to cool completely.

6. *Prepare Icing Sugar Glaze:* In a small bowl, mix together confectioner's sugar and cold water until the right drizzling consistency. Transfer half to a separate bowl. To one bowl, stir in chocolate and enough of the hot water for it to be the right consistency for drizzling.

7. Drizzle white glaze in a zigzag pattern on top of one loaf, and do the same with the chocolate glaze on the second loaf. Or do a zigzag pattern with white and chocolate glaze on each loaf. If not using both loaves immediately, they can be frozen for up to six months, well wrapped first in plastic wrap, then in a freezer bag.

TIP: Make a special pumpkin ice cream sundae: soften 2 cups (500 mL) of vanilla or butter pecan ice cream just slightly, stir in 1 can (19 oz/540 mL) of pumpkin purée, then cinnamon and nutmeg. Spoon into custard cups, sprinkle with some graham wafer crumbs, and then place in freezer for an hour.

Nut Loaf

Serves 8 to 10		
3 cups	all-purpose flour	750 ml
1 tbsp	baking powder	15 mL
¼ tsp	salt	1 mL
1 cup	butter or margarine, softened	250 mL
1¾ cups	granulated sugar	425 mL
3	eggs, separated	3
1 tsp	vanilla	5 mL
¼ cup	milk	50 mL
1 cup	chopped nuts (pecans or walnuts)	250 mL

Preheat oven to 350°F (180°C)

9- by 5-inch (1.5 L) metal loaf pan, well greased and floured

1. In a medium bowl, sift together flour, baking powder and salt.

2. In a large mixer bowl, cream butter and sugar on medium speed until smooth. Add egg yolks and vanilla and beat until light and fluffy.

3. Stir in flour mixture alternately with milk, making 3 additions of flour and 2 of milk, until well blended.

4. In a small mixer bowl with clean beaters, beat egg whites on high speed until stiff peaks form. Fold into batter gently. Add nuts, folding until well combined. Pour into prepared baking pan.

5. Bake in preheated oven for 50 to 60 minutes, or until a toothpick inserted in the center comes out clean and dry. Cool in pan on a wire rack for 10 minutes, then remove onto wire rack to cool completely.

VARIATION

Cranberry Nut Loaf: Use chopped pecans and add 1 cup (250 mL) cranberries to the nuts. Change granulated sugar to 1 cup (250 mL) granulated sugar and ¾ cup (175 mL) firmly packed brown sugar.

Raspberry Swirl Loaf

Serves 8 to 10

1½ cups	all-purpose flour	375 mL
¾ cup	firmly packed brown sugar	175 mL
2 tsp	baking powder	10 mL
1 tsp	ground cardamom	5 mL
½ cup	butter or margarine	125 mL
2	eggs	2
¾ cup	buttermilk	175 mL
6 tbsp	seedless raspberry jam	90 mL

Preheat oven to 350°F (180°C)

9- by 5-inch (1.5 L) metal loaf pan, greased and floured

1. In a large bowl, combine flour, brown sugar, baking powder and cardamom and mix well. Cut in butter with 2 knives or a pastry blender to form coarse crumb mixture.

2. In a small bowl, combine eggs and buttermilk and whisk until blended. Stir into flour mixture until well combined.

3. Spoon about ⅓ of the batter onto the bottom of the prepared baking pan. Drop 2 tbsp (25 mL) of the jam in two long strips lengthwise (1 tbsp/15 mL each) over the batter in the bottom of the pan. Swirl through with a knife or spatula.

4. Top with another ½ of the remaining batter, dropping another 2 tbsp (25 mL) of jam over top of that layer. Swirl through again with a knife or spatula. Top with the remaining batter and the remaining 2 tbsp (25 mL) of jam and swirl one more time with a knife.

5. Bake in preheated oven for 40 to 50 minutes, or until a toothpick inserted in the center comes out clean and dry. Cool in pan on a wire rack for 10 minutes and then remove onto wire rack to cool completely.

> **TIP:** If you have left your cake in the pan for too long, and it just won't come out, try dipping the pan quickly in hot water (like a gelatin mold), or put in a slow oven, 250°F (120°C), for 3 to 5 minutes. If all else fails, leave cake in pan and decorate with frosting, then slice.

Easy Baked Alaska Loaf

Serves 8 to 10

1	package (about 18.25 oz/515 g) chocolate cake mix	1
1	brick (1 qt/1 L) strawberry or Neapolitan ice cream (or any other favorite flavor), keep in freezer	1

WHITE FLUFFY FROSTING

1/4 tsp	cream of tartar	1 mL
2	egg whites	2
1 tbsp	water	15 mL
2 tbsp	light corn syrup	25 mL
1 1/2 tsp	vanilla	7 mL
1/2 tsp	lemon extract	2 mL
2 1/2 cups	confectioner's (icing) sugar, sifted	625 mL

Preheat oven according to cake mix instructions

9-inch (2.5 L) square metal baking pan, greased and floured

1. Prepare chocolate cake mix according to the directions on the package. Pour batter into prepared baking pan.

2. Bake in preheated oven for time indicated on cake mix package. Allow cake to cool in pan for about 10 minutes. Remove from pan and cool completely on wire rack.

3. Cut off top of cake to make flat, if necessary. Cut cake to 1/2-inch (1 cm) larger than the brick of ice cream on all sides and place on an ovenproof serving plate.

4. *Prepare White Fluffy Frosting:* In a medium mixer bowl, beat cream of tartar and egg whites on high speed until firm peaks form. In a small bowl, mix together water, corn syrup, vanilla and lemon extract. Add to the egg white mixture, alternating with the confectioner's sugar and beating well after each addition, until frosting is creamy, stiff and easy to spread.

5. Remove ice cream from freezer. Place in center of the trimmed cake layer. Quickly spread the frosting over the ice cream and cake, making sure that you seal the edges of the cake all around.

6. Raise temperature in oven to 500°F (260°C) and place frosted loaf into hot oven for 4 to 5 minutes, or until the meringue-type frosting is golden brown. Serve immediately.

TIP: To cut a 2 qt (2 L) brick of ice cream to fit this cake, open up one end and top of box and stand ice cream brick vertically on remaining closed end. Cut in half lengthwise. Freeze remaining ice cream for another use.

Layer Cakes and Tortes

Butterscotch Layer Cake

Serves 12 to 16		
2¼ cups	all-purpose flour	550 mL
1 tsp	baking soda	5 mL
1 tsp	salt	5 mL
½ tsp	baking powder	2 mL
⅔ cup	chopped butterscotch candies	150 mL
¼ cup	water	50 mL
1 cup	granulated sugar	250 mL
½ cup	butter or margarine, softened	125 mL
3	eggs	3
1 cup	buttermilk or sour cream	250 mL

COCONUT TOPPING

½ cup	granulated sugar	125 mL
⅔ cup	evaporated milk	150 mL
1 tbsp	cornstarch	15 mL
⅓ cup	butterscotch pieces	75 mL
2 tbsp	butter or margarine	25 mL
1 cup	flaked coconut (sweetened or unsweetened)	250 mL
½ cup	chopped nuts	125 mL
	Whipped cream or whipped topping	

Preheat oven to 375°F (190°C)

Two 9-inch (23 cm) round metal baking pans, greased and floured

1. In a medium bowl, sift together flour, baking soda, salt and baking powder.

2. In a small saucepan, over low heat, stir butterscotch and water, stirring constantly, until the pieces melt. Set aside to cool to room temperature, about 10 to 15 minutes.

3. In a large mixer bowl, on medium speed, cream sugar and butter until smooth. Add eggs, one at a time, beating after each addition, until well blended. Stir in cooled butterscotch mixture and mix well. Add flour mixture to creamed mixture alternately with the buttermilk, making 3 additions of flour and 2 of buttermilk, beating on low speed until well incorporated. Spoon into prepared baking pans, dividing evenly.

4. Bake in preheated oven for 25 to 30 minutes, or until a toothpick inserted in the center comes out clean and dry. Cool in pans on wire racks for 10 minutes, then remove from pans onto wire racks to cool completely.

5. *Prepare Coconut Topping:* In a medium saucepan, combine sugar, evaporated milk and cornstarch. Cook over medium heat, stirring until boiling and thickened. Remove from heat and stir in the butterscotch and butter, stirring until these have melted. Add coconut and nuts and mix well. Cool.

6. Spread the topping on each cake layer, dividing evenly. Place one cake layer on a serving plate. Top with the other cake layer. Frost the sides of the cake with whipped cream. Pipe some whipped cream around top edge of layered cake, making a border about ½ inch (1 cm) wide all around the top edges. Keep refrigerated until ready to serve.

TIP: When a recipe calls for flaked coconut, it means dried coconut. It is used in recipes where fresh coconut would add unwanted additional moisture.

Classic Red Devil's Cake

Serves 12 to 16

2½ cups	cake flour	625 mL
½ cup	unsweetened cocoa powder	125 mL
1½ tsp	baking soda	7 mL
1 tsp	salt	5 mL
1¾ cups	granulated sugar, divided	425 mL
½ cup	butter or margarine or shortening, softened	125 mL
1 tsp	vanilla	5 mL
1 tsp	red food coloring	5 mL
3	eggs, separated	3
1⅓ cups	water	325 mL

WHITE FROSTING

1 cup	milk	250 mL
⅓ cup	all-purpose flour	75 mL
1 cup	granulated sugar	250 mL
1 cup	butter or margarine, softened	250 mL
2 tsp	vanilla	10 mL

Sometimes called Red Velvet Cake

Preheat oven to 350°F (180°C)

Two 8-inch (20 cm) round metal baking pans, lightly greased and floured

1. In a medium bowl, sift together flour, cocoa, baking soda and salt.

2. In a large mixer bowl, on medium speed, cream 1 cup (250 mL) of the sugar and butter until smooth. Add vanilla, red food coloring and then egg yolks, one at a time, beating after each addition.

3. Add flour mixture to creamed mixture alternately with the water, making 3 additions of flour and 2 of water, beating on low speed until well blended.

4. In a small mixer bowl with clean beaters, on high speed, beat egg whites until soft peaks form. Gradually add the remaining ¾ cup (175 mL) of sugar, by spoonfuls, and beat until stiff peaks form. Gently fold into batter until well blended. Spoon into the two prepared baking pans, dividing evenly.

5. Bake in preheated oven for 35 to 45 minutes, or until a toothpick inserted in the center comes out clean and dry. Cool in pans on wire racks for 10 minutes, and then remove from pans onto wire racks to cool completely.

6. *Prepare White Frosting:* In a small saucepan, whisk milk and flour to blend. Bring to a boil over medium heat, stirring for 2 to 3 minutes, or until thickened. Cover and chill in refrigerator for at least 30 minutes.

7. In small mixer bowl, cream sugar and butter until smooth. Add the chilled milk mixture and beat for about 8 to 10 minutes, or until fluffy. Add vanilla and mix well. Spread ⅓ of the frosting on one cake layer, top with the other cake layer and frost top and sides.

TIP: Dust the layers of your cake lightly with confectioner's sugar before spreading on the filling to keep it from soaking into the cake.

Mom's Sour Cream Chocolate Layer Cake

	Serves 12 to 16	
2 cups	cake flour	500 mL
1¼ tsp	baking soda	6 mL
1 tsp	salt	5 mL
1 cup	water	250 mL
½ cup	butter or margarine	125 mL
4 oz	unsweetened chocolate, chopped	125 g
2 cups	granulated sugar	500 mL
1 cup	sour cream	250 mL
2	eggs	2
1½ tsp	vanilla	7 mL

CHOCOLATE SOUR CREAM FROSTING

1 cup	semi-sweet chocolate chips or pieces	250 mL
¼ cup	butter or margarine	50 mL
½ cup	sour cream	125 mL
2½ cups	confectioner's (icing) sugar, sifted	625 mL

Preheat oven to 350°F (180°C)

Two 8- or 9-inch (20 cm or 23 cm) round metal baking pans, greased and lightly floured

1. In a large mixer bowl, sift together flour, baking soda and salt.

2. Combine water, butter and chocolate in the top of a double boiler over simmering water, and heat until mixture is completely melted. Remove from heat and set aside to cool.

3. In another bowl, on medium speed, beat sugar, sour cream, eggs and vanilla until well blended. Stir in cooled chocolate mixture and beat until blended.

4. Pour chocolate mixture into flour mixture, gradually, and beat until smooth. Batter will be thin. Pour into prepared pans.

5. Bake in preheated oven for 35 to 40 minutes, or until top springs back when lightly touched, or a toothpick inserted in center comes out clean and dry. Cool in pans on wire racks for 10 minutes. Run a knife around edges to loosen cakes from pan. Remove from pans and leave to cool completely on wire racks.

6. *Prepare Chocolate Sour Cream Frosting:* In a saucepan over low heat, combine chocolate pieces and butter. Melt, stirring constantly. Set aside to cool for about 5 minutes.

7. Add sour cream and mix to blend. Gradually add the confectioner's sugar and beat until smooth and of the right consistency for spreading.

8. Place one cake layer on plate. Slice a small piece off of the top to make surface flat. Spread evenly with ⅓ of the frosting. Top with second cake layer. Spread remaining frosting over top and sides of layered cake.

> **TIP:** If your cake layer has sunk in the center, cut a circle out of the center of each layer. Stack your layers and frost as usual, thereby making a ring cake. You could fill the center with chopped fresh fruit or some whipped cream.

Hungarian Dobos Torte

Serves 12 to 16		
6	eggs, separated	6
⅔ cup	granulated sugar, divided	150 mL
1 cup	sifted all-purpose flour	250 mL
CHOCOLATE CREAM		
2 cups	milk	500 mL
1 tsp	vanilla	5 mL
6	egg yolks	6
¾ cup	granulated sugar	175 mL
⅓ cup	all-purpose flour, sifted	75 mL
Pinch	salt	Pinch
2 oz	unsweetened chocolate, melted	60 g
CARAMEL TOPPING		
½ cup	granulated sugar	125 mL

NOTE: The original, correct way to make this torte is to grease and flour cookie sheets with six 8-inch (20 cm) rounds by tracing around an 8-inch (20 cm) layer cake pan. If using the cookie sheet method, divide the batter into 6 portions and spread about 3/4 cup (175 mL) into each round traced on cookie sheets. Try to put 2 rounds on each sheet, and bake each separately at 350°F (180°C) for about 10 minutes, until lightly browned or cake springs back when touched lightly with your fingertip. Remove from sheets and then cool on wire racks.

Preheat oven to 350°F (180°C)

Three 8-inch (20 cm) round metal cake baking pans, greased and floured

1. In a large mixer bowl, on high speed, beat egg whites until frothy. Gradually add ⅓ cup (75 mL) of the sugar, by spoonfuls, beating until stiff, glossy peaks form.

2. In a small mixer bowl, beat egg yolks until frothy. Add remaining ⅓ cup (75 mL) of sugar, gradually, beating on high speed for about 5 to 6 minutes, or until mixture becomes lemon-colored and very thick. Fold gently into egg white mixture to blend. Then fold in the sifted flour, gently, just until blended. Spoon into the three prepared baking pans, dividing evenly.

3. Bake in preheated oven for 30 to 40 minutes, or until a toothpick inserted in the center comes out clean and dry. Cool in pans on wire racks for 10 minutes, then remove from pans onto wire racks to cool completely.

4. Slice each layer cake in half so that you have 6 layers, and slice off tops to flatten.

5. *Prepare Chocolate Cream:* In a double boiler over medium heat, heat milk just until steaming and bubbles form around edge of pan. In a mixer bowl, beat vanilla and egg yolks until foamy. Gradually add sugar and beat, on high speed, until lemon-colored and thick. Add the flour and salt, beating until blended. Beat in melted chocolate. Mix in scalded milk slowly. Return entire mixture to the double boiler and cook over simmering water, stirring constantly, for about 20 to 25 minutes, until thick. Strain, cover and refrigerate until completely cooled.

6. Set about ⅓ of the Chocolate Cream aside. Divide the remaining ⅔ of the Chocolate Cream into 4 equal portions, spread it evenly over each of 4 cake layers and stack, so that you have 5 stacked layers with cream between. Use the Chocolate Cream you set aside to frost over top and sides. Set in refrigerator to chill for at least 30 minutes.

7. *Prepare Caramel Topping:* In a heavy skillet over medium heat, melt sugar until golden. Spoon this quickly onto the remaining cake layer, spreading evenly. With a sharp, greased knife, mark into 8 or 12 wedges, cutting right through the sugar so that, when the topping hardens, this marking will make it easier to cut the cake.

8. Place this top onto chilled cake layers and chill until ready to serve.

Meringue Blitz Torte

1 cup	all-purpose flour	250 mL
1 tsp	baking powder	5 mL
Pinch	salt	Pinch
¾ cup	confectioner's (icing) sugar	175 mL
½ cup	butter or margarine, softened	125 mL
4	egg yolks	4
¼ cup	milk	50 mL
½ cup	sliced almonds	125 mL
2 tbsp	granulated sugar	25 mL
2 cups	ready-to-serve vanilla pudding	500 mL

MERINGUE TOPPING

4	egg whites	4
1 cup	granulated sugar	250 mL

Preheat oven to 350°F (180°C)

Two 8-inch (20 cm) round metal baking pans, greased and floured

1. *Prepare the Meringue Topping:* In a small mixer bowl, beat egg whites until foamy. Add the sugar, 1 tbsp (15 mL) at a time, beating until mixture is glossy and stiff peaks form. Set aside.

2. In a medium bowl, sift together flour, baking powder and salt.

3. In a large mixer bowl, combine the confectioner's sugar, butter, egg yolks and milk. Beat on low speed for 1 minute until blended.

4. Add flour mixture to the butter mixture and beat on medium speed for another 2 to 3 minutes, until well blended. Spoon batter into each prepared baking pan, dividing evenly.

5. Spread half of the meringue mixture on top of the batter in each pan, then sprinkle half of the almonds on top of each. Sprinkle the granulated sugar on top of the almonds in each pan.

6. Bake in preheated oven for 30 to 35 minutes, or until meringue is set and golden brown. Cool in pans for 10 minutes, then turn out on racks with meringue sides up and cool completely.

7. When cooled, place one cake on a serving plate, meringue side up, and spread the vanilla pudding evenly over top. Place the second cake on top of the pudding. Chill until ready to serve.

Mocha Hazelnut Torte

Serves 12 to 16		
4 tsp	instant coffee granules	20 mL
1¼ cups	milk	300 mL
3 cups	cake flour	750 mL
⅓ cup	sifted unsweetened cocoa powder	75 mL
1 tbsp	baking powder	15 mL
1 tsp	salt	5 mL
1½ cups	granulated sugar	375 mL
¾ cup	butter or margarine, softened	175 mL
6	egg yolks	6

MERINGUE TOPPING

6	egg whites	6
¾ cup	granulated sugar	175 mL
½ cup	chopped or sliced hazelnuts	125 mL

CREAM FILLING

1½ cups	whipping (35%) cream	375 mL
¼ cup	prepared strong coffee	50 mL

GLAZE

2 oz	semi-sweet chocolate, melted and cooled	60 g

Preheat oven to 350°F (180°C)

Three 9-inch (23 cm) round metal baking pans, lightly greased and floured

1. *Prepare coffee mixture first:* Mix together coffee granules and milk until dissolved. Set aside.

2. In a medium bowl, sift together cake flour, cocoa, baking powder and salt.

3. In a large mixer bowl, on medium speed, beat sugar and butter until smooth. Add egg yolks, one at a time, beating after each addition, until light and fluffy. Add flour mixture alternately with coffee mixture, making 3 additions of flour and 2 of coffee, beating on low speed until moistened and blended. Then beat on medium speed for 3 to 5 minutes until well blended. Pour batter into the three prepared baking pans, dividing evenly.

4. *Prepare Meringue Topping:* In a large, clean bowl, beat egg whites until soft peaks form. Gradually add sugar, by spoonfuls, beating until stiff peaks form. Spread lightly over top of the batter in each pan, dividing evenly. Sprinkle the hazelnuts over top in each pan.

5. Bake in preheated oven for 35 to 40 minutes, or until topping is a golden brown. Cool in pans on wire racks for 20 to 25 minutes and remove from pans onto wire racks to cool completely.

6. *Prepare Cream Filling:* In a mixer bowl, beat cream and coffee until stiff peaks form. Spread half of filling gently over the meringue side of one cake layer. Top with a second layer, meringue side up, and spread remaining filling on top. Top this with the remaining cake layer, with meringue side facing up.

7. Drizzle the melted chocolate over top and let it run down sides. Chill for at least 30 minutes, or until ready to serve.

> **TIP:** When whipping (35%) cream does not seem to whip properly, add 3 or 4 drops of lemon juice, or ½ tsp (2 mL) unflavored gelatin. Always use glass or metal mixing bowls to whip cream, and be sure that your beaters are thoroughly cleaned before whipping.

Peach Cream Torte

Serves 10 to 12		
1 cup	all-purpose flour, sifted	250 mL
¼ cup	granulated sugar	50 mL
6 tbsp	butter or margarine	90 mL
1	egg yolk, lightly beaten	1
2 cups	milk	500 mL
1	package (6 oz/175 g) coconut-cream pudding mix	1
4	medium-sized firm, ripe peaches, peeled, halved and pitted	4
	Water	
1 tsp	vanilla	5 mL
1½ cups	whipping (35%) cream	375 mL
GLAZE		
1½ tsp	cornstarch	7 mL
2 tbsp	light corn syrup	25 mL
1½ tsp	lemon juice	7 mL

1. In a medium bowl, sift together flour and sugar. Cut in butter with two knives, or a pastry blender, until mixture resembles coarse crumbs. Add beaten egg yolk and mix until a smooth, soft dough is formed and leaves side of bowl clean. Press into the bottom and up the side of baking pan, about 1½ inches (4 cm) high. Do not prick this shell.

2. Bake in preheated oven for 20 to 25 minutes or until golden brown. Cool completely in pan, on a wire rack.

3. In a medium saucepan over low heat, combine milk and pudding mix. Cook, following package directions, until thickened. Spoon into a large bowl, cover with plastic wrap and chill for about 2 hours.

4. Place peach halves in a single layer in a skillet. Add water to cover. Bring to a boil and then reduce to simmer for 2 to 3 minutes, until peaches are tender. Reserve 6 tbsp (90 mL) of this liquid in a small bowl. Drain the rest and set peaches aside to cool.

5. *Prepare glaze:* In a small saucepan over low heat, cook reserved liquid, cornstarch and corn syrup, stirring until mixture boils and becomes thick. Remove from heat and stir in lemon juice.

6. In a small mixer bowl, beat vanilla and whipping cream until stiff peaks form. Fold gradually into chilled pudding mixture in large bowl. Blend thoroughly and spoon over pastry in springform pan. Arrange peach halves, rounded side up, in a circle on top. Spoon glaze over top of peaches.

Angel Food, Chiffon and Sponge Cakes

Traditional Angel Food Cake

Serves 10 to 12		
1½ cups	confectioner's (icing) sugar	375 mL
1 cup	cake flour	250 mL
Pinch	salt	Pinch
10	egg whites, at room temperature (about 1¼ cups/300 mL)	10
1½ tsp	cream of tartar	7 mL
¾ cup	granulated sugar	175 mL
1 tsp	vanilla	5 mL
1 tsp	almond extract (optional)	5 mL

Preheat oven to 350°F (180°C)

10-inch (4 L) metal tube pan, ungreased

1. In a medium bowl, sift together confectioner's sugar, flour and salt.

2. In a large, clean mixer bowl, on high speed, beat egg whites and cream of tartar until foamy. Gradually add the granulated sugar, beating until stiff peaks form. Sift ⅓ of the flour mixture over the egg whites and fold in gently. Fold in remaining flour mixture, in two more portions, folding lightly just until well blended. Fold in vanilla and almond extract, if using. Spoon into baking pan. Tap pan on counter lightly to get rid of any air bubbles. Smooth top of batter.

3. Bake in preheated oven for 40 minutes, or until lightly browned and top of cake springs back when touched lightly with fingertip. Immediately invert pan and, using hole in tube, hang upside down on an inverted funnel, neck of a bottle or a wire rack until cooled completely.

4. With a long thin knife or metal spatula, loosen around the edges, and then remove cake from pan. Decorate as desired.

VARIATIONS

Pineapple Angel Food Cake: Add 19-oz (540 mL) can crushed pineapple and its juice to the batter with vanilla (omit almond extract), mixing in until well combined, and bake as above.

Coconut and Strawberry Angel Cake: Beat 2 cups (500 mL) whipping (35%) cream and ¼ cup (50 mL) confectioner's sugar on high speed until stiff peaks form. Spread over the sides and top of the plain angel food cake. Sprinkle ¼ cup (500 mL) toasted shredded sweetened coconut over the frosting. Arrange sliced strawberries on top (about 2 cups/500 mL). Chill cake for at least 30 minutes or for up to 4 hours.

Angel Cake Loaf: Spoon batter into 2 ungreased 9- by 5-inch (1.5 L) metal loaf pans and bake in preheated oven for 25 to 30 minutes, then proceed as above.

Burnt Sugar Angel Cake

Serves 10 to 12		
2 cups	granulated sugar, divided	500 mL
½ cup	water	125 mL
1 cup	cake flour	250 mL
¼ tsp	salt	1 mL
12	egg whites, at room temperature (about 1½ cups/375 mL)	12
1½ tsp	cream of tartar	7 mL
1 cup	chopped pecans, toasted	250 mL
1½ tsp	vanilla	7 mL
	Pecan halves	

BURNT SUGAR FROSTING

1 cup	confectioner's (icing) sugar, sifted	250 mL
2 tbsp	butter or margarine, softened	25 mL
2 tbsp	milk	25 mL

Preheat oven to 375°F (190°C)

10-inch (4 L) metal tube pan, ungreased

1. In a small saucepan, cook ¾ cup (175 mL) of the sugar until melted, stirring constantly, until golden brown. Stir in water, bring to a boil and boil for 5 to 10 minutes, or until mixture is syrupy and caramel-colored and reduced to about ⅓ cup (75 mL). Set aside to cool to room temperature, about 10 to 15 minutes.

2. In a bowl, sift together another ¾ cup (175 mL) of sugar and the cake flour and salt. Sift 3 or 4 times.

3. In a large, clean mixer bowl, on high speed, beat egg whites and cream of tartar until soft peaks form. Gradually beat in ¼ cup (50 mL) of the syrup mixture. Add the remaining ¾ cup (175 mL) of sugar, by spoonfuls, beating until stiff peaks form. Sift ⅓ of the flour mixture over the egg whites and fold in gently. Fold in remaining flour mixture in two portions, folding lightly just until well blended. Fold in chopped pecans and vanilla. Pour into baking pan. Tap pan on counter lightly to get rid of any air bubbles. Smooth top of batter.

4. Bake in preheated oven for 35 to 40 minutes, or until a toothpick inserted in the center comes out clean and dry. Immediately invert pan and, using hole in tube, hang upside down on an inverted funnel, the neck of a bottle or a wire rack, and cool completely. With a long thin knife or metal spatula, loosen around the edges and then remove cake from pan. Place on serving plate.

5. *Prepare Burnt Sugar Frosting:* In a medium bowl, mix confectioner's sugar, butter, the remaining syrup mixture and milk. Mix well and spoon over top of cake, allowing it to drip onto the sides. Decorate top with pecan halves, or as desired.

> **TIP:** To slice an angel food cake easily, freeze the whole cake overnight before frosting. The cake doesn't get squished by the knife and it slices up nicely.

Frosted Chocolate Angel Food Cake

½ cup	sifted unsweetened cocoa powder	125 mL
⅓ cup	hot water	75 mL
1½ cups	granulated sugar, divided	375 mL
¾ cup	cake flour	175 mL
¼ tsp	salt	1 mL
12	egg whites, at room temperature (about 1½ cups/375 mL)	12
1 tsp	cream of tartar	5 mL
1 tsp	vanilla	5 mL

COCOA FROSTING

¾ cup	confectioner's (icing) sugar	175 mL
3 tbsp	sifted unsweetened cocoa powder	45 mL
2 cups	whipping (35%) cream	500 mL
1 tsp	vanilla	5 mL

NOTE: Sprinkle some confectioner's sugar or some chopped nuts over top, or alternating strips of both to create a pattern.

Preheat oven to 350°F (180°C)

10-inch (4 L) metal tube pan, ungreased

1. In a small bowl, combine cocoa powder and hot water and mix until well blended. Let cool completely.

2. In another bowl, sift together ¾ cup (175 mL) of the sugar, the flour and salt.

3. In a large, clean mixer bowl, on high speed, beat egg whites and cream of tartar until foamy. Gradually add the remaining ¾ cup (175 mL) sugar, by spoonfuls, beating until stiff peaks form. Sift ⅓ of the flour mixture over the egg whites and fold in gently. Fold in remaining flour mixture in two portions, folding lightly just until well blended. Fold in vanilla.

4. Take 1 cup (250 mL) of the egg white mixture and stir into the cocoa mixture. Mix well and then gently fold this cocoa mixture into the remaining egg white mixture, folding until well blended. Spoon into the baking pan. Tap pan lightly on counter to remove any air bubbles. Smooth top of batter.

5. Bake in preheated oven for 45 to 50 minutes, or until a toothpick inserted in the center comes out clean and dry. Immediately invert pan and, using hole in tube, hang upside down on an inverted funnel, the neck of a bottle or a wire rack, and cool completely. With a long thin knife or metal spatula, loosen around the edges and then remove cake from pan.

6. *Prepare Cocoa Frosting:* In a mixer bowl, sift together confectioner's sugar and cocoa powder. Add whipping cream and vanilla and beat on medium speed until stiff and of spreading consistency. Cut cake in half horizontally and place the bottom layer on a serving plate, cut side up. Spread evenly with about ⅓ of the frosting. Top with second layer, cut side down, and frost top and sides.

Lemon Swirl Angel Cake

	Serves 10 to 12	
1½ cups	granulated sugar, divided	375 mL
1 cup	cake flour	250 mL
¼ tsp	salt	1 mL
12	egg whites, at room temperature (about 1½ cups/375 mL)	12
1½ tsp	cream of tartar	7 mL
6	egg yolks	6
1 tbsp	grated lemon zest	15 mL
1½ tsp	vanilla	7 mL
½ tsp	almond extract (optional)	2 mL

NOTE: If desired, make a lemon glaze (see recipe, page 28) and drizzle over top and sides of cooled cake.

Preheat oven to 375°F (190°C)
10-inch (4 L) metal tube pan, ungreased

1. In a medium bowl, sift together ¾ cup (175 mL) of the sugar, the flour and salt.

2. In a large, clean mixer bowl, on high speed, beat egg whites and cream of tartar until foamy. Gradually add the remaining ¾ cup (175 mL) sugar, by spoonfuls, beating until stiff peaks form.

3. In a small mixer bowl, beat egg yolks until lemon-colored and very thick. Fold in lemon zest, vanilla and almond extract, if using.

4. Sift $\frac{1}{3}$ of the flour mixture over the egg whites and fold in gently. Fold in remaining flour mixture in two portions, folding lightly just until well blended. Spoon half of this batter into another bowl and gently fold in the egg yolk mixture. Spoon the plain batter and the egg yolk batter alternately in spoonfuls around the baking pan and in layers. Cut through batters with a knife or thin spatula, making a swirl pattern.

5. Bake in preheated oven for 40 to 45 minutes or until top springs back when touched lightly with fingertip. Immediately invert pan and, using hole in tube, hang upside down on an inverted funnel, the neck of a bottle or a wire rack, and cool completely. With a long thin knife or metal spatula, loosen around the edges and then remove cake from pan.

Surprise Angel-Sponge Cake

	Serves 10 to 12	
1½ cups	granulated sugar, divided	375 mL
1 cup	cake flour	250 mL
¼ tsp	salt	1 mL
11	egg whites (about 1⅓ cups/325 mL)	11
1¼ tsp	cream of tartar	6 mL
4	egg yolks, well beaten	4
1 tsp	grated orange zest	5 mL
2 tbsp	orange juice	25 mL
2 tbsp	cake flour, sifted	25 mL
½ tsp	vanilla	2 mL

Preheat oven to 375°F (190°C)

10-inch (4 L) metal tube pan, ungreased

1. In a medium bowl, sift together ½ cup (125 mL) of the sugar, 1 cup (250 mL) cake flour and salt.

2. In a large, clean mixer bowl, on high speed, beat egg whites and cream of tartar until soft peaks form. Gradually add the remaining 1 cup (250 mL) of sugar , by spoonfuls, beating until stiff peaks form. Sift ⅓ of the flour mixture over the egg whites and fold in gently. Fold in remaining flour mixture in two portions, folding lightly just until well blended. Transfer half of batter to another bowl. Set both aside.

3. In a small mixer bowl, combine egg yolks, orange zest and orange juice and beat until lemon-colored and very thick. Fold this mixture and the 2 tbsp (25 mL) cake flour into one bowl of batter. Fold the vanilla into the other bowl of batter. Spoon batters alternately in spoonfuls around the baking pan. Tap pan lightly on counter to remove any air bubbles. Smooth top of batter.

4. Bake in preheated oven for 35 to 40 minutes, or until a toothpick inserted into the center comes out clean and dry. Immediately invert pan and, using hole in tube, hang upside down on an inverted funnel, the neck of a bottle or a wire rack, and cool completely. With a long thin knife or metal spatula, loosen around the edges and then remove cake from pan. Decorate as desired.

> **TIP:** If you need eggs at room temperature but have forgotten to remove them from the refrigerator, put them in warm water for several minutes before cracking.

Three-Egg Angel Cake

Serves 10 to 12		
1 cup	all-purpose flour	250 mL
2 tsp	baking powder	10 mL
½ tsp	cream of tartar	2 mL
¾ cup	granulated sugar	175 mL
⅔ cup	milk	150 mL
3	egg whites	3
Pinch	salt	Pinch
½ tsp	vanilla	2 mL
½ tsp	almond extract (optional)	2 mL

Preheat oven to 350°F (180°C)

10-inch (4 L) metal tube pan, ungreased

1. In a large bowl, sift together flour, baking powder and cream of tartar. Sift 3 or 4 more times.

2. In a small saucepan, heat sugar and milk over medium heat just until steaming. Remove from heat.

3. In a large, clean mixer bowl, on high speed, beat egg whites and salt until stiff peaks form. Slowly add the hot milk mixture, beating until well blended. Set aside to cool.

4. Fold sifted flour mixture into egg white mixture. Fold in vanilla and almond extract, if using, until well combined. Pour into baking pan, smoothing top.

5. Bake in preheated oven for 30 to 35 minutes, or until cake springs back when touched lightly with fingertip. Immediately invert pan and, using hole in tube, hang upside down on an inverted funnel, the neck of a bottle or a wire rack, and cool completely. With a long thin knife or metal spatula, loosen around the edges and then remove cake from pan. Decorate as desired.

TIP: After you have beaten the egg whites to perfection, keep foam cakes light and airy by always folding in the dry ingredients with a rubber spatula, using a circular motion and never stirring.

Traditional Chiffon Cake

Serves 12 to 16		
6	eggs, separated	6
½ tsp	salt	2 mL
1½ cups	granulated sugar, divided	375 mL
½ cup	warm water	125 mL
1½ cups	all-purpose flour	375 mL
1 tsp	vanilla	5 mL
½ tsp	cream of tartar	2 mL

Preheat oven to 325°F (160°C)
10-inch (4 L) metal tube pan, ungreased

1. In a large mixer bowl, beat egg yolks and salt for 2 to 3 minutes, until lemon-colored and thick. Beat in 1 cup (250 mL) of sugar gradually and continue beating. Gradually add the water and beat until mixture is frothy.

2. Slowly beat in ¾ cup (175 mL) of the flour and vanilla until blended. Beat in the remaining flour and blend well.

3. In a clean mixer bowl with clean blades, on high speed, beat egg whites and cream of tartar until soft peaks form. Gradually add the remaining ½ cup (125 mL) of sugar, by spoonfuls, beating until stiff peaks form. Fold egg white mixture into the egg yolk mixture, gently, until well combined. Spoon into baking pan. Tap pan lightly on counter to remove any air bubbles. Smooth top of batter.

4. Bake in preheated oven for 55 to 60 minutes, or until top springs back when touched lightly with fingertip. Immediately invert pan and, using hole in tube, hang upside down on an inverted funnel, the neck of a bottle or a wire rack, and cool completely. With a long thin knife or metal spatula, loosen around the edges and then remove cake from pan. Serve plain or decorate as desired.

VARIATION

Banana Chiffon Cake: Add 1 cup (250 mL) of mashed, ripe bananas to the egg yolk mixture before combining with egg whites.

Coconut Chiffon Cupcakes

Makes 30 cupcakes		
2¼ cups	cake flour	550 mL
1½ cups	granulated sugar, divided	375 mL
1 tbsp	baking powder	15 mL
1 tsp	salt	5 mL
⅓ cup	vegetable oil	75 mL
1 cup	milk, divided	250 mL
1½ tsp	vanilla	7 mL
2	eggs, separated	2
1 cup	flaked or shredded coconut (sweetened or unsweetened)	250 mL

Preheat oven to 400°F (200°C)

30 muffin cups, lined with paper baking cups

1. In a large mixer bowl, sift together flour, 1 cup (250 mL) of the sugar, baking powder and salt. Mix until well combined and make a well in the center. Add the oil, ½ cup (125 mL) of the milk and vanilla and beat, on medium speed, for 1 to 2 minutes until blended.

2. Add the remaining milk and the egg yolks and beat for another 1 to 2 minutes.

3. In a small, clean mixer bowl with clean beaters, on high speed, beat the egg whites until soft peaks form. Gradually add the remaining ½ cup (125 mL) sugar, by spoonfuls, beating until stiff peaks form.

4. Fold egg white mixture into the batter, gently, until fully blended. Spoon into muffin cups, filling about ¾ full. Sprinkle coconut on top of each.

5. Bake in preheated oven for 15 minutes, or until golden and a toothpick inserted in the centers comes out clean and dry. Cool completely in pans on wire racks.

Glazed Chocolate Chiffon Cake

Serves 12 to 16		
2¼ cups	cake flour	550 mL
1¾ cups	granulated sugar	425 mL
1 tbsp	baking powder	15 mL
1 tsp	salt	5 mL
½ cup	vegetable oil	125 mL
5	egg yolks, beaten	5
¾ cup	cold water	175 mL
1 tsp	vanilla	5 mL
7	egg whites	7
½ tsp	cream of tartar	2 mL
3 oz	semi-sweet chocolate, grated	90 g
CHOCOLATE GLAZE		
4 oz	semi-sweet chocolate, chopped	125 g
¼ cup	whipping (35%) cream	50 mL
1 tsp	vanilla	5 mL

Preheat oven to 325°F (160°C)

10-inch (4 L) metal tube pan, ungreased

1. In a large bowl, sift together flour, sugar, baking powder and salt. Make a well in the center. Pour oil, egg yolks, water and vanilla into well. Mix well until blended.

2. In a large, clean mixer bowl with clean blades, on high speed, beat egg whites and cream of tartar until stiff peaks form. Slowly and gently fold into batter. Quickly fold in the grated chocolate. Pour into baking pan. Tap pan lightly on counter to remove any air bubbles. Smooth top of batter.

3. Bake in preheated oven for 55 minutes. Increase temperature to 350°F (180°C) and bake for another 10 to 15 minutes, or until top springs back when touched lightly with fingertip. Immediately invert pan and, using hole in tube, hang upside down on an inverted funnel, the neck of a bottle or a wire rack, and cool completely. With a long thin knife or metal spatula, loosen around the edges and then remove cake from pan.

4. *Prepare Chocolate Glaze:* In a small saucepan, combine chocolate and whipping cream, stirring on low heat until chocolate is completely melted. Stir in vanilla. Drizzle immediately over top and sides of cooled cake.

Maple Nut Chiffon Cake

Serves 12 to 16		
2¼ cups	cake flour	550 mL
¾ cup	granulated sugar	175 mL
¾ cup	packed brown sugar	175 mL
1 tbsp	baking powder	15 mL
1 tsp	salt	5 mL
½ cup	vegetable oil	125 mL
5	egg yolks	5
¾ cup	cold water	175 mL
2 tsp	maple extract	10 mL
8	egg whites	8
½ tsp	cream of tartar	2 mL
1 cup	finely chopped walnuts or other nuts	250 mL
	Buttercream Frosting (see recipe, page 113, optional)	

Preheat oven to 325°F (160°C)
10-inch (4 L) metal tube pan, ungreased

1. In a large mixer bowl, sift together flour, granulated sugar, brown sugar, baking powder and salt.
2. In another bowl, whisk oil, egg yolks, water and maple extract, beating until smooth.
3. Add egg mixture to the flour mixture and beat, on low speed, until well blended.
4. In a small, clean mixer bowl with clean beaters, on high speed, beat egg whites and cream of tartar until very stiff peaks form. Fold into the batter gently, until blended. Fold in nuts. Spoon into baking pan. Tap pan lightly on counter to remove any air bubbles. Smooth top of batter.
5. Bake in preheated oven for 55 minutes. Increase heat to 350°F (180°C) and bake for an additional 10 to 15 minutes, or until top springs back when touched lightly with fingertip. Immediately invert pan and, using hole in tube, hang upside down on an inverted funnel, the neck of a bottle or a wire rack, and cool completely. With a long thin knife or metal spatula, loosen around the edges and then remove cake from pan.
6. Frost, if desired, with Butter Frosting or another frosting.

> **TIP:** When baking calls for mostly egg whites, drop the yolks into a pan of boiling, salted water and cook for about 10 minutes, until firm. You'll have hard-boiled egg yolks to use in sandwiches or salads.

Traditional Sponge Cake

Serves 12 to 16		
1¾ cups	all-purpose flour	425 mL
1½ cups	granulated sugar, divided	375 mL
2½ tsp	baking powder	12 mL
4	eggs, separated	4
1 tsp	vanilla	5 mL
1 cup	milk	250 mL
2 tbsp	butter or margarine, softened	25 mL

NOTE: I often use a Bundt pan for this particular cake, and do not invert the pan to cool. I leave the cake in the pan for 20 to 25 minutes to cool and then remove from the pan to cool completely on a wire rack.

Preheat oven to 325°F (160°C)

10-inch (4 L) metal tube pan, ungreased

1. In a medium bowl, sift together flour, 1 cup (250 mL) of the sugar and baking powder.

2. In a large, clean mixer bowl, on high speed, beat egg whites until foamy. Gradually add the remaining ½ cup (125 mL) of sugar, by spoonfuls, beating until sugar is dissolved and stiff peaks form.

3. In another mixer bowl, on high speed, beat egg yolks and vanilla until lemon-colored and thick.

4. In a small saucepan over medium heat, heat milk and butter until the butter is melted, but do not bring to a boil. Gradually beat into the egg yolk mixture. Add flour mixture and beat on low speed until well blended. Fold into the egg white mixture, blending until well combined. Pour into baking pan.

5. Bake in preheated oven for 55 to 60 minutes, or until top of cake springs back when touched lightly with fingertip. Immediately invert pan and, using hole in tube, hang upside down on an inverted funnel, the neck of a bottle or a wire rack, and cool completely. With a long thin knife or metal spatula, loosen around the edges and then remove cake from pan.

Chocolate Sponge Cake Roll

Serves 10 to 12		
1/3 cup	sifted unsweetened cocoa powder	75 mL
1/3 cup	all-purpose flour	75 mL
1/2 tsp	baking powder	2 mL
1/4 tsp	salt	1 mL
4	eggs	4
3/4 cup	granulated sugar	175 mL
1 tsp	vanilla	5 mL
	Unsweetened cocoa powder	

CHOCOLATE CREAM FILLING

1	package (4 oz/125 g) chocolate whipped dessert mix	1
1/2 cup	milk	125 mL
1/2 cup	water	125 mL
1/2 cup	whipping (35%) cream	125 mL

NOTE: You could decorate by sprinkling confectioner's sugar or shaving chocolate curls over top, or any other decoration desired.

Preheat oven to 350°F (180°C)

15- by 10-inch (38 by 25 cm) rimmed baking sheet, greased and lined with greased waxed or parchment paper

1. In a medium bowl, sift together cocoa powder, flour, baking powder and salt.

2. In a large mixer bowl, beat eggs until thick and lemon-colored. Gradually add sugar, a spoonful at a time, and vanilla, beating for about 10 to 12 minutes, until very thick. Gently fold in flour mixture until blended. Spoon into prepared baking pan, spreading evenly.

3. Bake in preheated oven for 20 to 25 minutes, or until cake springs back when touched lightly with fingertip. Let cool in pan on a wire rack for about 10 minutes. Cut off a 1/4-inch (0.5 cm) strip from the edges of cake. Invert cake onto a clean tea towel sprinkled with unsweetened cocoa powder and remove the waxed paper. Starting at the narrow end, roll up cake and wrap in towel. Set aside to cool completely on a wire rack.

4. *Prepare Chocolate Cream Filling:* In a bowl, mix dessert mix with the milk and water and follow the directions on the package. Chill in refrigerator for at least 30 minutes, or until ready to serve.

5. When ready to serve, in a small mixer bowl, beat the whipping cream until stiff. Spoon half of the chilled chocolate dessert into another small bowl and beat until smooth. Gently fold in the whipped cream until well combined.

6. Unroll cake carefully and spread chocolate cream filling over top, spreading evenly. Re-roll, using the towel as a guide. Remove towel and place roll on a serving plate. Whisk the remaining chocolate dessert until smooth and frost the roll, top and sides.

VARIATION

Lemon Sponge Cake Roll: Omit cocoa powder and chocolate cream filling ingredients. Separate eggs into yolks and whites. Add 2 tbsp (25 mL) lemon juice and 1 tsp (5 mL) lemon extract to the egg yolks. Fold the flour mixture into the egg yolk mixture, as above. Beat the egg whites with 1/2 tsp (2 mL) cream of tartar until stiff and fold into the batter, as above. Bake and cool as directed. Fill with crabapple jelly or any other jam or jelly you desire.

Orange Sponge Cake

	Serves 12 to 16	
6	eggs, separated	6
1¾ cups	sifted all-purpose flour	425 mL
¼ tsp	salt	1 mL
1½ cups	granulated sugar, divided	375 mL
1 tbsp	grated orange zest	15 mL
6 tbsp	freshly squeezed orange juice	90 mL
	Confectioner's (icing) sugar	

NOTE: Decorate with an orange frosting (see recipe variation, page 110) or orange glaze, or leave plain and serve with sherbet or a raspberry sauce.

Preheat oven to 350°F (180°C)

10-inch (4 L) metal tube pan, ungreased

1. Place egg whites in a large, clean mixer bowl to come to room temperature.

2. In another bowl, sift together flour and salt and set aside.

3. Beat the egg whites, on medium speed, until foamy. Gradually beat in ½ cup (125 mL) of the sugar, a spoonful at a time, beating until stiff peaks form.

4. In a small mixer bowl, on high speed, beat egg yolks until lemon-colored and thick, about 2 to 3 minutes. Do not under-beat. Beat in remaining sugar, gradually, until mixture is smooth and blended.

5. Beat in flour mixture alternately with orange juice, making 3 additions of flour and 2 of orange juice, on low speed, just to blend. Add orange zest. Gently fold into egg white mixture until well combined. Pour into baking pan.

6. Bake in preheated oven for 50 to 55 minutes, or until top springs back when touched lightly with fingertip. Immediately invert pan and, using hole in tube, hang upside down on an inverted funnel, the neck of a bottle or a wire rack, and cool completely. With a long thin knife or metal spatula, loosen around the edges and then remove cake from pan. Sift confectioner's sugar over top.

Sabbath Sponge Cake

	Serves 12 to 16	
½ cup	cake flour	125 mL
Pinch	salt	Pinch
7	eggs, separated	7
	Grated zest of 1 lemon	
	Juice of 1 lemon	
¾ cup	fine granulated sugar, divided	175 mL
½ tsp	cream of tartar	2 mL
	Confectioner's (icing) sugar	

NOTE: This cake is usually topped with confectioner's sugar, sprinkled over top.

Preheat oven to 325°F (160°C)
10-inch (4 L) metal tube pan, ungreased

1. In a medium bowl, sift flour and salt 2 to 3 times.

2. In a large mixer bowl, on high speed, beat the egg yolks until lemon-colored and thick. Beat in lemon zest, lemon juice and ½ of the sugar.

3. In a clean mixer bowl with clean beaters, on high speed, beat egg whites and cream of tartar until soft peaks form. Gradually add the remaining sugar, by spoonfuls, beating until stiff peaks form.

4. Fold egg white mixture gently into egg yolk mixture. Sift the flour mixture over top, and fold in. Pour into baking pan.

5. Bake in preheated oven for 55 to 60 minutes, or until top springs back when touched lightly with fingertip. Immediately invert pan and, using hole in tube, hang upside down on an inverted funnel, the neck of a bottle or a wire rack, and cool completely. With a long thin knife or metal spatula, loosen around the edges and then remove cake from pan.

Cheesecakes

New York Style Cheesecake

Serves 10 to 12

CRUST

1/4 cup	finely chopped walnuts	50 mL
1/2 tsp	ground cinnamon	2 mL
1 3/4 cups	graham wafer crumbs (about 20 whole wafers)	425 mL
1/2 cup	butter or margarine, melted	125 mL

FILLING

1 1/2 lbs	cream cheese, softened	750 g
1 cup	granulated sugar	250 mL
2 tbsp	all-purpose flour	25 mL
1 tsp	vanilla	5 mL
1/2 tsp	finely grated lemon zest (optional)	1 mL
2	eggs	2
1	egg yolk	1
1/4 cup	milk	50 mL

Preheat oven to 375°F (190°C)

9-inch (23 cm) springform pan, greased

1. *Prepare crust:* In a medium bowl, combine walnuts, cinnamon and crushed graham wafer crumbs. Mix well to combine and stir in melted butter. Set aside 1/4 cup (50 mL) of this mixture, if you wish to use as topping. Press the remaining crumb mixture on the bottom of the pan, spreading evenly, and pressing about 2 inches up the sides. Set aside.

2. *Prepare filling:* In a large mixer bowl, combine cream cheese, sugar, flour, vanilla and lemon zest, if using. Beat on medium speed until well combined. Reduce speed to low and add eggs and egg yolk until blended. Stir in the milk and mix well. Pour filling mixture over crust in pan and sprinkle remaining crumb mixture evenly over top, if desired.

3. Bake in preheated oven for 40 to 50 minutes, until firm around the edges and center is set.

4. Cool in pan on a wire rack for 15 minutes, then run a knife around edge to loosen the crust from the pan. Cool a bit longer, about 30 minutes, and then remove sides of pan.

5. Cover and chill in refrigerator for 4 to 6 hours before serving.

VARIATIONS

Fruit Topping: Before chilling, spread 1 can (19 oz/540 mL) of blueberry, cherry or any other flavor of pie filling over top.

Streusel Topping: Spread a streusel topping (see recipe, page 22) over top of filling and then bake as above.

Raspberry Sauce: Combine 1 1/2 cups (375 mL) frozen raspberries, 1/4 cup (50 mL) granulated sugar, 1 tsp (5 mL) lemon juice and, if desired, 1 tbsp (15 mL) raspberry liqueur in a blender. Blend until smooth. Pour mixture into a sieve over a bowl to remove seeds. Spread evenly over top of filling and then bake as above.

Praline Topping: Put 1/2 cup (125 mL) granulated sugar in a heavy frying pan and cook over medium heat until melted and a darker, golden color. Add 1/3 cup (75 mL) of whole blanched almonds and mix well so that the nuts become well coated. Lightly grease a baking sheet and pour mixture onto it. Set aside to cool completely, then break into pieces and place into a plastic bag. Roll with a rolling pin until coarsely crushed. Spread over top of cheesecake before chilling.

> **TIP:** To blanch almonds, cover them with boiling water. Let stand a few minutes and then rinse with cold water. Pinch each nut and the skin will slip right off.

Classic Cheesecake

GRAHAM CRUST

1½ cups	graham wafer crumbs (about 18 whole wafers)	375 mL
⅓ cup	confectioner's (icing) sugar	75 mL
½ cup	butter or margarine, melted	125 mL
1 tsp	ground cinnamon (optional)	5 mL

FILLING

1 lb	creamed cottage cheese	500 g
1 lb	cream cheese, softened	500 g
1½ cups	granulated sugar	375 mL
4	eggs, lightly beaten	4
3 tbsp	all-purpose flour	45 mL
3 tbsp	cornstarch	45 mL
1 tsp	vanilla	5 mL
1 tsp	grated lemon zest	5 mL
1½ tbsp	lemon juice	22 mL
2 cups	sour cream	500 mL
½ cup	butter or margarine, melted	125 mL
	Canned or fresh fruit	

NOTE: Another method is to set aside sour cream and bake the cheesecake for 65 minutes. Remove from oven and spread the sour cream evenly over top. Return to oven and bake for another 5 minutes. Then proceed as above. To prevent cracking on top, let the sour cream come to room temperature first and place a shallow pan, half full of water, underneath on the lower rack while baking.

Preheat oven to 325°F (160°C)

9-inch (23 cm) springform pan, greased

1. *Prepare Graham Crust:* In a small bowl, mix together graham crumbs, confectioner's sugar, melted butter and cinnamon, if using. Press into the bottom of prepared baking pan.

2. *Prepare filling:* In a large mixer bowl, on high speed, beat cottage cheese and cream cheese. Add sugar gradually and then beat in eggs, one at a time, beating after each addition.

3. Add the flour, cornstarch, vanilla, lemon zest and lemon juice, and beat on low speed until blended. Add the sour cream and melted butter and continue beating just until smooth and well blended. Pour over crust, spreading evenly.

4. Bake in preheated oven for 70 minutes, or until firm around the edges and center is set. Cool on a wire rack for 20 to 25 minutes, then chill in refrigerator for 3 hours, or overnight. Before serving, run a spatula around the sides of cake, then release the clasp and remove. Leave bottom of springform in place and transfer over to a serving plate.

5. When ready to serve, top with fruit, such as peach slices or raspberries, kiwi and strawberries.

Layered Chocolate-Vanilla Cheesecake

Serves 10 to 12		
CRUST		
1¼ cups	graham wafer crumbs (about 16 whole wafers)	300 mL
⅓ cup	butter or margarine, melted	75 mL
FILLING		
½ cup	granulated sugar	125 mL
1 lb	cream cheese, softened	500 g
4	eggs	4
½ cup	whipping (35%) cream	125 mL
1 tbsp	cornstarch	15 mL
1 tsp	grated lemon zest	5 mL
1 tbsp	lemon juice	15 mL
1 tsp	vanilla	5 mL
3 tbsp	unsweetened cocoa powder	45 mL
	Chocolate curls or shavings (optional)	

Preheat oven to 325°F (160°C)

9-inch (23 cm) springform pan, greased

1. *Prepare crust:* In a bowl, mix together graham crumbs and the melted butter. Set aside ¼ cup (50 mL) of the crumb mixture for garnish, if desired. Press remaining crumb mixture firmly onto bottom of prepared baking pan. Bake in preheated oven for 10 minutes, or until golden. Cool completely.

2. *Prepare filling:* In a large mixer bowl, on medium speed, cream sugar and cream cheese until smooth. Add eggs, one at a time, beating well after each addition. Beat in whipping cream, cornstarch, lemon zest, lemon juice and vanilla, beating until smooth and thoroughly blended.

3. Place about ⅓ of the mixture in a small bowl. Sift cocoa powder over top and then fold in until well blended.

4. Spread half of the remaining vanilla mixture over top of crust. Top with the cocoa mixture, spreading evenly. Then spread the remaining vanilla mixture over top of the cocoa mixture.

5. Bake in preheated oven for 50 to 60 minutes, or until firm around the edges and center is set. Turn off oven and keep oven door ajar to let cake cool for about 1 hour. Remove from oven and then chill in refrigerator for at least 6 to 8 hours before serving. Before serving, run a spatula around the sides of cake, then release the clasp and remove. Leave bottom of springform in place and transfer over to a serving plate.

6. If desired, to garnish, spread the reserved crumb mixture around edge of top of cake in a strip about 1 inch (2.5 cm) deep and place chocolate curls or shavings, if using, in the middle.

TIP: Here's how to make chocolate curls: For each square of chocolate you use, place square in microwave, on defrost, for 1 minute, until slightly soft. Draw a vegetable peeler over the flat bottom surface and carefully lift curls with a toothpick. Place curls right onto your cake or on a plate to use when ready.

All Chocolate Cheesecake

CHOCOLATE CRUST

1 cup	finely crushed chocolate wafer crumbs (about 25 wafers)	250 mL
2 tbsp	granulated sugar	25 mL
3 tbsp	butter or margarine, melted	45 mL

CHOCOLATE FILLING

¾ cup	granulated sugar	175 mL
1½ lbs	cream cheese, softened	750 g
1 tsp	vanilla	5 mL
3	eggs	3
3 oz	white chocolate, melted and cooled	90 g
2 tbsp	raspberry liqueur or syrup (optional)	25 mL
3 oz	semi-sweet chocolate, melted and cooled	90 g
	White and semi-sweet chocolate curls or shavings	

CHOCOLATE GLAZE

6 oz	semi-sweet chocolate, chopped	175 g
¾ cup	whipping (35%) cream	175 mL

Preheat oven to 350°F (180°C)

9-inch (23 cm) springform pan, lightly greased

1. *Prepare crust:* In a small bowl, mix together wafer crumbs, sugar and melted butter, until blended and crumbly. Press firmly onto bottom of your prepared baking pan. Bake in preheated oven for 10 minutes, or until golden. Cool completely. Increase oven temperature to 425°F (220°C).

2. *Prepare filling:* In a large mixer bowl, on medium speed, cream sugar and cream cheese until smooth. Add vanilla and then eggs, one at a time, beating well after each addition. Place half of this batter in another bowl and stir in the melted white chocolate and liqueur, if using, and set aside.

3. To the remaining batter, add the melted semi-sweet chocolate and stir until well blended. Spoon this chocolate batter into the crust, spreading evenly. Slowly spoon the white chocolate batter over top, spreading evenly.

4. Bake for 10 minutes, then lower heat to 250°F (120°C) and bake for 35 to 40 minutes more, or until firm around the edges and center is set. Set on a wire rack and cool completely in the pan. Run a spatula around the sides of cake, then release the clasp and remove. Leave bottom of springform in place and transfer over to a serving plate.

5. *Prepare glaze:* In a small saucepan over low heat, heat chocolate and whipping cream, stirring until melted and smooth. Spread over top of cake to cover completely and allow mixture to drizzle over the sides.

6. Garnish with white and semi-sweet chocolate curls or shavings. Chill in refrigerator for at least 30 minutes, or until ready to serve.

> **TIP:** To melt large amounts of chocolate, use your slow cooker on low heat. It keeps the chocolate warm for as long as you need it.

Caramel Apple Cheesecake

Serves 10 to 12

CRUST

1½ cups	all-purpose flour	375 mL
¼ cup	granulated sugar	50 mL
½ cup	butter or margarine, softened	125 mL
1	egg yolk	1

FILLING

2 tbsp	butter or margarine	25 mL
2	apples (Granny Smith or any type preferred), peeled, thinly sliced	2
1½ tsp	milk	7 mL
20	soft vanilla caramels	20
½ cup	granulated sugar	125 mL
1 lb	cream cheese, softened	500 g
1 tsp	vanilla	5 mL
2	eggs	2
½ cup	finely chopped pecans, hazelnuts or other nut	125 mL
	Vanilla ice cream (optional)	

Preheat oven to 400°F (200°C)

9-inch (23 cm) springform pan, lightly greased

1. *Prepare crust:* In a small bowl, combine flour, sugar, butter and the egg yolk. Mix well and then press into bottom and about 1 inch (2.5 cm) up the sides of prepared baking pan. Bake in preheated oven for 15 minutes, or until golden. Cool completely. Reduce oven temperature to 325°F (160°C).

2. *Prepare filling:* In a large skillet, melt butter. Add apples and cook, over low heat, until tender. Arrange apples on top of baked crust.

3. In a small saucepan, over low heat, combine milk and caramels, and cook until melted. Drizzle this mixture over the apples.

4. In a large mixer bowl, on medium speed, cream sugar and cream cheese until smooth. Add vanilla and beat in eggs, one at a time, beating until well blended. Spoon over the caramel-apple mixture.

5. Bake for 30 to 35 minutes, or until firm around the edges and center is set. Cool in pan for 20 to 25 minutes. Run a spatula around the sides of cake, then release the clasp and remove. Leave bottom of springform in place and cool completely.

6. Chill in refrigerator for at least 30 minutes, or until ready to serve. Sprinkle the nuts over top. Place a scoop of vanilla ice cream over each slice of cake, if desired.

Speedy Blueberry Cheesecake

Serves 6 to 8

CRUST

½ cup	butter or margarine, softened	125 mL
¾ cup	granulated sugar, divided	175 mL
1¼ cups	finely crushed graham wafer crumbs (about 16 whole wafers)	300 mL

FILLING

2	eggs	2
1 tsp	vanilla	5 mL
8 oz	cream cheese, softened	250 g
Pinch	ground cinnamon	Pinch

TOPPING

1	can (19 oz/540 mL) blueberry pie filling	1
2 tbsp	lemon juice	25 mL
	Whipped Topping	

Preheat oven to 300°F (150°C)

9-inch (2.5 L) square baking pan or dish, ungreased

1. *Prepare crust:* In a small bowl, combine butter, ¼ cup (50 mL) of the sugar and the graham wafer crumbs. Press into bottom of baking pan, evenly and firmly.

2. *Prepare filling:* In a large mixer bowl, on medium speed, beat eggs until thick and pale yellow in color. Add the remaining ½ cup (125 mL) of sugar, vanilla and cream cheese, and beat until smooth and blended. Spoon over crumb crust.

3. Bake in preheated oven for 30 to 35 minutes or until firm around the edges and center is set. Cool in pan on a wire rack, sprinkle cinnamon over top, and let cool completely.

4. *Prepare topping:* In a small bowl, mix blueberry pie filling and lemon juice to blend. Pour over top of the cheesecake, spreading evenly, and chill in refrigerator for 3 to 4 hours, or preferably overnight. To serve, top a slice with a dollop of whipped topping.

TIP: Most cakes can be frozen for up to 6 months if completely cooled and not frosted, and if wrapped tightly in plastic wrap and then in foil. Cheesecakes and butter cakes are the best choices, because the higher the fat content, the better they take to the deep freeze. Thaw overnight in the refrigerator.

Mini Cheesecakes

Makes 12 mini cheesecakes		
12	chocolate wafer cookies	12
¾ cup	granulated sugar	175 mL
1 lb	cream cheese, softened	500 g
1 tsp	vanilla	5 mL
2	eggs	2
1 cup	canned fruit pie filling (peach, blueberry, cherry)	250 mL

Preheat oven to 300°F (150°C)

12-cup muffin pan, lined with paper baking cups

1. Place 1 chocolate wafer in the bottom of each muffin cup. Trim wafers to fit into bottom of cups, if necessary.

2. In a large mixer bowl, on medium speed, cream sugar and cream cheese until smooth. Add vanilla and then eggs, and beat until smooth and well blended. Spoon into muffin cups, over the wafer, filling each cup about ¾ full.

3. Bake in preheated oven for 20 to 25 minutes, or until set. Cool in cups on a wire rack for about 20 minutes, and then remove carefully and cool completely. Store in refrigerator for up to 3 days. Just before serving, top each cheesecake with a spoonful of pie filling.

Deluxe Lemon Cheesecake

Serves 12 to 16		
CRUST		
2½ cups	crushed gingersnap cookies (about 40 cookies)	625 mL
⅓ cup	butter or margarine, melted	75 mL
FILLING		
¾ cup	granulated sugar	175 mL
2 lbs	cream cheese, softened	1 kg
4	eggs	4
2 tsp	lemon juice	10 mL
1 tsp	vanilla	5 mL

Preheat oven to 350°F (180°C)

10-inch (25 cm) springform pan, greased

1. *Prepare crust:* In a small bowl, mix together cookie crumbs and butter. Mix well and press onto the bottom and up the sides of the prepared baking pan.

2. *Prepare filling:* In a large mixer bowl, on medium speed, cream sugar and cream cheese. Add eggs, lemon juice and vanilla, and beat until smooth and well blended. Pour over crust, spreading evenly.

3. Bake in preheated oven for 45 to 55 minutes, or until firm around the edges and center is set. Turn off oven, leave door ajar, and let cake cool for about 1 hour. Cool completely in pan on a wire rack. Run a spatula around the sides of cake, then release the clasp and remove. Leave bottom of springform in place and chill in refrigerator several hours before serving.

Eggnog Cheesecake

Serves 12 to 16

CRUST

1¾ cups	graham wafer crumbs (about 20 whole wafers)	425 mL
¼ cup	granulated sugar	50 mL
½ cup	butter or margarine, melted	125 mL

FILLING

1 cup	granulated sugar	250 mL
2 lbs	cream cheese, softened	1 kg
3 tbsp	all-purpose flour	45 mL
½ tsp	ground nutmeg	2 mL
3 tbsp	rum	45 mL
1 tsp	vanilla	5 mL
2	eggs	2
1 cup	whipping (35%) cream	250 mL
4	egg yolks	4
	Whipped cream	
	Ground cinnamon or nutmeg	

Preheat oven to 325°F (160°C)

9-inch (23 cm) springform pan, lightly greased

1. *Prepare crust:* In a small bowl, combine wafer crumbs, sugar and melted butter. Mix well until mixture is crumbly. Press firmly onto bottom and up the sides of prepared baking pan. Bake in preheated oven for 10 minutes, or until golden. Cool completely.

2. *Prepare filling:* In a large mixer bowl, on medium speed, beat sugar and cream cheese until smooth. Add flour, nutmeg, rum and vanilla, and beat until well blended. Add the eggs, one at a time, beating after each addition, until blended. Beat in the whipping cream and egg yolks until well combined. Pour over crust, spreading evenly.

3. Bake for 70 to 75 minutes, or until firm around the edges and the center is almost set. Cool completely in pan on a wire rack. Run a spatula around the sides of cake, then release the clasp and remove. Leave bottom of springform in place and chill in refrigerator for 4 to 5 hours, or overnight.

4. Garnish with whipped cream and then sprinkle with cinnamon or nutmeg, or decorate as desired.

No-Bake Mocha Cheesecake

Serves 12 to 16

CRUST

1¼ cups	finely crushed chocolate wafer cookies (about 36 wafers)	300 mL
¼ cup	granulated sugar	50 mL
⅓ cup	butter or margarine, melted	75 mL

FILLING

1 lb	cream cheese, softened	500 g
1	can (10 oz/300 mL) sweetened condensed milk	1
⅔ cup	chocolate syrup	150 mL
2 tbsp	instant coffee granules	25 mL
1 tbsp	hot water	15 mL
1 cup	whipping (35%) cream, whipped	250 mL

13- by 9-inch (3 L) metal baking pan, lightly greased

1. *Prepare crust:* In a small bowl, mix together wafer crumbs, sugar and melted butter, until mixture is crumbly. Set aside ¼ cup (50 mL) of the crumb mixture for garnish later. Spread remaining crumb mixture evenly onto bottom of prepared baking pan. Chill in refrigerator.

2. *Prepare filling:* In a large mixer bowl, on medium speed, beat cream cheese until smooth. Add milk and chocolate syrup, beating just until well blended.

3. In another bowl, dissolve the coffee granules in the water. Stir into cheese mixture and mix well. Gently fold in the whipped cream until mixture is well combined.

4. Pour into crust in pan, cover, and freeze for 6 to 8 hours, until firm. Sprinkle the reserved crumb mixture over top. Freeze for up to 6 months. Serve frozen.

TIP: To minimize cracking in cheesecakes, put a shallow pan half full of hot water on the rack below your cake during baking. Then turn oven off, leave door ajar, and let cheesecake stand in oven for about 30 minutes. Remove from oven and refrigerate overnight.

Cool Key Lime Cheesecake

Serves 10 to 12

CRUST

1¾ cups	graham wafer crumbs (about 20 whole wafers)	425 mL
¼ cup	granulated sugar	50 mL
½ cup	butter or margarine, melted	125 mL

FILLING

¾ cup	granulated sugar	175 mL
1½ lbs	cream cheese, softened	750 g
3 tbsp	all-purpose flour	45 mL
1 cup	sour cream	250 mL
3	eggs	3
1 tbsp	grated key lime zest (optional)	15 mL
⅔ cups	key lime juice	150 mL
1 tsp	vanilla	5 mL
	Drop of green food coloring (optional)	
	Whipping (35%) cream, whipped (optional)	
	Key limes, thinly sliced (optional)	

Preheat oven to 375°F (190°C)

9-inch (23 cm) springform pan, greased

1. *Prepare crust:* In a small bowl, combine wafer crumbs, sugar and melted butter. Mix well until crumbly. Press firmly onto the bottom and about 1½ inches (3.5 cm) up the sides of your prepared baking pan. Bake in preheated oven for 8 minutes, or until golden. Cool completely. Reduce oven temperature to 325°F (160°C).

2. *Prepare filling:* In a large mixer bowl, on medium speed, cream sugar and cream cheese until smooth. Beat in flour and sour cream until well blended. Add eggs, one at a time, beating until well blended. Stir in lime zest, if using, lime juice, vanilla and food coloring, if using. Mix well. Pour over crust, spreading evenly.

3. Bake for 50 to 60 minutes, or until firm around the edges and center is almost set. Cool completely in pan on a wire rack. Run a spatula around the sides of cake, then release the clasp and remove. Leave bottom of springform in place and chill in refrigerator several hours or overnight before serving. Garnish with dollops of whipped cream and very thin slices of key lime, if desired.

TIP: Key limes, grown mainly in Florida, are smaller and have a more yellow color than the more common Persian lime. Key limes can be found at specialty produce markets. To substitute for key lime juice, use ½ Persian lime juice and ½ lemon juice.

Tropical Pineapple Cheesecake

Serves 12 to 16

CRUST

1 cup	finely crushed graham wafer crumbs (about 14 whole wafers)	250 mL
1/4 cup	packed brown sugar	50 mL
1/2 tsp	ground cinnamon	2 mL
1/2 cup	butter or margarine, melted	125 mL

FILLING

1 cup	granulated sugar	250 mL
1 lb	cream cheese, softened	500 g
5	eggs, separated	5
1	can (19 oz/540 g) crushed pineapple, well-drained	1

TOPPING

2 tbsp	granulated sugar	25 mL
2 cups	sour cream	500 mL
1 tsp	vanilla	5 mL

Preheat oven to 350°F (180°C)

13- by 9-inch (3 L) metal baking pan, lightly greased

1. *Prepare crust:* In a small bowl, combine wafer crumbs, brown sugar, cinnamon and melted butter. Reserve 1/4 cup (50 mL) and set aside. Spread remaining crumb mixture evenly onto bottom of prepared baking pan.

2. *Prepare filling:* In a large mixer bowl, on medium speed, cream sugar, cream cheese and egg yolks until smooth.

3. In a small, clean mixer bowl with clean beaters, beat the egg whites on high speed, until stiff peaks form. Fold gently into the creamed mixture. Fold in pineapple and blend thoroughly. Pour onto crust, spreading evenly, and bake in preheated oven for 30 minutes. Sprinkle some of the reserved crumbs over top.

4. *Prepare topping:* In a small bowl, combine sugar, sour cream and vanilla and mix with a fork or spoon. Spoon over top of cake. Sprinkle the remainder of reserved crumb mixture over top.

5. Reduce oven temperature to 300°F (150°C) and bake for another 5 to 10 minutes. Cool in pan on a wire rack and then chill in refrigerator for at least 30 minutes, or until ready to serve. Cut into squares.

TIP: To make sour cream last longer, turn its container upside down in the refrigerator. This prevents air from filling the top.

Fancy and Specialty Cakes

Black Forest Cake

Serves 12 to 16

¾ cup	sifted cake flour	175 mL
¼ cup	sifted unsweetened cocoa powder	50 mL
¼ tsp	salt	1 mL
5	eggs, separated	5
½ tsp	cream of tartar	2 mL
⅔ cup	granulated sugar, divided	150 mL
3 tbsp	water	45 mL
1 tsp	vanilla	5 mL

CHERRY FILLING

2½ cups	canned sweetened black cherries with juice	625 mL
3 tbsp	granulated sugar	45 mL
2½ tbsp	cornstarch	32 mL
1 tbsp	cherry liqueur or brandy (kirsch)	15 mL

CHOCOLATE BUTTERCREAM FILLING

½ cup	granulated sugar	125 mL
Pinch	salt	Pinch
2 tbsp	water	25 mL
1	egg white	1
Pinch	cream of tartar	Pinch
½ tsp	vanilla	2 mL
⅓ cup	butter, softened	75 mL
1 oz	semi-sweet chocolate, melted and cooled	30 g

CHOCOLATE CREAM FROSTING

3 tbsp	granulated sugar	45 mL
3 tbsp	sifted unsweetened cocoa powder	45 mL
1 cup	whipping (35%) cream	250 mL
1 tsp	vanilla	5 mL
	Chocolate shavings or curls	
	Whole maraschino cherries, stemmed	

Preheat oven to 325°F (160°C)

Two 9-inch (23 cm) round metal cake pans, ungreased

1. In a medium bowl, mix together flour, cocoa powder and salt.

2. In a small, clean mixer bowl, beat the egg whites and cream of tartar until frothy. Beat in ⅓ cup (75 mL) of the sugar until stiff peaks are formed.

3. In a large mixer bowl, beat the egg yolks and the remaining sugar until light and fluffy. Stir in the vanilla and water. Sift flour mixture over this egg yolk mixture in thirds, gently folding in after each addition. Then gently fold in the egg white mixture and blend well. Pour into the two baking pans, dividing evenly

4. Bake in preheated oven for 30 to 35 minutes, or until a toothpick inserted in the center comes out clean and dry. Invert pans onto wire racks and cool for 10 minutes. Remove from pans and cool completely.

5. *Prepare Cherry Filling:* Remove pits from the cherries, if necessary. In a medium saucepan, combine sugar and cornstarch. Stir in the cherries and their juice and cook, over medium heat, stirring until mixture comes to a boil and is clear and thickened. Cover and cook, over low heat, for 5 minutes, stirring occasionally. Remove from heat to cool. Stir in the liqueur. Cool completely.

6. *Prepare Chocolate Buttercream Filling*: In another saucepan, over medium heat, combine sugar, salt and water. Stir until sugar is dissolved, then allow to boil, without stirring, until a small amount of this syrup forms a soft ball when dropped into water.

7. In a clean mixer bowl with clean beaters, beat the egg white and cream of tartar until soft peaks form. Slowly pour the hot, syrupy mixture into the egg white mixture in a thin stream, beating until mixture becomes thick. Cool slightly, then beat in vanilla. Cool completely.

8. In another bowl, cream butter until smooth. Beat in egg white mixture, by spoonfuls, and then the melted chocolate, blending well. Cool or chill until the right consistency, if necessary.

9. Place one cake layer on a serving plate. Spread a 1-inch (2.5 cm) border of buttercream filling around the edge of the cake and then spread the remainder in a 1¼-inch (4 cm) circle in the center. Spread the cooled cherry mixture between the buttercream border and center. Place second cake layer on top, pressing down gently.

10. *Prepare Chocolate Cream Frosting:* In a small mixer bowl, beat sugar, cocoa, cream and vanilla until stiff peaks form. Do not over-beat. Frost top and sides of cake. Decorate with chocolate shavings and cherries, or any other desired decoration. Refrigerate for at least 1 hour, or until chilled, or for up to 1 day.

> **TIP:** $1\frac{1}{2}$ cans (each 14 oz/398 mL) of cherries is about $2\frac{1}{2}$ cups (625 mL). Drain extra cherries from second can and pat dry to use as garnish, if desired.

Passover Wine Cake

Serves 10 to 12		
$\frac{1}{2}$ cup	matzo cake meal	125 mL
$\frac{1}{4}$ cup	potato starch or cornstarch	50 mL
6	eggs, separated, at room temperature	6
1 cup	granulated sugar, divided	250 mL
1 tsp	vanilla	5 mL
$\frac{1}{4}$ cup	vegetable oil	50 mL
$\frac{1}{2}$ cup	apricot preserves	125 mL
2 tbsp	lemon juice	25 mL

WINE SAUCE

$\frac{1}{4}$ cup	granulated sugar	50 mL
2 tbsp	water	25 mL
2 tbsp	lemon juice	25 mL
$\frac{1}{4}$ cup	sweet white wine	50 mL

Preheat oven to 350°F (180°C)

10-inch (3 L) Bundt pan, heavily greased

1. In a small bowl, combine cake meal and potato starch.
2. In a small, clean mixer bowl, beat egg whites until foamy. Gradually add $\frac{1}{2}$ cup (125 mL) of the sugar and beat until stiff peaks form.
3. In a large mixer bowl, beat egg yolks, vanilla and the remaining $\frac{1}{2}$ cup (125 mL) of sugar until mixture is thick. Gently fold in egg white mixture and then the starch mixture. Drizzle the oil over the batter and mix gently into batter until well incorporated. Spoon into prepared baking pan.
4. Bake in preheated oven for 35 to 40 minutes, or until a toothpick inserted in the center comes out clean and dry. Cool in pan on a wire rack for 10 minutes and then remove and place on wire rack to cool completely.
5. *Prepare Wine Sauce:* In a small saucepan, combine sugar, water and lemon juice, bring to a simmer over low heat, and simmer for 2 to 3 minutes. Remove from heat and stir in wine.
6. Place cake on a serving plate and spoon wine sauce over cake until it is absorbed. Combine the apricot preserves and lemon juice and heat until melted, then brush over cake.

> **TIP:** Cooling cakes in their pans on a rack will prevent sogginess, because the bottom of the pans will be cooled by the air.

Boston Cream Pie

Serves 12 to 16		
2	eggs, separated	2
1½ cups	granulated sugar, divided	375 mL
2¼ cups	cake flour	550 mL
1 tbsp	baking powder	15 mL
1 tsp	salt	5 mL
⅓ cup	vegetable oil	75 mL
1½ tsp	vanilla	7 mL
1 cup	milk	250 mL

CUSTARD FILLING

⅓ cup	granulated sugar	75 mL
2 tbsp	all-purpose flour	25 mL
1 tbsp	cornstarch	15 mL
¼ tsp	salt	1 mL
1½ cups	milk	375 mL
1	egg	1
1	egg yolk	1
1 tsp	vanilla	5 mL

CHOCOLATE GLAZE

1 oz	unsweetened chocolate, chopped	30 g
1 tbsp	butter or margarine	15 mL
1 cup	confectioner's (icing) sugar, sifted	250 mL
½ tsp	vanilla	2 mL
3 to 4 tsp	boiling water or milk	15 to 20 mL

Not really a pie, but a cake

Preheat oven to 350°F (180°C)

Two 9-inch (23 cm) round metal cake pans, lightly greased

1. In a small, clean mixer bowl, beat the egg whites until soft peaks form. Add ½ cup (125 mL) of the sugar, slowly, and continue beating until stiff peaks form.

2. In the large mixer bowl, sift together cake flour, baking powder, salt and the remaining 1 cup (250 mL) of sugar. Add the oil and ½ cup (125 mL) of the milk and beat on medium speed for about 2 minutes. Gradually add the egg yolks and the remaining ½ cup (125 mL) of milk, and beat for another 2 minutes.

3. Fold in the beaten egg white mixture only until well blended. Spoon into prepared cake pans, dividing equally.

4. Bake in preheated oven for 25 to 30 minutes, or until a toothpick inserted in center comes out clean and dry. Cool in pans on wire racks for 10 minutes. Remove from pans and place on wire rack to cool completely.

5. *Prepare Custard Filling:* In a medium saucepan, over medium heat, combine sugar, flour, cornstarch and salt. Slowly add the milk and cook until it boils and becomes thickened. Continue cooking for another 2 to 3 minutes. In a small bowl, combine the egg, egg yolk and vanilla and beat with a fork to mix. Pour a few spoonfuls of the hot mixture into the egg mixture and then add this mixture to the saucepan, stirring constantly until mixture comes to a boil again. Remove from heat, cover with lid, foil or waxed paper, and set aside to cool to room temperature, about 10 to 15 minutes.

6. *Meanwhile, prepare Chocolate Glaze:* In a small saucepan, over low heat, combine chocolate and butter, stirring until completely melted. Remove from heat and stir in the confectioner's sugar and vanilla. Stir in the boiling water, one spoonful at a time, until the glaze is the right consistency to spread over top of the cake.

7. Place one cake layer on a plate. If necessary, cut off a bit from the top to make it flat and even. Spread custard filling evenly over top. Place second cake layer on top of the custard. Spread the chocolate glaze over top and allow it to drizzle over the sides. Chill in refrigerator until glaze sets.

> **TIP:** To cool a cake that has just come out of the oven, place the pan on a wet towel. Your cake will not stick to the pan if you cool it this way.

Lady Baltimore Cake

Serves 12 to 16

2½ cups	sifted cake flour	625 mL
1 tbsp	baking powder	15 mL
½ tsp	salt	2 mL
2 cups	granulated sugar	500 mL
¾ cup	shortening, softened	175 mL
1 tsp	vanilla	5 mL
¼ tsp	lemon extract	1 mL
½ cup	milk	125 mL
½ cup	water	125 mL
6	egg whites	6

LADY BALTIMORE FILLING

½ cup	finely chopped pecans	125 mL
⅓ cup	chopped raisins	75 mL
⅓ cup	chopped dried figs	75 mL
3 tbsp	chopped drained maraschino cherries	45 mL
2 tsp	grated orange zest	10 mL

PINK MOUNTAIN CREAM FROSTING

1 cup	granulated sugar	250 mL
⅓ cup	light corn syrup	75 mL
¼ cup	maraschino cherry liquid	50 mL
¼ tsp	salt	1 mL
4	egg whites	4
Pinch	cream of tartar	Pinch
½ tsp	vanilla	2 mL
	Red food coloring	

NOTE: If desired, substitute water for the cherry liquid and omit the red food coloring for a white frosting.

Preheat oven to 350°F (180°C)

Two 9-inch (23 cm) round metal cake pans, greased on bottom, then lined with wax paper that has been greased and floured

1. In a medium bowl, sift together flour, baking powder and salt.

2. In a large mixer bowl with clean beaters, on medium speed, cream sugar and shortening until smooth. Beat in vanilla and lemon extract until light and fluffy.

3. Add flour mixture to creamed mixture alternately with the milk and water, making 3 additions of flour and 1 each of milk and water, on low speed, beating well after each addition.

4. In a small, clean mixer bowl with clean beaters, on high speed, beat egg whites until stiff peaks form. Fold into batter, gently, until well blended. Pour into prepared baking pans, dividing evenly.

5. Bake in preheated oven for 25 to 30 minutes, or until center springs back when touched lightly with a fingertip. Cool in pan on wire racks for 10 minutes, loosen around edges with a knife and turn out onto wire rack to cool completely.

6. *Prepare Lady Baltimore Filling:* In a medium bowl, combine pecans, raisins, figs, cherries and zest, and toss to mix well.

7. *Prepare Pink Mountain Cream Frosting:* In a small saucepan, over medium heat combine sugar, corn syrup, cherry liquid and salt. Heat to boiling and boil gently until a small amount of the syrup mixture falls threadlike from a spoon. In a large, clean mixer bowl with clean beaters, beat egg whites and cream of tartar. Pour the hot syrup mixture onto egg whites, very slowly, in a thin stream, beating on high speed until stiff and glossy. Beat in vanilla and a few drops of the red food coloring. Fold in the filling mixture and mix well.

8. Place one layer of cake on a serving plate. Spread filling over top. Place second cake layer on top of the first. Frost sides and top of cake with remaining frosting. Decorate further as desired.

Petit Four Cakes

Makes about 54 tiny cakes		
2 cups	sifted cake flour	500 mL
1 tbsp	baking powder	15 mL
¼ tsp	salt	1 mL
¼ cup	butter or margarine, softened	50 mL
¼ cup	shortening	50 mL
1¼ cups	granulated sugar, divided	300 mL
½ tsp	vanilla	2 mL
¼ tsp	almond extract	1 mL
¾ cup	milk	175 mL
6	egg whites	6

Preheat oven to 350°F (180°C)

13- by 9-inch (3 L) metal baking pan, greased and floured

1. In a medium bowl, sift together flour, baking powder and salt.

2. In a large mixer bowl, cream butter and shortening until smooth. Gradually add 1 cup (250 mL) of the sugar, vanilla and almond extract, and beat until light and fluffy. Beat in flour mixture alternately with the milk, making 3 additions of flour and 2 of milk, on low speed, beating well after each addition.

3. In a small, clean mixer bowl with clean beaters, beat egg whites until foamy. Gradually beat in the remaining ¼ cup (50 mL) of sugar and beat until soft peaks form. Fold gently into the batter. Pour into prepared baking pan.

4. Bake in preheated oven for 40 to 45 minutes, or until a toothpick inserted in the center comes out clean and dry. Cool in pan on a wire rack for 10 minutes, then remove from pan and cool completely on wire rack.

5. Cut cooled cake into 1½-inch (4 cm) squares or diamonds. Place squares into paper baking cups and decorate as desired.

> **TIP:** To measure solid shortening, line your measuring cup with plastic wrap and then fill it with shortening. To remove the shortening, lift out with the plastic wrap. It will come out easily, and the cup will still be clean.

Sally Lunn Cake

Serves 12 to 16		
3½ cups	all-purpose flour, divided	875 mL
¼ cup	granulated sugar	50 mL
1	package (¼ oz/7 g) quick-rise (instant) yeast (or 2¼ tsp/11 mL)	1
1 tsp	salt	5 mL
1 cup	milk	250 mL
½ cup	butter or margarine, cut into chunks	125 mL
¼ cup	water	50 mL
3	eggs, room temperature	3

Preheat oven to 400°F (200°C)

10-inch (3 L) Bundt pan, greased and floured

1. In a large mixer bowl, combine 1 cup (250 mL) of the flour, sugar, yeast and salt. Set aside.

2. In a medium saucepan over low heat, combine milk, butter and water until liquids are warm, but butter does not need to melt.

3. Add butter mixture to flour mixture, beating on medium speed for about 2 to 3 minutes. Add eggs and another 1 cup (250 mL) of flour, beating on high speed for 2 to 3 minutes. Stir in enough of the remaining flour to make a stiff batter. Cover and let rise in a warm place for about 1 hour, or until doubled in size.

4. Stir down and spoon into prepared baking pan. Cover and let rise in a warm place for about 45 minutes, or until doubled in size again.

5. Bake in preheated oven for 30 to 35 minutes, or until top is golden brown. Remove from pan onto a wire rack and cool completely, or serve when just warm.

> **TIP:** To test if yeast is still good, dissolve a bit of it in ¼ cup (50 mL) of warm water that has about 1 tsp (5 mL) of sugar dissolved in it. It should start bubbling in a few minutes. If it doesn't, or is slow, throw it away.

Très Leches Cake

Serves 12 to 16		
1½ cups	all-purpose flour	375 mL
1 tsp	baking powder	5 mL
1 cup	granulated sugar	250 mL
½ cup	butter or margarine, softened	125 mL
½ tsp	vanilla	2 mL
5	eggs	5
1 cup	milk (whole/homogenized)	250 mL
1 cup	sweetened condensed milk	250 mL
¾ cup	evaporated milk	175 mL
⅓ cup	liqueur or brandy (optional)	75 mL

TOPPING		
1 cup	granulated sugar	250 mL
1½ cups	whipping (35%) cream	375 mL
1 tsp	vanilla	5 mL

Preheat oven to 350°F (180°C)

13- by 9-inch (3 L) metal baking pan, greased and floured

1. In a large bowl, combine flour and baking powder. Set aside.

2. In a large mixer bowl, on medium speed, cream sugar and butter until smooth. Beat in vanilla and then eggs, one at a time, beating well after each addition.

3. Gradually, by spoonfuls, add flour mixture to the creamed mixture, on low speed, mixing until well combined. Pour into prepared baking pan, spreading evenly.

4. Bake in preheated oven for 30 to 35 minutes, or until a toothpick inserted in the center comes out clean and dry. Pierce top of cake with a fork, or skewer, in about 10 places. Cool completely in pan on wire rack.

5. In another bowl, combine milk, condensed milk, evaporated milk and liqueur, if using. Pour over top of the cooled cake and allow to soak in while chilling for at least 2 hours.

6. *Prepare topping:* In a small bowl, whisk sugar, whipping cream and vanilla until thick. Spread over top of cake. Store in refrigerator until ready to serve (up 1 week).

> **TIP:** If you want leftover whipped cream to retain its lightness, height and texture for a day or more, add 1 tsp (5 mL) of light corn syrup to each 1 cup (250 mL) of cream while whipping.

Esther's Favorite Cakes

Felicia's Apple Cake

Serves 12 to 16		
1¾ cups	all-purpose flour	425 mL
2 tsp	baking powder	10 mL
Pinch	salt	Pinch
2	eggs	2
¾ cup	granulated sugar	175 mL
¾ cup	vegetable oil	175 mL
½ cup	cold water	125 mL
1	can (21 oz/625 mL) apple pie filling	1
	Cinnamon sugar	

Preheat oven to 350°F (180°C)

13- by 9-inch (3 L) metal baking pan, greased

1. In a medium bowl, sift together flour, baking powder and salt.

2. In a large mixer bowl, on medium speed, beat eggs until well beaten. Add the sugar slowly, beating until blended. Beat in oil. Add flour mixture alternately with water, making 3 additions of flour and 2 of water, beating on low speed until well blended.

3. Spread about half, or a little more, of the batter on the bottom of your prepared baking pan. Spread apple pie filling over top, in spoonfuls, evenly. Top with remaining batter, spreading evenly, to cover apple filling. Sprinkle cinnamon-sugar mixture over top of cake.

4. Bake in preheated oven for 45 to 55 minutes, or until a toothpick inserted in the center comes out clean and dry. Cool completely in pan on a wire rack.

Mildred's Banana Cake

Serves 8 to 10		
2 cups	all-purpose flour	500 mL
2 tsp	baking powder	10 mL
¼ tsp	salt	1 mL
1 tsp	baking soda	5 mL
⅓ cup	buttermilk or sour cream	75 mL
1 cup	granulated sugar	250 mL
½ cup	butter or margarine, softened	125 mL
2	eggs, well beaten	2
1 cup	mashed, ripe bananas, (2 to 3 medium)	250 mL
1 tsp	vanilla	5 mL

Preheat oven to 350°F (180°C)

9- by 5-inch (1.5 L) metal loaf pan, greased and floured

1. In a medium bowl, sift together flour, baking powder and salt. In a small bowl, dissolve the baking soda in the buttermilk. Set aside.

2. In a large mixer bowl, on medium speed, cream sugar and butter until light and fluffy. Add beaten eggs, beating until blended. Add bananas and vanilla, beating until well blended.

3. Beat in flour mixture alternately with the buttermilk mixture on low speed, making 3 additions of flour and 2 of buttermilk, mixing until thoroughly combined. Spoon into prepared baking pan.

4. Bake in preheated oven for 50 to 55 minutes, or until a toothpick inserted in the center comes out clean and dry. Cool in pan on wire rack for 10 minutes and remove from pan onto wire rack to cool completely.

Betty's Carrot Cake

Serves 12 to 16		
3 cups	all-purpose flour	750 mL
1 tbsp	baking powder	15 mL
1 tsp	salt	5 mL
½ tsp	baking soda	2 mL
4	eggs	4
2 cups	granulated sugar	500 mL
1 cup	vegetable oil	250 mL
1 tsp	vanilla	5 mL
2 cups	grated carrots (about 4 medium)	500 mL
½ cup	chopped nuts	125 mL

TOPPING

½ cup	packed brown sugar	125 mL
2 tbsp	butter or margarine, softened	25 mL
2 tbsp	milk	25 mL
¼ cup	chopped nuts	50 mL

NOTE: When spreading topping on a hot cake, it is not as important to spread it evenly, as it melts and forms a glaze when put back into oven.

Preheat oven to 375°F (190°C)

10-inch (4 L) tube pan, ungreased

1. In a medium bowl, combine flour, baking powder, salt and baking soda.
2. In a large mixer bowl, combine eggs, sugar, oil and vanilla. Beat on medium speed until well combined.
3. Add flour mixture to egg mixture, mixing until well blended. Fold in carrots and chopped nuts. Pour batter into baking pan.
4. Bake in preheated oven for 45 minutes, or until tester inserted in the center comes out just slightly moist.
5. *Prepare topping:* Cream together brown sugar and butter until smooth. Add milk and nuts and mix well.
6. Remove cake from oven, spread topping over top of cake, and bake for 15 minutes more, or until tester inserted in center of cake comes out clean and dry and topping is golden. Immediately invert pan and, using hole in tube, hang upside down on an inverted funnel, the neck of a bottle or a wire rack, and cool completely. With a long thin knife or metal spatula, loosen around the edges and then remove cake from pan. Place on serving plate.

Sima's Cheesecake

Serves 12 to 16		
¾ cup	granulated sugar	175 mL
½ cup	butter, melted	125 mL
2	eggs	2
	Juice of 1 orange	
	Grated zest from ½ lemon	
1 tsp	vanilla	5 mL
2½ cups	all-purpose flour	625 mL
¼ cup	milk	50 mL

CHEESE FILLING

½ cup	granulated sugar	125 mL
1 lb	pressed cottage cheese	500 g
1 lb	cream cheese, softened	500 g
1	egg	1
⅓ cup	butter, melted	75 mL
	Juice of ½ lemon	
1 tsp	vanilla	5 mL

Preheat oven to 350°F (180°C)

13- by 9-inch (3 L) metal baking pan, greased

1. In a large mixer bowl, combine sugar, butter, eggs, orange juice and lemon zest. Beat on medium speed until well blended. Stir in vanilla, then flour alternately with the milk, making 3 additions of flour and 2 of milk. Mix until soft dough is formed. Set aside ¼ of the dough. Press remaining dough onto bottom and up sides of prepared baking pan.

2. *Prepare Cheese Filling:* In a large mixer bowl, combine sugar, pressed cheese and cream cheese. Beat on low speed until blended. Add egg, butter, lemon juice and vanilla, and mix until well blended. Spoon cheese filling over top of dough.

3. Roll out reserved dough into 10 long strips, about ½ inch (1 cm) wide. Arrange strips over top of cheese filling in a lattice pattern (see tip, page 131).

4. Bake in preheated oven for 50 to 60 minutes, until golden brown. Cool completely in pan on a wire rack.

> **TIP:** Keep a plastic sandwich bag in your shortening container, or close by, and use like a mitten to grease baking pans and sheets. I also use the wrappers from the shortening or margarine to grease pans.

Ann's Cheesecake Torte

Serves 10 to 12		
1	package (6.5 oz/200 g) chocolate wafers	1
2 tbsp	butter or margarine, melted	25 mL
8 oz	cream cheese, softened	250 g
1 cup	confectioner's (icing) sugar, sifted	250 mL
2 cups	frozen whipped topping, thawed	500 mL
1	can (14 oz/398 mL) crushed pineapple, well drained	1
1	can (19 oz/540 mL) cherry pie filling	1

9-inch (23 cm) springform pan, greased

1. Set aside 14 chocolate wafers. Crush the remaining wafers and put into a small bowl. Add the butter and mix well. Press firmly onto bottom of prepared baking pan. Stand the reserved 14 wafers on end around the pan.

2. In a large mixer bowl, on medium speed, beat cream cheese and confectioner's sugar until smooth and blended. Fold in whipped topping, gently, until well combined. Fold in pineapple. Spoon into baking pan.

3. Wrap pan in foil and freeze until it feels firm, at least 2 to 3 hours or overnight. About 2 hours before serving, spread cherry pie filling evenly over top and remove springform ring. Keep in fridge until ready to serve.

Baba Mary's Favorite Chocolate Roll

Serves 10 to 12		
5	eggs, separated	5
1 cup	sifted confectioner's (icing) sugar	250 mL
3 tbsp	unsweetened cocoa powder, sifted	45 mL
1 tsp	vanilla	5 mL
	Chocolate Buttercream Filling (optional, see recipe, page 90)	
	Sweetened whipping (35%) cream, whipped (optional)	
	Confectioner's (icing) sugar (optional)	
	Chocolate sauce (optional)	

Preheat oven to 350°F (180°C)

15- by 10-inch (38 by 25 cm) rimmed baking sheet, greased and floured

1. In a clean mixer bowl, on high speed, beat egg whites until foamy. Gradually add sugar, a spoonful at a time, until stiff peaks form. Add cocoa powder.

2. In another bowl, beat egg yolks until lemon-colored and thick. Add vanilla and blend.

3. Fold egg yolk mixture gently into the egg white mixture until well combined. Spoon batter into prepared baking pan, spreading evenly with a spatula.

4. Bake in preheated oven for 20 minutes, or until top springs back when lightly touched. Spread a damp tea towel over cake and cool in pan on a wire rack for 15 minutes.

5. Sprinkle a clean tea towel with cocoa powder. When cake has almost cooled, remove damp towel and loosen edges carefully with a spatula. Invert onto cocoa-dusted towel. Roll up the cake, jelly roll-style, using the towel as a guide, and set aside to cool completely.

6. When completely cooled, unroll and spread with any filling you desire, such as Chocolate Buttercream Filling (see recipe, page 90) or sweetened whipped cream. Re-roll and place on a serving plate. Sprinkle with icing sugar, if desired, or drizzle a hot or cold chocolate sauce over top.

Esther's Chocolate Pound Cake

Serves 8 to 10		
2 cups	all-purpose flour	500 mL
1 tsp	baking soda	5 mL
1½ cups	firmly packed brown sugar	375 mL
½ cup	butter or margarine, softened	125 mL
2	eggs	2
1 cup	sour cream	250 mL
1 tsp	vanilla	5 mL
2 oz	unsweetened chocolate, melted and cooled	60 g

Preheat oven to 325°F (160°C)

9- by 5-inch (1.5 L) metal loaf pan, greased and dusted with unsweetened cocoa powder

1. In a medium bowl, combine flour and baking soda.

2. In a large mixer bowl, on medium speed, cream sugar and butter until smooth and blended. Add eggs, one at a time, beating well after each addition. Gradually add flour mixture, on low speed, beating until well combined. Add sour cream and vanilla and beat until well blended. Add chocolate and continue beating until thoroughly combined. Pour into prepared baking pan.

3. Bake in preheated oven for 60 to 70 minutes, or until a toothpick inserted in the center comes out clean and dry. Cool in pan for 10 minutes, then loosen around edges with a knife and remove carefully from pan onto wire rack to cool completely.

Mom's Chocolate Chip Chiffon Cake

Serves 12 to 16		
2¼ cups	sifted cake flour	550 mL
1⅓ cups	granulated sugar	325 mL
1 tbsp	baking powder	15 mL
1 tsp	salt	5 mL
¾ cup	cold water	175 mL
½ cup	vegetable oil	125 mL
5	egg yolks	5
2 tsp	vanilla	10 mL
8	egg whites	8
½ tsp	cream of tartar	2 mL
3 oz	unsweetened chocolate, grated	90 g

Preheat oven to 325°F (160°C)

10-inch (4 L) tube pan, ungreased, or a 10-inch (3 L) Bundt pan, lightly greased

1. In a large mixer bowl, sift together flour, sugar, baking powder and salt. Mix well and make a well in the center. Pour in water, oil, egg yolks and vanilla. Beat on medium speed for about 3 minutes, and then on high speed for another 2 minutes, until mixture bubbles.

2. In a clean mixer bowl with clean beaters, beat egg whites and cream of tartar on high speed until stiff peaks form. Gently fold into egg yolk mixture until well incorporated. Do not stir.

3. Sprinkle the grated chocolate over top of batter, gently folding in with few strokes. Pour into prepared baking pan. Tap pan lightly on counter to remove any air bubbles. Smooth top of batter.

4. Bake in preheated oven for 55 minutes, then increase temperature to 350°F (180°C) and bake for another 10 to 15 minutes, or until cake springs back when lightly touched. Immediately invert pan and, using hole in tube, hang upside down on an inverted funnel, the neck of a bottle or a wire rack, and cool completely. With a long thin knife or metal spatula, loosen around the edges and then remove cake from pan.

Christine's Honey Cake

Serves 10 to 12		
3 cups	all-purpose flour	750 mL
1 tsp	baking powder	5 mL
1 tsp	ground cinnamon	5 mL
1 tsp	ground allspice	5 mL
1 cup	cold, strong coffee	250 mL
1 tsp	baking soda	5 mL
1¼ cups	packed brown sugar	300 mL
1 cup	liquid honey	250 mL
4	eggs, at room temperature	4
¾ cup	vegetable oil	175 mL

Preheat oven to 325°F (160°C)

9- by 5-inch (1.5 L) metal loaf pan, greased and floured

1. In a medium bowl, sift together flour, baking powder, cinnamon and allspice. In a small bowl, combine coffee with baking soda and mix well.

2. In a large mixer bowl, on medium speed, beat together brown sugar and honey. Add the eggs and beat well. Beat in oil until blended.

3. Stir in flour mixture alternately with the coffee mixture, making 3 additions of flour and 2 of coffee, until well blended. Pour into prepared baking pan.

4. Bake in preheated oven for 1 hour, or until a toothpick inserted in the center comes out clean and dry. Cool completely in pan on a wire rack.

Mom's Ice-Box Cake

Serves 6 to 8		
3 oz	gelatin, any flavor	90 g
1 cup	graham wafer crumbs (about 12 whole wafers)	250 mL
1 cup	chopped walnuts	250 mL
½ cup	packed brown sugar	125 mL
	Grated zest of 1 lemon	
	Whole graham wafers	
FILLING		
½ cup	packed brown sugar	125 mL
1½ cups	sour cream	375 mL
2 tsp	lemon juice	10 mL
1 tsp	vanilla	5 mL

NOTE: Originally, a creative cook quickly put together a reasonable facsimile of a cake by alternating layers of cookies and flavored whipped cream. This creation was placed in an old-fashioned ice-box to mellow, hence the name ice-box cake.

9-inch (2.5 L) square metal baking pan, ungreased

1. Prepare gelatin as directed on package. Chill in refrigerator until set.
2. In a medium bowl, combine graham crumbs, walnuts, brown sugar and lemon zest. Mix well until thoroughly combined.
3. *Prepare filling:* In another bowl, combine brown sugar, sour cream, lemon juice and vanilla. Mix well until thoroughly blended.
4. Arrange whole graham wafers on bottom of baking pan. Spread half of the filling mixture evenly on top of wafers. Place another layer of whole graham wafers on top of filling. Top with the remaining filling mixture, spreading evenly.
5. Spoon half of the crumb mixture on top of the filling mixture. Spread the gelatin over top and then spread the remaining crumb mixture on top of the gelatin. Chill in refrigerator for at least 30 minutes, or until ready to serve. Store any remaining cake in the refrigerator.

Arlene's Pumpkin Pecan Cake

Serves 12 to 16		
1	package (18.25 oz/ 515 g) spice cake mix	1
1 cup	canned pumpkin purée (not pie filling)	250 mL
½ cup	vegetable oil	125 mL
1	package (4-serving size) vanilla instant pudding mix	1
3	eggs	3
1 tsp	ground cinnamon	5 mL
½ cup	water	125 mL
½ cup	chopped pecans	125 mL
	Whipped cream or ice cream (optional)	

Preheat oven to 350°F (180°C)

10-inch (3 L) Bundt pan, greased and floured

1. In a large mixer bowl, combine cake mix, pumpkin, oil and pudding mix, beating until blended. Add eggs, one at a time, beating well after each addition. Beat in cinnamon and water, beating until well blended.
2. Fold in pecans, gently, and mix until thoroughly combined. Pour into prepared baking pan.
3. Bake in preheated oven for 40 to 45 minutes, or until a toothpick inserted in the center comes out clean and dry. Cool in pan on a wire rack for 10 minutes, then turn out of pan onto wire rack to cool completely. Serve with whipped cream or ice cream, if desired.

Shauna's Passover Chiffon Cake

Serves 12 to 16		
10	eggs, separated	10
3 tbsp	unsweetened cocoa powder	45 mL
½ cup	hot water	125 mL
1½ cups	granulated sugar	375 mL
½ cup	vegetable oil	125 mL
1 tsp	vanilla	5 mL
½ tsp	cream of tartar	2 mL
¾ cup	matzo cake meal	175 mL
¼ cup	potato starch	50 mL

Preheat oven to 325°F (160°C)

10-inch (4 L) tube pan, ungreased

1. Set aside egg whites, in a large mixer bowl, to come to room temperature.

2. In a small bowl, mix together cocoa powder and hot water.

3. In another large mixer bowl, combine egg yolks, cocoa mixture, sugar, oil and vanilla, beating until well blended.

4. With clean beaters, on high speed, beat egg whites and cream of tartar until stiff peaks form. Fold gently into the egg yolk mixture until well combined. Gently fold in cake meal, and then potato starch, until thoroughly blended. Spoon into baking pan. Tap pan lightly on counter to remove any air bubbles. Smooth top of batter.

5. Bake in preheated oven for 75 minutes, or until cake springs back when lightly touched. Immediately invert pan and, using hole in tube, hang upside down on an inverted funnel, the neck of a bottle or a wire rack, and cool completely. With a long thin knife or metal spatula, loosen around the edges and then remove cake from pan.

Esther's Sour Cream Coffee Cake

Serves 12 to 16		
1½ cups	all-purpose flour	375 mL
1½ tsp	baking powder	7 mL
1 cup	sour cream	250 mL
1 tsp	baking soda	5 mL
1 cup	granulated sugar	250 mL
¼ cup	butter or margarine, softened	50 mL
2	eggs, lightly beaten	2
1 tbsp	vanilla	15 mL
TOPPING		
½ cup	chopped nuts	125 mL
¼ cup	granulated sugar	50 mL
½ tsp	ground cinnamon	2 mL
1 to 1½ tbsp	butter	15 to 22 mL

Preheat oven to 350°F (180°C)

10-inch (3 L) Bundt pan, lightly greased

1. *Prepare topping:* In a small bowl, mix together nuts, sugar and cinnamon.

2. In another bowl, combine flour and baking powder. In a small bowl, mix sour cream and baking soda. Set aside.

3. In a large mixer bowl, cream sugar, butter and eggs until smooth and fluffy. Add sour cream mixture to the egg mixture and beat on low speed until well blended.

4. Stir flour mixture into creamed mixture. Add vanilla and mix well until combined. Pour into prepared baking pan. Sprinkle nut mixture evenly over top of batter and dot with butter.

5. Bake in preheated oven for 45 to 50 minutes, or until a toothpick inserted in the center comes out clean and dry. Turn off oven and keep door ajar, allowing cake to remain in oven until slightly cooled, about 15 to 20 minutes. Remove cake from pan onto a wire rack to cool completely.

> **TIP:** If your recipe calls for chopped nuts, put whole nuts in a plastic bag and roll them with a rolling pin. Then just pour them from the bag into your mixing bowl.

Frostings and Glazes

Basic Frosting Base

	Makes about 2¼ cups (550 mL)	
3 cups	confectioner's (icing) sugar, sifted	750 mL
½ cup	butter or margarine, softened	125 mL
¼ cup	(approx) milk	50 mL
½ tsp	vanilla	2 mL

Note: To this basic recipe, you can add whatever you desire, such as melted chocolate, food coloring, nuts, etc.

1. In a large mixer bowl, combine sugar, butter, milk and vanilla. Beat on medium speed until smooth. Add more milk, if necessary, 1 tsp (5 mL) at a time, so that frosting is fairly thin but of spreading consistency.

TIP: To frost a cake easily, place cake on a plate and then on a lazy Susan.

Banana Frosting

	Makes about 2½ cups (625 mL)	
½ cup	butter or margarine, softened	125 mL
½ cup	mashed, ripe bananas (1 to 2 medium)	125 mL
3½ cups	sifted confectioner's (icing) sugar	825 mL
1 tbsp	lemon juice	15 mL
1 tsp	vanilla	5 mL

1. In a large mixer bowl, cream butter and bananas until blended. Gradually add the sugar, lemon juice and vanilla, and mix well. Chill until mixture is the right consistency for spreading.

VARIATION

Banana Filling: Chop 2 bananas with a little pulverized sugar and lemon juice and mix together. Spread in between layers of cake and cover top and sides with Banana Frosting.

Brown Butter Frosting

	Makes about 1¾ cups (425 mL)	
¼ cup	butter or margarine	50 mL
2 cups	sifted confectioner's (icing) sugar	500 mL
2 tbsp	half-and-half (10%) or table (18%) cream	25 mL
1 tsp	vegetable oil	5 mL
1 tsp	vanilla	5 mL
	Hot water	

1. Put butter in a medium saucepan, over low heat, and heat slowly until liquid bubbles up, is very foamy, and then settles and is golden brown, about 3 to 5 minutes. Remove from heat and add sugar, cream, oil and vanilla. Stir until right consistency for spreading. If mixture is too thick, add some hot water.

Buttercream Frosting

Makes about 1 cup (250 mL)		
¼ cup	butter, softened	50 mL
1½ cups	sifted confectioner's (icing) sugar	375 mL
1 tsp	vanilla	5 mL
2 to 3 tbsp	whipping (35%) cream	25 to 45 mL

1. In a mixer bowl, cream butter until smooth. Gradually add in sugar and vanilla and beat until light and fluffy. If necessary, add a little cream, a spoonful at a time, until mixture is of the right consistency.

VARIATIONS

Chocolate Buttercream Frosting: Add 2 oz (60 g) melted unsweetened chocolate to the recipe. If desired, add some chopped nuts.

Orange Buttercream Frosting: Add grated zest and juice of half an orange and 1½ tsp (7 mL) of lemon juice. If mixture is too thin, add a little more icing sugar and beat well.

Caramel Candy Frosting

Makes about 3½ cups (875 mL)		
28	soft vanilla caramels (8 oz/250 g)	28
½ cup	water	125 mL
½ cup	butter or margarine, softened	125 mL
Pinch	salt	Pinch
4 cups	sifted confectioner's (icing) sugar	1 L
¼ cup	chopped walnuts (optional)	50 mL

1. In the top of a double boiler, over boiling water, melt caramels in water, stirring constantly. Cool to room temperature, about 10 to 15 minutes.
2. In a large mixer bowl, cream butter, add salt, and then add icing sugar alternately with the caramel mixture, making 4 additions of sugar and 3 of caramel, beating on low speed until smooth and creamy. Stir in walnuts, if desired. Chill until of the right consistency for spreading.

White Chocolate Buttercream Frosting

Makes about 1¾ cups (425 mL)		
6 oz	white chocolate, chopped	175 g
¼ cup	milk or cream (half-and-half (10%) or table (18%))	50 mL
1 cup	cold, unsalted butter, cut into chunks	250 mL
1 cup	confectioner's (icing) sugar	250 mL

1. In a small saucepan, melt chocolate in milk, over low heat, stirring just until melted. Let cool for about 15 minutes, until just warm to the touch.
2. In a large mixer bowl, cream butter until soft and smooth. Gradually add sugar and blend. Add cooled chocolate and beat on high speed until smooth and fluffy, about 2 to 3 minutes.

Chocolate Glaze

Makes about 1½ cups (325 mL)		
¼ cup	unsweetened cocoa powder	50 mL
3 tbsp	water	45 mL
2 tbsp	butter or shortening	25 mL
2 tbsp	light corn syrup	25 mL
2 cups	sifted confectioner's (icing) sugar	500 mL
¼ tsp	vanilla	1 mL

1. In a medium saucepan, over low heat, combine cocoa powder, water, butter and corn syrup, stirring until butter melts and mixture is smooth. Remove from heat and gradually beat in sugar and vanilla. If mixture is too thick to drizzle, add another spoonful of water.

Dark Chocolate Glaze

Makes about ⅔ cup (150 mL)		
2 oz	unsweetened chocolate, chopped	60 g
⅓ cup	granulated sugar	75 mL
¼ cup	water	50 mL
1 tsp	butter	5 mL
1 tbsp	milk	15 mL

1. In a double boiler, over hot water, melt chocolate.
2. In a small saucepan, combine sugar and water, and bring to a boil. Boil for 1 minute, stirring constantly.
3. Put melted chocolate in a mixer bowl. Slowly stir in sugar mixture, then the butter. Add milk and beat, on low speed, until of drizzling consistency. While glaze is still warm, drizzle over cake.

Coffee Frosting

Makes about 1½ cups (375 mL)		
2 cups	sifted confectioner's (icing) sugar, divided	500 mL
½ cup	butter or margarine, softened	125 mL
3 tbsp	coffee liqueur	45 mL
2 tbsp	milk	25 mL
1 tbsp	instant coffee granules	15 mL

1. In a small mixer bowl, cream 1 cup (250 mL) of the sugar and butter until smooth and fluffy.
2. In a measuring cup, mix together liqueur, milk and instant coffee until blended. Add to the creamed mixture alternately with the remaining icing sugar, beating until smooth.

TIP: To prevent crust from forming on prepared icings and frostings, press a piece of plastic wrap against the surface until ready to use.

Cherry Frosting

	Makes about 2 cups (500 mL)	
3 cups	confectioner's (icing) sugar, sifted	750 mL
⅓ cup	butter or margarine, softened	75 mL
2 tbsp	chopped drained maraschino cherries	25 mL
2 tbsp	milk	25 mL
1½ tsp	vanilla	7 mL
2	drops red food coloring	2

1. In a large mixer bowl, cream sugar and butter until smooth. Stir in cherries, milk, vanilla and food coloring. Beat on medium speed until the right consistency for spreading.

Coconut Frosting and Filling

	Makes about 2½ cups (625 mL)	
⅔ cup	granulated sugar	150 mL
Pinch	salt	Pinch
1	can (6 oz/175 mL) evaporated milk	1
¼ cup	butter or margarine	50 mL
1	egg, lightly beaten	1
1⅓ cups	flaked coconut (sweetened or unsweetened)	325 mL
½ cup	chopped pecans	125 mL
1 tsp	vanilla	5 mL

1. In a medium saucepan, over medium heat, combine sugar, salt, milk, butter and egg. Cook and stir until mixture thickens and begins to boil, 12 to 15 minutes. Remove from heat. Stir in coconut, pecans and vanilla, and mix well. Cool completely before frosting or filling cake.

Cream Filling

Makes about 2 cups (500 mL)		
½ cup	granulated sugar	125 mL
⅓ cup	all-purpose flour	75 mL
½ tsp	salt	2 mL
2 cups	milk	500 mL
2	eggs, slightly beaten	2
1 tsp	vanilla	5 mL

1. In a medium saucepan, over medium heat, combine sugar, flour and salt. Slowly stir in milk and cook until mixture boils and thickens, then cook for 2 minutes longer. Stir a little of this hot mixture into the eggs, then stir back into remaining hot mixture and bring just to boiling, stirring constantly until thick. Remove from heat. Add vanilla and set aside to cool.

VARIATIONS

Chocolate Filling: Add 1½ oz (45 g) of unsweetened chocolate, chopped, with the milk. Increase the sugar to ¾ cup (175 mL).

Lemon Filling: Substitute ⅔ cup (150 mL) water for the milk. Add 1 tbsp (15 mL) grated lemon zest and 2 tbsp (25 mL) lemon juice to the sugar mixture. Omit the vanilla.

Butterscotch Filling: Use ⅔ cup (150 mL) packed brown sugar instead of the granulated sugar. Add ¼ cup (50 mL) butter with the vanilla.

Lemon Butter Icing

Makes about 1¼ cups (300 mL)		
½ cup	butter, softened	125 mL
1¾ cups	sifted confectioner's (icing) sugar	425 mL
1 tbsp	grated lemon zest	15 mL
1 tbsp	lemon juice	15 mL

1. In a large mixer bowl, cream butter until soft and smooth. Gradually add sugar, lemon zest and lemon juice, and beat on low speed, just until well blended.

VARIATION

Orange Butter Frosting: Substitute orange juice and zest for the lemon juice and zest.

Fluffy Mocha Frosting

Makes about 1½ cups (375 mL)		
2¾ cups	confectioner's (icing) sugar	675 mL
¼ cup	unsweetened cocoa powder, sifted	50 mL
6 tbsp	butter or margarine, softened	90 mL
2 tbsp	milk	25 mL
2 tbsp	cold, strong brewed coffee	25 mL
1 tsp	vanilla	5 mL

1. In a large mixer bowl, on low speed, cream sugar, cocoa powder and butter until smooth. Gradually add milk, coffee and vanilla, beating until well blended.

TIP: To keep cake crumbs from ruining your frosting, spread a thin layer of frosting on your cake first. Let this set and then frost as usual.

Seven-Minute Frosting

Makes about 2 cups (500 mL)		
1½ cups	granulated sugar	375 mL
¼ tsp	cream of tartar (or use 2 tsp/10 mL light corn syrup)	1 mL
2	egg whites	2
⅓ cup	cold water	75 mL
Pinch	salt	Pinch
1 tsp	vanilla	5 mL

1. In the top of a double boiler, before placing on stove, combine sugar, cream of tartar, egg whites, cold water and salt. Beat with a hand mixer or whisk to blend.
2. Place over boiling water and cook, whisking constantly, until mixture forms stiff peaks, about 7 minutes.
3. Remove from the boiling water and pour into a mixing bowl. Add vanilla and whisk for 2 to 3 minutes, or until mixture is the right consistency for spreading.

VARIATIONS
Chocolate Fluff Frosting: Fold in 2 oz (60 g) of unsweetened chocolate, melted and cooled, just before spreading on cake.
Brown Sugar Frosting: Substitute brown sugar for the granulated sugar and, if desired, replace vanilla with ½ tsp (2 mL) maple extract.

TIP: An easy way to frost an angel food cake, or any cake, is to thaw 2 cups (500 mL) frozen whipped topping. Fold in one package of any flavor gelatin powder. It mixes up in seconds and tastes great.

PART TWO

Pies

Introduction to Pies

After mastering the art of cake making, it seemed only logical to attempt pie baking, but creating a perfect pie crust seemed an even more insurmountable challenge than baking a cake. Many people shy away from pie-making because they can't make good pastry. It is important to remember two things: keep all the ingredients as cold as possible, and work the dough as little as possible.

The principal ingredients in a pie crust are flour, fat and liquid. My greatest problem was in adding the liquid to the flour-fat mixture. It is nearly impossible for a recipe to tell you the exact amount of liquid to use, mainly because flours vary. If you use too little, your crust may be crumbly instead of flaky, and if you use too much you will end up with a tough crust. Pie dough should be soft and semi-dry — not sticky or doughy, but moist enough to hold its shape.

All-purpose flour is the most popular choice, as it makes a tender, flaky crust. It should be sifted once before measuring. The choice of fat is more varied. Lard makes excellent pastry, but most people steer away from it because we're all trying to reduce our fat intake. I like to use shortening. Whichever fat is used, it should be well chilled before you add it. Using your fingers to work the fat into the flour sometimes works best. Pastries made with lard or shortening usually do not require chilling, but pastries made with a large amount of butter do require chilling to make a flakier crust.

Once you have found the right combination, stick to it. Trying to find this combination is what causes people to give up. As my mom used to say, just add enough that it feels or looks right. Her pies were delicious. You have to be flexible to be a good pastry maker, as the dough you have always used may, at times, handle differently because of room temperature, humidity or a slight variation in measuring your ingredients. So persevere!

There are pre-made crusts for busy days or unexpected company: baked crusts, oven-ready frozen crusts, crumb crusts in foil pans and prepared tart shells. Today's fillings are also easier and more readily available. For a homemade look, there are canned fruit fillings, pumpkin fillings, packaged pie fillings and custard mixes, and frozen whipped toppings. What could be easier than opening a can of prepared pudding, ready to spoon right into your crust?

But I still feel there is nothing more rewarding than a homemade crust and filling. Topped with real, heavy whipping cream — now that is a real culinary accomplishment! That is why I have sought out so many recipes for pie crusts, many from good friends. I want to share with you some of the variations, so that you can find the best combination for you. Enjoy!

Making a Perfect Pie Crust

1. While preheating the oven, place a cookie sheet on the rack where you will be baking the pie. When pie is ready for baking, place it on the cookie sheet and bake for the required time. This helps the baking process.
2. Sift the flour once and then measure accurately into the mixing bowl with the other dry ingredients.
3. Cut in the shortening (or fat) with a pastry blender or two knives until the pieces are the size of small peas. An experienced pie baker may want to do this by hand.
4. To make your pastry extra tender and flaky, divide the shortening in half. Cut in the first half until the mixture resembles cornmeal. Then cut in the remaining half until mixture resembles small peas.
5. Add liquid slowly. Sprinkle 1 tbsp (15 mL) of the water over part of the flour-shortening mixture. Gently toss with a fork and push to one side of the bowl. Sprinkle the next tablespoon of water over the dry part, mix lightly and push over to the moistened part. Repeat until all of the mixture is moistened. Gather up mixture with your fingers and form into a ball. If you are making a two-crust pie, divide the dough into lower and upper crust and form each of these into a ball.

6. If using a food processor, place the flour and salt, if used, into the bowl and pulse once or twice, just to blend. Cut the cold shortening into chunks and add to bowl. Process briefly, in intervals, until the mixture resembles coarse crumbs. Add the water and pulse the dough until it holds together in a ball and feels like the right consistency.

7. Turn the dough out onto a lightly floured working surface, flatten ball slightly and roll out to $\frac{1}{8}$-inch (0.25 cm) thickness. Roll the dough from the center out to the edge, using light strokes. Never roll completely across. Dust with more flour underneath as required, but do not turn dough over. If your dough is sticky, chill for 15 to 30 minutes before rolling.

8. Roll dough on waxed paper or between two sheets of waxed paper to prevent sticking. If any tears occur, do not re-roll your pastry. Just patch it up.

9. To transfer your pastry to the pie plate, roll it carefully over your rolling pin, then unroll over the pie plate, fitting it loosely onto the bottom and sides. You can also fold the pastry in half, place it gently into your pan, and then open up and fit into your pie plate. Lift the edges while easing into pan to avoid shrinking, but do not stretch the dough to fit.

10. For a single crust, fit the dough loosely into the bottom and sides of the pan. Trim the dough $\frac{1}{2}$ to 1 inch (1 to 2.5 cm) beyond the edge. Fold under and flute the edge, or press all around the rim with the tines of a fork. If your recipe calls for a baked pie shell, prick the bottom and sides well with a fork so the shell won't puff up while baking. If the crust and filling are to be baked together, do not prick the pastry.

11. For a double crust, fit the lower crust into the pan. Trim it even with the rim of your pie plate and moisten the edge. After adding the pie filling, add the top crust and trim $\frac{1}{2}$ inch (1 cm) beyond the edge. Tuck top under the edge of the lower crust to seal in the juices. Crimp or flute the edges, making sure the edges are hooked onto the rim of the pan. Slash the upper crust with several slits to allow steam to escape, using whatever design you wish.

12. Some people like to cover the edges of the pie plate with a strip of tin foil to prevent over-browning, but be sure to remove the foil about 15 minutes before the end of the baking time.

13. If pre-baking the crust, place a sheet of aluminum foil over the dough and put pie weights, rice or beans onto the foil to prevent bubbles. Bake as directed in recipe, then remove the weights and foil, brush crust with a beaten egg and return to oven to bake for 1 to 2 minutes more, until golden.

Making a Perfect Meringue

1. Use a small, deep bowl unless you are using more than 4 egg whites. Clean the bowl and beaters first to make sure there isn't any grease or oil on them.

2. Separate your eggs carefully so that there is not even a tiny bit of egg yolk in the whites.

3. For maximum volume, egg whites should be at room temperature before you beat them.

4. Beat egg whites with cream of tartar, as this stabilizes the whites. Beat on high speed until foamy and soft peaks form when the beaters are lifted. If you don't have any cream of tartar, use a teaspoon of lemon juice, unless you have more than 2 or 3 whites.

5. When adding sugar, do so gradually, and on medium speed, adding sugar a spoonful at a time. When all of the sugar has been added, increase speed and beat until stiff, but still glossy, and pliable peaks form.

6. Pour your hot filling into a baked, cooled crust. Set aside and allow a thin film to form on the filling. Spoon the meringue onto the hot filling around the edge of the crust so that there is less chance of the meringue shrinking and weeping. Then gently spread the meringue with a spatula around the inner edge of the pie crust until it is well sealed.

7. Using the spatula, spread the meringue from the edges toward the center, swirling but not making high peaks. Cover the entire pie.

8. After baking, cool your meringue pie on a wire rack, at room temperature, for 3 hours before cutting. To cut slices easily, be sure to use a sharp knife. After each cut, dip your knife into hot water.

Pie Crusts

To mix and roll out the dough, follow the steps in "Making a Perfect Pie Crust," page 112, unless otherwise directed.

Single-Crust Plain Pastry

Makes enough for one 9-inch (23 cm) single-crust pie		
1½ cups	all-purpose flour	375 mL
½ tsp	salt	2 mL
½ cup	cold shortening, cubed	125 mL
2 to 4 tbsp	cold water	25 to 50 mL

Preheat oven to 450°F (230°C)
9-inch (23 cm) pie plate

1. In a large bowl, sift together flour and salt. Cut in the shortening with a pastry blender or two knives, until mixture resembles coarse meal.

2. Sprinkle 1 tbsp (15 mL) of the water over part of the flour mixture and toss lightly with a fork. Push this to the side of the bowl. Repeat this procedure, using just enough water until all of the flour mixture is moistened. Form dough into a ball. Flatten slightly into a circle and wrap in plastic wrap. Chill in refrigerator for about 30 minutes.

3. On a lightly floured surface, roll the dough out and transfer to the pie plate. Turn edges under and flute or crimp as desired. Refrigerate for about 15 minutes, or until chilled.

4. If a baked pie shell is needed, prick the bottom and sides well with a fork so that your pastry does not puff up while baking. If your recipe requires the filling and crust to be baked together, do not prick the pastry. Just add the filling and bake as directed.

5. Bake in preheated oven for 10 to 12 minutes, or until golden brown.

VARIATIONS

Poppy Seed Pastry: Add 1 tsp (5 mL) poppy seeds to the flour mixture before adding the water.

Pecan Pastry: Add 3 tbsp (45 mL) finely chopped pecans to the flour mixture before adding the water.

Lemon Pastry: Add ½ tsp (2 mL) grated lemon zest to the flour mixture, and substitute 1 tbsp (15 mL) lemon juice for 1 tbsp (15 mL) of the water.

TIP: To add great flavor and color to a plain pastry crust, add 1 tbsp (15 mL) of minced, fresh parsley to the flour mixture before cutting in the butter.

Double-Crust Pie Pastry

**Makes enough for
one 9-inch (23 cm)
double-crust pie or
24 2½-inch (6 cm) tarts**

2 cups	all-purpose flour	500 mL
1 tsp	salt	5 mL
¾ cup	cold shortening, cubed	175 mL
3 to 5 tbsp	cold water	45 to 75 mL

9-inch (23 cm) pie plate

1. In a large bowl, combine flour and salt. Cut in shortening, using a pastry blender or two knives, until mixture resembles coarse crumbs or large peas.
2. Sprinkle with cold water, 1 tbsp (15 mL) at a time, tossing lightly with a fork. Add just enough water, a spoonful at a time, to form dough into a ball.
3. Divide dough in half. Shape each half into a ball and flatten slightly into a circle with the palm of your hand. Wrap each separately in plastic wrap and chill in refrigerator for 15 to 30 minutes for easier rolling.
4. On lightly floured surface, roll half the dough out and transfer it to the pie plate. To repair any tears, moisten edges and press together. Trim edge even with pie plate. Dampen edges of dough and fill with desired filling .
5. Roll out remaining dough 1 inch (2.5 cm) larger than the pie plate and place on top of filling. Fold under and flute or crimp as desired. Cut slits in top to allow steam to escape.
6. Bake as directed in recipe.

TIP: Get a rich, flaky, melt-in-your-mouth pie crust by substituting the same amount of sour cream for any water in the recipe.

Flaky Double-Crust Pastry

Makes enough for one 9-inch (23 cm) double-crust pie

2 cups	cake flour	500 mL
¾ tsp	salt	4 mL
¼ tsp	granulated sugar	1 mL
⅔ cup	cold shortening, cut in chunks	150 mL
1 tsp	white vinegar or lemon juice	5 mL
3 tbsp	ice water	45 mL

Note: This pastry is too fragile for deep tarts such as Classic Butter Tarts, Chocolate Butter Tarts or Old-fashioned Chess Tarts.

9-inch (23 cm) deep-dish pie plate

1. In a large bowl, combine flour, salt and sugar, and mix well to blend. Cut in the chunks of shortening, using a pastry blender or two knives, until the mixture resembles small peas.

2. Sprinkle the vinegar and ice water over the flour mixture, 1 spoonful at a time. Stir with a fork.

3. Press together with your hand until particles begin to cling and can be formed into a rough ball that cleans the bowl. If the dough is too dry, break open the ball and sprinkle a few more drops of water, then press together again. Dough should not be wet and sticky.

4. Divide dough in half, with a little more in one portion. The larger half will be used for the bottom crust, and the other for the top crust. Flatten each slightly into a round circle and wrap separately in waxed paper. Chill in freezer until dough is firm but still pliable, about 15 minutes.

5. Set the larger portion on a floured surface, lightly flour your rolling pin and roll out the dough into a circle wide enough to fit your pie plate. Press down lightly into the plate and trim off excess. Dampen the edge and fill with the filling.

6. Roll out remaining dough 1 inch (2.5 cm) larger than the pie plate and place on top of filling. Fold under and flute or crimp as desired. Cut slits in top to allow steam to escape.

7. Bake as directed in recipe.

All-Purpose No-Fail Pie Pastry

	Makes enough for two 9-inch (23 cm) double-crust pies and one 9-inch (23 cm) single-crust pie	
4 cups	all-purpose flour	1 L
1 tbsp	granulated sugar	15 mL
2 tsp	salt	10 mL
1¾ cups	shortening, at room temperature (no substitutes)	425 mL
½ cup	water	125 mL
1 tbsp	vinegar (white or cider)	15 mL
1	egg	1

1. In a large bowl, combine flour, sugar and salt. Mix with a fork to blend. Add the shortening and mix again with the fork, or a pastry blender, until mixture is crumbly.

2. In another bowl, whisk water, vinegar and egg. Pour into flour mixture and mix together until moistened and blended.

3. Divide dough into 5 portions and shape each portion with your hands into a flat, round patty. Wrap each separately in plastic wrap. Chill in refrigerator for at least ½ hour or freeze in airtight container for up to 3 months. Thaw in refrigerator before using.

VARIATIONS

Lemon-Lime Soda Pie Pastry: Use 5½ cups (1.375 L) flour, ¾ tsp (4 mL) baking soda, ½ tsp (2 mL) salt, 1 lb (500 g) cold shortening and 1 can (12 oz/340 mL) cold lemon-lime soda in place of the above ingredients, and then follow the same instructions.

Brown Sugar Pastry: Use 5½ cups (1.375 L) flour, 1¼ tsp (6 mL) salt, 1 tsp (5 mL) baking powder, 1 lb (500 g) lard, 1 egg (lightly beaten with a fork), 2 tbsp (25 mL) packed brown sugar and 1 tbsp (15 mL) vinegar. Proceed as above, but put egg into a 1-cup (250 mL) measuring cup, add the brown sugar and vinegar, and then fill with cold water to the top. Then add to the flour and lard mixture.

Dry Pastry Mix

	Makes enough for six 9-inch (23 cm) single-crust pies	
6 cups	all-purpose flour	1.5 L
1 tbsp	salt	15 mL
1 lb	lard or shortening, cut into cubes	500 g

This recipe is convenient and economical

1. In a large bowl, combine the flour and salt. Cut in the lard with a pastry blender, or two knives, until mixture resembles coarse crumbs.

2. Cover and keep on a cupboard shelf until ready to use, or for up to 1 month.

3. Use 2 cups (500 mL) of the mix (unsifted) and 2½ tbsp (32 mL) of water for a single-crust pie.

4. For a double-crust pie, use 2⅔ cups (660 mL) of the mix, and ¼ cup (50 mL) of water.

Sweet Dough Crust

Makes enough for two 9-inch (23 cm) single-crust pies or 24 2½-inch (6 cm) tarts		
1	egg, separated	1
Pinch	cream of tartar	Pinch
½ cup	butter, softened	125 mL
¼ cup	granulated sugar	50 mL
¼ tsp	salt	1 mL
2 cups	sifted all-purpose flour	500 mL
	Milk	

1. In a small mixer bowl, beat egg white and cream of tartar just until foamy.
2. In a warm bowl, with a wooden spoon, mash butter into a smooth paste. Stir in the sugar and salt. Gradually stir in the flour, mashing until mixture resembles fine particles.
3. Add the egg yolk and egg white mixture to the flour mixture, and work it with your hands or wooden spoon until soft dough forms. Shape dough into a ball, adding a little milk, if necessary, to soften dough enough to be manageable. Press into a flat, round patty.
4. If not using immediately, wrap in plastic and keep chilled in refrigerator for up to 2 days, or freeze for up to 3 months. Before using pastry, bring to room temperature. If frozen, thaw in refrigerator.

Rich Pastry

Makes enough for two 9-inch (23 cm) single-crust pies		
½ cup	butter	125 mL
¼ cup	shortening	50 mL
3 tbsp	granulated sugar	45 mL
1 tsp	grated lemon zest	5 mL
2 cups	all-purpose flour	500 mL

Two 9-inch (23 cm) pie plates

1. In a large bowl, cream butter, shortening and sugar until smooth. Add lemon zest.
2. Stir in flour gradually, until well blended, and shape into a ball.
3. Divide dough in half. Press each into the bottom and up the sides of the pie plates.
4. If not using immediately, wrap in plastic and keep chilled in refrigerator for up to 2 days, or freeze for up to 3 months. Before using pastry, bring to room temperature. If frozen, thaw in refrigerator.
5. Bake as directed in recipe.

Hot-Water Pastry

Makes enough for one 9-inch (23 cm) double-crust pie		
½ cup	shortening	125 mL
½ cup	boiling water	125 mL
2¾ cups	all-purpose flour	675 mL
½ tsp	baking powder	2 mL
½ tsp	salt	2 mL

1. In a small bowl, melt shortening with the boiling water. Set aside to cool.
2. In a large bowl, sift together flour, baking powder and salt, mixing until well blended. Add cooled shortening mixture and mix well until mixture is very moist.
3. Divide dough in half and press each into a flat, round patty. Wrap in plastic wrap and chill in refrigerator for several hours or overnight before rolling.

Egg Yolk Pastry

Makes enough for three 9-inch (23 cm) double-crust pies or six 9-inch (23 cm) single-crust pies		
5 cups	sifted all-purpose flour	1.25 L
4 tsp	granulated sugar	20 mL
½ tsp	salt	2 mL
½ tsp	baking powder	2 mL
1½ cups	lard or shortening	375 mL
2	egg yolks	2
	Cold water	

1. In a large bowl, combine flour, sugar, salt and baking powder. Cut in lard with a pastry blender, or two knives, until mixture is crumbly.
2. In a measuring cup, beat egg yolks lightly with a fork, then beat in enough cold water to bring the measure to just under 1 cup (250 mL).
3. Sprinkle the egg yolk and water mixture over the flour mixture, 1 tbsp (15 mL) at a time, tossing with the fork, just until dough is moist and will hold together.
4. Divide into 6 even balls and press each into a flat, round patty. Wrap in plastic wrap and chill for at least 30 minutes or freeze for up to 3 months. Thaw in refrigerator overnight before rolling, if necessary.
5. Roll out dough as directed in recipe.

Oil Pastry

Makes enough for one 9-inch (23 cm) double-crust pie		
2½ cups	all-purpose flour	625 mL
1 tsp	baking powder	5 mL
3	eggs	3
1 cup	granulated sugar	250 mL
⅔ cup	vegetable oil	150 mL

1. In a large bowl, combine flour and baking powder until blended.
2. In another bowl, whisk eggs and sugar until well blended. Add oil and beat until thoroughly blended.
3. Add egg mixture to flour mixture, stirring until mixture forms a dough.
4. Follow recipe instructions.

> **TIP:** Re-roll any scraps of leftover pie dough and cut into shapes. Sprinkle with sugar and ground cinnamon and bake at 475°F (240°C) for 8 to 10 minutes, or until lightly browned.

Cheese Pastry

Makes enough for one 9-inch (23 cm) double-crust pie		
2 cups	all-purpose flour	500 mL
1 tsp	salt	5 mL
¾ cup	shortening	175 mL
⅓ cup	shredded Cheddar cheese	75 mL
5 to 6 tbsp	cold water	75 to 90 mL

1. In a large bowl, combine flour and salt and mix with a fork. Cut in shortening, using a pastry blender or two knives, until mixture resembles coarse crumbs.
2. Stir in the cheese. Sprinkle water, 1 tbsp (15 mL) at a time, into the mixture, mixing lightly with a fork after each addition.
3. Shape mixture into a ball with your hands, then divide dough into two portions and shape each into a flat, round patty. Wrap in plastic wrap or waxed paper, and chill until ready to use. Roll out as directed in recipe.

Chocolate Crumb Crust

Makes one 9-inch (23 cm) single pie crust		
1¼ cups	finely crushed chocolate wafer crumbs (about 30 wafers)	300 mL
¼ cup	packed brown sugar	50 mL
¼ cup	butter or margarine, melted	50 mL

Preheat oven to 350°F (180°C)

9-inch (23 cm) pie pan

1. In a medium bowl, combine cookie crumbs, brown sugar and melted butter. Mix until well blended.
2. Press firmly onto the bottom and sides of the pie plate.
3. Bake in preheated oven for 8 to 10 minutes, or until lightly browned. Cool.

Coconut Crumb Crust

Makes one 9-inch (23 cm) single pie crust		
1 cup	flaked coconut (sweetened or unsweetened)	250 mL
1 cup	vanilla wafer crumbs (about 25 cookies)	250 mL
2 tbsp	butter or margarine, softened	25 mL
2 tbsp	granulated sugar	25 mL

Preheat oven to 375°F (190°C)

Cookie sheet and 9-inch (23 cm) pie plate

1. Spread the flaked coconut on the cookie sheet and bake in preheated oven for 10 minutes, until lightly browned. Stir once or twice during baking. Cool.
2. In a medium bowl, combine coconut, crumbs, melted butter and sugar. Mix well until thoroughly combined.
3. Press firmly into bottom and sides of pie plate, making a small rim. Bake in preheated oven for 6 to 8 minutes, or until golden brown. Cool.

Corn Flake Crust

Makes one 9-inch (23 cm) single pie crust		
1 cup	corn flake crumbs	250 mL
¼ cup	granulated sugar	50 mL
½ tsp	ground cinnamon (optional)	2 mL
¼ cup	butter or margarine, melted	50 mL

9-inch (23 cm) pie plate

1. In a bowl, combine crumbs, sugar, cinnamon, if using, and melted butter. Mix well.
2. Press firmly into pie plate. Chill.

Cornmeal Pastry

Makes enough for one 9-inch (23 cm) single-crust pie		
1 cup	all-purpose flour	250 mL
½ cup	cornmeal	125 mL
½ tsp	salt	2 mL
½ cup	shortening	125 mL

1. In a medium bowl, combine flour, cornmeal and salt.
2. Cut in shortening with a pastry blender, or two knives, until mixture resembles coarse crumbs.
3. Sprinkle with water, 1 tbsp (15 mL) at a time, stirring with a fork until mixture forms a dough. Pat dough into a ball and press into a flat, round patty. Wrap in plastic wrap or waxed paper, and chill until ready to use. Roll out as directed in recipe.

Graham Cracker Crust

Makes one 9-inch (23 cm) single pie crust		
1½ cups	finely crushed graham wafer crumbs (about 18 whole wafers)	375 mL
3 tbsp	granulated sugar	45 mL
⅓ cup	butter or margarine, melted	75 mL

Preheat oven to 350°F (180°C)

9-inch (23 cm) pie plate

1. In a medium bowl, combine wafer crumbs, sugar and melted butter. Mix well to blend. Set aside about 2 to 3 tbsp (25 to 45 mL) for topping.
2. Press remaining mixture onto bottom and sides of pie plate.
3. Bake in preheated oven for 10 minutes, or until firm. You can also chill in refrigerator until firm. Either method will work well.

> **TIP:** To make your graham wafer crust even more special, use half graham wafer crumbs and half vanilla, chocolate or shortbread cookie crumbs, or any other favorite cookies.

Gingersnap Crust

Makes one 9-inch (23 cm) single pie crust		
1½ cups	fine gingersnap crumbs (about 24 gingersnaps)	375 mL
¼ cup	butter or margarine, softened	50 mL

Preheat oven to 375°F (190°C)

9-inch (23 cm) pie plate, greased

1. In a medium bowl, combine crumbs and butter until well mixed.
2. Press into bottom and sides of prepared pie pan.
3. Bake in preheated oven for about 8 minutes. Cool.

Lemon Juice Pastry

Makes enough for two 9-inch (23 cm) single-crust pies or 24 2½-inch (6 cm) tarts		
3 cups	sifted pastry flour	750 mL
1 cup	shortening	250 mL
1	egg, lightly beaten	1
3 tbsp	lemon juice	45 mL
1 tsp	salt	5 mL
2 tbsp	ice water	25 mL

Best used for tarts and fancy pies

1. In a medium bowl, sift flour again. Cut in shortening and mix until mixture resembles coarse crumbs.
2. Add in egg and lemon juice and blend. Add salt to the ice water and gradually add this to the mixture until it holds together to form a dough.
3. Shape dough into a ball and press into a flat, round patty. Wrap in plastic wrap or waxed paper, and chill in refrigerator for 2 hours. Roll out pastry as directed in recipe.

Crunchy Oatmeal Crust

Makes one 9-inch (23 cm) single pie crust		
1 cup	quick-cooking rolled oats	250 mL
⅓ cup	sifted all-purpose flour	75 mL
⅓ cup	packed brown sugar	75 mL
¼ tsp	salt	1 mL
Pinch	ground cinnamon (optional)	Pinch
Pinch	ground nutmeg (optional)	Pinch
⅓ cup	butter or margarine	75 mL

Preheat oven to 375°F (190°C)

9-inch (23 cm) pie plate, greased

1. In a medium bowl, combine oats, flour, brown sugar and salt, and cinnamon and nutmeg, if using. Mix together well.
2. Cut in butter until mixture resembles coarse crumbs. Press into prepared pie plate.
3. Bake in preheated oven for 15 minutes, or until golden brown. Cool.

Poppy Seed Crust

Makes one 9-inch (23 cm) single pie crust		
1⅓ cups	all-purpose flour	325 mL
1 tbsp	poppy seeds	15 mL
¼ tsp	salt	1 mL
½ cup	shortening	125 mL
3 tbsp	cold water	45 mL

9-inch (23 cm) pie plate

1. In a medium bowl, combine flour, poppy seeds and salt. Cut in shortening until mixture resembles coarse crumbs.
2. Add water 1 tbsp (15 mL) at a time, tossing with a fork until dough forms a ball. Press into a flat, round patty. Refrigerate for at least 30 minutes.
3. Roll out as directed in recipe.

> **TIP:** Chill your rolling pin in the freezer before using so the dough won't stick to it.

Shortbread Crust

Makes one 9-inch (23 cm) single pie crust or 18 2½-inch (6 cm) tart shells		
1 cup	butter or margarine, softened	250 mL
½ cup	granulated sugar	125 mL
2 cups	all-purpose flour	500 mL
Pinch	salt	Pinch

Preheat oven to 300°F (150°C)

9-inch (23 cm) pie plate or 14 to 18 tart tins

1. In a large bowl, cream butter and sugar until smooth. Add flour and salt and work in with your fingers to form a dough.
2. Press into bottom and sides of pie plate.
3. Bake in preheated oven for 30 to 40 minutes, or until golden brown. Cool.

Sour Cream Pastry

Makes enough for three 9-inch (23 cm) single-crust pies		
3 cups	all-purpose flour	750 mL
1 tsp	baking powder	5 mL
Pinch	salt	Pinch
1 cup	butter, softened	250 mL
¼ cup	granulated sugar	50 mL
1	egg yolk	1
½ cup	sour cream	125 mL

1. In a medium bowl, sift flour, baking powder and salt. Mix to blend.
2. In a large mixer bowl, cream butter and sugar until smooth and blended. Add egg yolk and beat. Add sour cream, beating until well blended.
3. Add flour mixture to batter, stirring until well combined. Knead into a smooth ball. Divide dough into 3 equal parts and press each into a flat, round patty. Wrap in plastic and chill for at least 30 minutes.
4. Roll out as directed in recipe. Dough can be wrapped and frozen for up to 3 months. If you are only using one pie crust, the extra dough may be frozen until needed.

Vanilla Wafer Crumb Crust

Makes one 9-inch (23 cm) single pie crust		
1⅓ cups	finely crushed vanilla wafers (about 38 cookies)	325 mL
2 tbsp	granulated sugar	25 mL
½ tsp	vanilla	2 mL
⅓ cup	unsalted butter, melted	75 mL

Preheat oven to 350°F (180°C)

9-inch (23 cm) pie pan, greased

1. In a medium bowl, combine cookie crumbs, sugar and vanilla until blended.
2. Add melted butter and mix together until well blended.
3. Press firmly into bottom and sides of prepared pie pan. Bake in preheated oven for 8 minutes, or until lightly browned. Cool.

TIP: To shape a graham wafer or cookie crust evenly, heap the crumb mixture into your 9-inch (23 cm) pie plate and press an 8-inch pie plate on top, into the crumbs. This is a much easier and quicker method than pressing by hand.

Walnut Crumb Crust

Makes one 9-inch (23 cm) single pie crust

1 cup	finely crushed graham wafer crumbs (about 14 whole wafers)	250 mL
½ cup	finely chopped walnuts	125 mL
¼ tsp	salt	1 mL
¼ cup	butter or margarine, softened	50 mL
1 tbsp	liquid honey	15 mL

Preheat oven to 350°F (180°C)

9-inch (23 cm) pie plate

1. In a medium bowl, combine wafer crumbs, walnuts and salt. Mix well.
2. Add butter and honey and mix together until thoroughly combined.
3. Press into bottom and sides of pie plate and bake in preheated oven for 6 to 8 minutes, or until lightly browned. Cool.

Whole Wheat Crust

Makes one 9-inch (23 cm) single pie crust

1¼ cups	whole wheat flour	300 mL
½ tsp	salt	2 mL
½ cup	shortening	125 mL
	Cold water	

Preheat oven to 450°F (230°C)

9-inch (23 cm) pie plate

1. In a medium bowl, mix together flour and salt. Cut in shortening with a pastry blender, or two knives, until mixture resembles coarse crumbs.
2. Add water 1 tbsp (15 mL) at a time, just until mixture holds together and forms a dough. Shape into a ball. Press into a flat, round patty.
3. Roll out and transfer to pie plate. Bake in preheated oven for 10 to 12 minutes, or until lightly browned. Cool.

Zwieback Crust

1 cup	zwieback crumbs (about 6 biscuits)	250 mL
¼ cup	confectioners' (icing) sugar	50 mL
2 tbsp	butter or margarine, melted	25 mL

9-inch (23 cm) pie plate, buttered on the bottom only

1. In a bowl, combine crumbs, sugar and butter.
2. Press firmly into bottom and sides of prepared pie plate. Chill until set.

Regular Pastry for Tarts

Preheat oven to 475°F (245°C)

Four tart or muffin pans, fluted or unfluted, or 24 tart tins

1. Use your favorite recipe for a double-crust pie.
2. Roll out thin, then cut into twenty-four 2½-inch (6 cm) rounds, using the rim of a glass or a cookie cutter.
3. Line tart or muffin tins with the rounds of dough.
4. If the shells are to be baked before filling, prick the bottoms with a fork and bake in preheated oven for 8 to 10 minutes, or until golden brown. If the shells are to be filled before baking, follow the instructions in your recipe.

> **TIP:** Freeze unbaked tart shells for handy future baking. Cut your pastry into 5-inch (12.5 cm) circles, prick thoroughly with a fork and stack with wax paper between each circle. Wrap securely in foil and freeze. When ready to use, place the frozen circles of dough over inverted muffin cups. Bake in preheated oven for 8 to 10 minutes, then fill as desired.

Icing Sugar Pastry for Tarts

Makes 12 2½-inch (6 cm) tart shells		
2 cups	cake flour	500 mL
½ cup	confectioner's (icing) sugar	125 mL
½ tsp	salt	2 mL
1 cup	shortening, softened	250 mL
1	egg, lightly beaten	1
1 tsp	vanilla (or other flavoring)	5 mL

Preheat oven to 350°F (180°C)

Two tart or muffin pans, fluted or unfluted, or 12 tart tins

1. In a medium bowl, combine flour, sugar and salt. Mix to blend.
2. Add shortening, egg and vanilla, and mix until thoroughly combined.
3. Press into bottoms and sides of tart or muffin tins.
4. If the shells are to be baked before filling, prick bottoms with a fork and bake in preheated oven for 10 to 15 minutes, or until golden brown. If baking first is not necessary, follow recipe instructions.

Meringue Pie Shells

Makes 8 small pie shells		
3	egg whites, at room temperature	3
¼ tsp	cream of tartar	1 mL
1 tsp	vanilla	5 mL
Pinch	salt	Pinch
1 cup	granulated sugar	250 mL
¼ cup	flaked coconut (sweetened or unsweetened, optional)	50 mL

Preheat oven to 275°F (140°C)

Baking sheet, lined with foil or waxed paper or parchment

1. In a mixer bowl, beat egg whites and cream of tartar. Add vanilla and salt and beat until frothy. Add sugar gradually, and beat until stiff, but not dry, peaks form.
2. Fold in coconut, if desired. Drop meringue in eight 3- to 3½-inch (7.5 to 8.5 cm) rounds onto prepared baking sheet, at least 2 inches (5 cm) apart. Press the middle of each round with the back of a spoon to make a shell, pushing around the edges to make soft sides.
3. Bake in preheated oven for 1 hour. Turn off the oven, keep the door closed and leave shells inside to dry for 1 hour. Fill as desired.

Mini Cheesecakes *(page 84)* ➤

Fruit Pies

(continued on next page)

Old-fashioned Cookie Sheet Apple Pie *(page 133)*

Pumpkin Pies

Other Fruit Pies

Applecot Lattice Pie

Serves 6 to 8

	Pastry for a 9-inch (23 cm) double-crust pie	
$\frac{1}{3}$ cup	granulated sugar	75 mL
2 tbsp	all-purpose flour	25 mL
1 cup	milk	250 mL
4	egg yolks, divided	4
$\frac{1}{2}$ tsp	vanilla	2 mL
4 cups	tart cooking apples, peeled and sliced (about 2 lbs/1 kg)	1 L
1 tbsp	lemon juice	15 mL
2 tbsp	butter or margarine	25 mL
2 tbsp	granulated sugar	25 mL
Pinch	ground nutmeg	Pinch
$\frac{3}{4}$ cup	apricot preserves	175 mL
1 tbsp	water	15 mL

Preheat oven to 425°F (220°C)

9-inch (23 cm) pie plate

1. In a small saucepan, combine the $\frac{1}{3}$ cup (75 mL) of sugar and flour, and mix to blend. Stir in milk and bring to a boil, stirring constantly. Reduce heat and simmer, stirring, until mixture is slightly thickened, about 1 to 2 minutes.

2. In a small bowl, whisk 3 of the egg yolks lightly, then stir in vanilla. Whisk some of the hot mixture into this and then pour back into the saucepan and stir to blend. Set aside to cool.

3. Sprinkle the apples with lemon juice. In a skillet, over low heat, combine butter, the 2 tbsp (25 mL) of sugar and nutmeg. Add the apples and sauté, stirring until apples are almost tender, about 5 minutes. Remove from heat.

4. In a small saucepan, melt the apricot preserves.

5. On lightly floured surface, roll out half of pastry and fit into pie plate. Spoon the egg yolk filling into the bottom crust. Arrange the apple slices on top, piling up slightly in the center. Spread melted preserves over top.

6. Roll out remaining pastry and cut into strips to make a lattice top (see tip, this page). Bring the overhang of bottom pastry up over the ends of the strips and crimp edges. Whisk the final egg yolk with water and brush over top of lattice, but not the edges. Bake in preheated oven for 40 to 45 minutes, or until golden brown. Cool completely.

> **TIP:** To make a lattice top, roll out pastry and cut into ten $\frac{1}{2}$-inch (1 cm) strips. Arrange five pastry strips, about $1\frac{1}{2}$ inches (3.5 cm) apart, over your filling. Fold back every other strip. Place another strip across, then unfold strips. To finish, fold back the alternate strips and place next strip the same distance from the other strip. Unfold strips and continue weaving until lattice top is completed.

Cranapple Pie

	Serves 6 to 8	
	Pastry for a 9-inch (23 cm) double-crust pie	
6 cups	Granny Smith apples, peeled and thinly sliced (about 5 apples)	1.5 L
1 cup	fresh or frozen cranberries	250 mL
¾ cup	granulated sugar	175 mL
3 tbsp	all-purpose flour	45 mL
1 tsp	ground cinnamon	5 mL
1 tbsp	lemon juice	15 mL

Preheat oven to 450°F (230°C)

9-inch (23 cm) pie plate

1. In a large bowl, combine apples and cranberries.
2. In a small bowl, combine sugar, flour and cinnamon. Sprinkle over the apples and cranberries, and mix well until fruit is coated.
3. On lightly floured surface, roll out half of pastry and fit into pie plate. Spoon filling into bottom crust in pie plate, spreading evenly, as it will seem very full. Sprinkle the lemon juice over top.
4. Roll out remaining pastry to fit over filling. Make some slits in the top of your second crust and place over top. Be sure to seal and then crimp or flute the edges.
5. Bake in preheated oven for 10 minutes. Reduce temperature to 350°F (180°C) and bake for another 40 to 50 minutes, or until crust is golden brown and apples are tender.

Deep-Dish Apple Pie

	Serves 8 to 10	
	Pastry for a 9-inch (23 cm) single-crust pie	
12 cups	tart cooking apples (Granny Smith or any other type preferred), peeled and thinly sliced (8 to 10 apples)	3 L
1½ cups	granulated sugar	375 mL
½ cup	all-purpose flour	125 mL
1 tsp	ground cinnamon	5 mL
1 tsp	ground nutmeg	5 mL
¼ tsp	salt	1 mL
2 tbsp	butter or margarine	25 mL

Preheat oven to 425°F (220°C)

9-inch (2.5 L) square metal baking pan

1. In a large bowl, combine apples, sugar, flour, cinnamon, nutmeg and salt. Toss together to mix well.
2. Spoon into baking pan. Dot over top with the butter. Place the pastry crust over top, make some slits near center, and fold edges under, just inside the edge of pan.
3. Bake in preheated oven for 1 hour, or until juice begins to bubble through the slits in the crust and apples are tender. Serve warm.

Old-fashioned Cookie Sheet Apple Pie

Serves 6 to 8

CHEDDAR CRUST

2 cups	all-purpose flour	500 mL
½ tsp	salt	2 mL
½ cup	cold butter, cut into cubes	125 mL
1 cup	shredded aged cheddar cheese	250 mL
½ cup	milk	125 mL

FILLING

5	Granny Smith apples, peeled and sliced	5
¼ cup	granulated sugar	50 mL
1 tbsp	all-purpose flour	15 mL
½ tsp	ground cinnamon	2 mL
Pinch	salt	Pinch
2 tbsp	butter or margarine	25 mL

GLAZE

1	egg	1
2 tbsp	milk	25 mL
	Confectioner's (icing) sugar (optional)	

Preheat oven to 400°F (200°C)

Rimmed baking sheet, lightly greased and dusted with flour

1. *Prepare Cheddar Crust:* In a large bowl, combine flour and salt, and mix with a fork. Cut in butter with a pastry blender, or two knives, until mixture resembles coarse crumbs. Stir in the cheese. Sprinkle milk, 1 tbsp (15 mL) at a time, into the mixture, mixing lightly with a fork after each addition. Shape mixture into a ball with your hands. Chill in refrigerator.

2. *Prepare filling:* In a large bowl combine apples, sugar, flour, cinnamon and salt, and mix well to coat.

3. Flatten pastry out onto the prepared baking sheet. Roll out to ¼-inch (0.5 cm) thickness and trim to make a 14-inch (35 cm) square. Roll out the trimmings and cut into strips.

4. Arrange apples in rows over the crust, overlapping slightly, and leaving an empty border about 2 inches (5 cm) wide at the edges. Dot apple mixture with butter. Fold the border edges over the filling and pinch the corners to seal. Place the strips of dough over top in a crisscross pattern.

5. *Prepare glaze:* In a small bowl, whisk the egg and milk, and brush over top of the pastry.

6. Bake in preheated oven for 30 to 35 minutes, or until crust is golden brown and apples are tender. Sprinkle with confectioner's sugar before serving, if desired.

Traditional Apple Pandowdy

Serves 6		
	Pastry for an 8-inch (20 cm) double-crust pie	
1	can (20 oz/600 g) apple slices, drained	1
½ cup	firmly packed brown sugar	125 mL
3 tbsp	butter or margarine, melted	45 mL
5 to 6 tbsp	maple syrup, divided	75 to 90 mL

Preheat oven to 425°F (220°C)

8-inch (20 cm) pie plate

1. In a medium bowl, mix together apple slices and brown sugar to blend.
2. On lightly floured surface, roll out half of pastry and fit into pie plate. Spoon apple mixture onto bottom crust. Dot with the butter and top with 3 tbsp (45 mL) of the syrup.
3. Roll out remaining pastry to fit over filling. Place top crust over the filling and make slits in the crust to allow steam to escape. Seal and crimp or flute the edges.
4. Bake in preheated oven for 15 minutes, then remove from the oven and make crisscross cuts about 1 inch (2.5 cm) apart through the top crust and filling. Drizzle the remaining maple syrup over top and bake for another 25 minutes. If crust browns too quickly, place a strip of foil around edge. Best when served warm.

TIP: To determine when a fruit pie is done, bake until the top crust is golden brown and insert a paring knife into one of the slits in your top crust. If the knife can easily pierce a piece of the fruit, it is soft and tender, and the filling is bubbly, your pie is done.

Impossible Apple Pie

Serves 6 to 8		
1	can (19 oz/540 mL) apple pie filling	1
1 tsp	ground cinnamon	5 mL
1 cup	all-purpose flour	250 mL
½ cup	firmly packed brown sugar	125 mL
1 tsp	baking powder	5 mL
¼ tsp	salt	1 mL
1	egg	1
1 tsp	vanilla	5 mL
½ cup	butter or margarine, melted	125 mL

This pie makes its own crust

Preheat oven to 375°F (190°C)

9-inch (23 cm) pie plate, greased

1. Spoon pie filling into prepared pie plate. Sprinkle cinnamon over top.
2. In a medium bowl, combine flour, sugar, baking powder and salt. Mix well.
3. In a small bowl, whisk egg and vanilla. Add to flour mixture and stir until mixture becomes crumbly. Sprinkle evenly over apple filling. Drizzle melted butter over top.
4. Bake in preheated oven for 30 minutes, or until golden brown and crisp. Serve warm with scoop of vanilla ice cream or whipped topping.

Upside-down Apple Pie

Serves 8 to 10

CRUST

1¼ cups	all-purpose flour	300 mL
½ tsp	salt	2 mL
¼ cup	cold butter or margarine	50 mL
2 tbsp	cold shortening	25 mL
4 to 5 tbsp	ice water	50 to 75 mL

APPLE FILLING

6	tart cooking apples, peeled and sliced	6
¾ cup	granulated sugar	175 mL
¼ cup	firmly packed brown sugar	50 mL
2 tbsp	all-purpose flour	25 mL
½ tsp	ground cinnamon	2 mL
¼ tsp	ground nutmeg	1 mL
¼ tsp	salt	1 mL
½ cup	chopped walnuts	125 mL
⅓ cup	packed brown sugar	75 mL
2 tbsp	butter or margarine, melted	25 mL

NOTE: Delicious when served warm with ice cream.

Preheat oven to 375°F (190°C)

9-inch (23 cm) deep-dish pie plate

1. *Prepare crust:* In a large bowl, sift together flour and salt. Cut in the chilled butter and shortening with a pastry blender, or two knives, until mixture resembles coarse meal. Sprinkle the ice water, 1 tbsp (15 mL) at a time, into the mixture, mixing lightly with a fork after each addition. Form dough into a ball and flatten slightly. Wrap in plastic. Chill in refrigerator for 1 hour, or overnight.

2. *Prepare filling:* In a large bowl, combine apples, granulated sugar, the ¼ cup (50 mL) of brown sugar, flour, cinnamon, nutmeg and salt. Mix well until blended.

3. Pour the melted butter over bottom of pie pan. Spread chopped walnuts over top and sprinkle the ⅓ cup (75 mL) brown sugar over the walnuts. Pour in apple mixture and spread evenly in pan.

4. On a lightly floured surface, roll out pastry to fit over filling. Place pastry over top of the apple mixture, turn edges under and crimp and seal to the edge of the pie plate. With a fork, prick the dough in several places.

5. Bake in preheated oven for 30 to 40 minutes, or until pastry is nicely browned and apples are tender. Cool in pie plate for about 5 minutes. Then invert onto a rimmed serving plate and remove the pie pan.

TIP: When preparing apples for an apple pie, use the small end of a melon baller to neatly and easily scoop out the core from apples that have been halved.

Cranberry Cherry Crumb Pie

Serves 6 to 8		
	Pastry for a 9-inch (23 cm) single-crust pie	
2 cups	fresh or frozen cranberries	500 mL
1	can (19 oz/540 mL) cherry pie filling	1
2 tbsp	cornstarch	25 mL
1 tbsp	lightly packed brown sugar	15 mL
8 oz	cream cheese, softened	250 g
1	can (10 oz/284 mL) sweetened condensed milk	1
¼ cup	lemon juice	50 mL

TOPPING

½ cup	all-purpose flour	125 mL
⅓ cup	packed brown sugar	75 mL
1 tsp	ground cinnamon	5 mL
½ cup	butter or margarine, softened	125 mL
½ cup	chopped nuts (optional)	125 mL

Preheat oven to 375°F (190°C)
9-inch (23 cm) pie plate

1. In a large bowl, combine cranberries, cherry pie filling, cornstarch and brown sugar. Mix well until thoroughly combined.

2. In a mixer bowl, beat cream cheese until light and fluffy. Add milk and lemon juice gradually, beating until smooth and blended.

3. On a lightly floured surface, roll out pastry and fit into pie shell. Spoon cream cheese mixture into prepared pie crust. Spoon fruit mixture over cheese mixture, spreading evenly.

4. *Prepare topping:* In a medium bowl, combine flour, brown sugar and cinnamon, and mix to blend. Add butter and mix with a fork until mixture resembles coarse crumbs. Mix in nuts, if using. Sprinkle over top of fruit mixture.

5. Bake in preheated oven for 50 to 55 minutes, or until golden brown. Cool on wire rack.

Classic Blueberry Pie

Serves 6 to 8		
Pastry for a 9-inch (23 cm) double-crust pie		
4 cups	fresh or frozen blueberries	1 L
¾ cup	granulated sugar	175 mL
3 tbsp	all-purpose flour	45 mL
½ tsp	grated lemon zest	2 mL
Pinch	salt	Pinch
½ tsp	ground cinnamon (optional)	2 mL
½ tsp	ground nutmeg (optional)	2 mL
2 tsp	lemon juice	10 mL
1 tbsp	butter or margarine, softened	15 mL

Preheat oven to 400°F (200°C)

9-inch (23 cm) pie plate

1. In a large bowl, combine blueberries, sugar, flour, lemon zest and salt. If desired, add cinnamon and nutmeg. Mix together well until thoroughly blended.

2. On a lightly floured surface, roll out half of pastry and fit into pie plate. Spoon blueberry mixture into bottom pie crust. Sprinkle with lemon juice and dot with butter.

3. Roll out remaining pastry to fit over filling. Cut several slits near the center, to allow steam to escape, and place over fruit filling. Trim, seal and flute edges or press with a fork all around.

4. Bake in preheated oven for 35 to 40 minutes, or until top is golden brown. Cool on a wire rack. Serve warm or cold.

> **TIP:** When making a juicy berry pie, sprinkle the bottom crust lightly with sugar and flour mixed in equal proportions.

Fresh Gooseberry Pie

Serves 6 to 8		
Pastry for a 9-inch (23 cm) double-crust pie		
3 cups	fresh gooseberries	750 mL
3 tbsp	quick-cooking tapioca	45 mL
1½ cups	granulated sugar	375 mL
¼ tsp	salt	1 mL
2 tbsp	butter or margarine, softened	25 mL

Preheat oven to 450°F (230°C)

9-inch (23 cm) pie plate

1. In a large bowl, crush about ½ cup (125 mL) of the gooseberries and add the tapioca, sugar and salt. Put into a large saucepan.

2. Add the remaining whole berries to the crushed mixture. Cook over medium heat, stirring, until mixture thickens.

3. On a lightly floured surface, roll out half of pastry and fit into pie plate. Spoon gooseberry mixture into bottom pie crust and dot with the butter.

4. Roll out remaining pastry to fit over filling. Make several slits in the top crust to allow steam to escape. Place over top of filling and trim, seal and flute or crimp edge.

5. Bake in preheated oven for 10 minutes. Reduce heat to 350°F (180°C) and continue baking for 30 to 35 minutes, until top crust is lightly browned. Cool slightly on a wire rack and serve warm, or cool completely.

Chocolate Raspberry Pie

Serves 6 to 8

	Chocolate Crumb Crust (see recipe, page 128), baked and cooled	
3 tbsp	granulated sugar	45 mL
1 tbsp	cornstarch	15 mL
2 cups	fresh raspberries	500 mL
1/3 cup	granulated sugar	75 mL
8 oz	cream cheese, softened	250 g
1/2 tsp	vanilla	2 mL
1/2 cup	whipping (35%) cream	125 mL
3 tbsp	butter or margarine	45 mL
2 oz	semi-sweet chocolate, chopped	60 g

9-inch (23 cm) pie plate

1. In a small saucepan, over medium heat, stir together the 3 tbsp (45 mL) sugar and the cornstarch.
2. Add raspberries and bring to a boil, stirring constantly. Boil for 2 to 3 minutes, or until thickened. Cool for 15 minutes. Then spoon into prepared pie crust and place in refrigerator.
3. In a large mixer bowl, on medium speed, cream sugar, cream cheese and vanilla until smooth, light and fluffy.
4. In a small mixer bowl, on high speed, beat whipping cream until stiff peaks form. Fold whipped cream into creamed mixture, and spread evenly over raspberry layer in crust. Cover with waxed paper and chill in refrigerator for 1 to 2 hours.
5. In a small saucepan, over low heat, melt butter and chocolate. Cool for 5 minutes. Pour over top of chilled pie. Cover loosely and set in refrigerator to chill for 3 hours, or overnight. Garnish with raspberries, if desired.

Raspberry Swirl Cream Pie

Serves 6 to 8

	Graham Cracker Crust (see recipe, page 123), baked and cooled	
1	package (3 oz/90 g) raspberry-flavored gelatin	1
1/2 cup	milk	125 mL
8 oz	white, regular size marshmallows	250 g
2 cups	frozen whipped topping, thawed	500 mL
1	package (10 oz/300g) frozen whole raspberries, thawed and drained	1

9-inch (23 cm) pie plate

1. Prepare gelatin as directed on the package. Chill in refrigerator until partially set.
2. In a small saucepan, over low heat, combine milk and marshmallows, stirring constantly, until melted, smooth and well blended. Set aside to cool. Then fold in whipped topping.
3. Fold raspberries into partially set gelatin. Spoon gelatin mixture into pie crust. Top with marshmallow mixture and swirl through with a knife or spatula for a marbled effect. Chill in refrigerator for 5 hours, or preferably overnight.

Saskatoon Berry Pie

Serves 6 to 8		
	Pastry for a 9-inch (23 cm) double-crust pie	
5 cups	Saskatoon berries	1.25 L
1 tbsp	quick-cooking tapioca	15 mL
½ to ¾ cup	granulated sugar	125 to 175 mL

Preheat oven to 375°F (190°C)

9-inch (23 cm) pie plate

1. On a lightly floured surface, roll out half of pastry and fit into pie plate. Spread berries over bottom of pie crust. Sprinkle tapioca and then sugar to taste over top of berries.

2. Roll out remaining pastry to fit over filling. Make several slits near the center of top crust. Place over top of berries. Trim overhang, fold under to fit rim, and seal, fluting edges.

3. Bake in preheated oven for 40 to 45 minutes, until fruit is bubbly and top is golden brown. Cool on wire rack.

> **TIP:** For even browning on double-crust pies, brush a beaten egg white or milk on the crust prior to baking.

Double Strawberry Pie

Serves 6		
	9-inch (23 cm) single-crust pie shell, baked and cooled	
1	package (3 oz/90 g) strawberry-flavored gelatin	1
1 cup	boiling water	250 mL
1	package (1 lb/500 g) frozen, sliced strawberries	1

NOTE: Serve with whipped cream, ice cream or whatever you desire.

9-inch (23 cm) pie plate

1. In a bowl, dissolve gelatin in the boiling water. Stir until completely dissolved.

2. Add frozen strawberries, stirring to break berries apart. When mixture is partially set, spoon into prepared pie crust. Chill in refrigerator until completely set.

> **TIP:** It is best to make your pie dough the day before and let it rest overnight in the refrigerator. You will find you have a much better dough, and there will be less shrinkage.

Strawberry Baked Alaska Pie

Serves 8

	9-inch (23 cm) single-crust pie shell, baked and well chilled	
1 cup	strawberry jam or sundae topping	250 mL
6 cups	strawberry ice cream, softened to room temperature	1.5 L

MERINGUE TOPPING

3	egg whites	3
Pinch	cream of tartar	Pinch
¼ cup	granulated sugar	50 mL
	Fresh strawberries	

9-inch (23 cm) pie plate

1. Set aside about ¼ cup (50 mL) of the strawberry jam. Spread remaining strawberry jam evenly over bottom of pie crust.

2. In a mixer bowl, beat ice cream until creamy and smooth. Spread over strawberry jam, mounding ice cream in the center. Freeze until firm, about 2 hours.

3. Preheat oven to 450°F (230°C).

4. *Prepare Meringue Topping:* In a small mixer bowl, on high speed, beat egg whites and cream of tartar until frothy. Gradually add sugar, a spoonful at a time, beating until stiff peaks form. Spread evenly over ice cream in crust, right to the edges, to seal pie.

5. Bake in preheated oven for 5 minutes, until meringue is lightly browned. Heat the reserved strawberry jam in a small saucepan, over low heat, for 2 to 3 minutes, until the right consistency to drizzle. Drizzle over the meringue and serve garnished with fresh strawberries.

TIP: When you bake a pie topped with meringue, always spread the meringue so that it extends out to the edge of your crust. This will prevent the meringue from pulling away and coming up short during baking.

Strawberry Marshmallow Pie

Serves 6 to 8

	Graham Cracker Crust (see recipe, page 123), baked and cooled	
¾ cup	orange juice	175 mL
1½ cups	white miniature marshmallows	375 mL
1½ cups	whipping (35%) cream, whipped	375 mL
2 cups	sliced fresh strawberries	500 mL
	Whipped cream (optional)	
	Fresh strawberries (optional)	

9-inch (23 cm) pie plate

1. In a double boiler, heat orange juice over simmering water. Add marshmallows, stirring constantly, until melted. Set aside to cool, then chill in refrigerator until partially set, stirring occasionally, about 30 minutes.

2. Fold in the whipped cream, then the strawberries, until thoroughly combined.

3. Spoon into prepared pie crust and chill in refrigerator for at least 1 hour or for up to 1 day. Garnish with whipped cream and whole strawberries, if desired.

Strawberry Peach Pie

	Pastry for a 9-inch (23 cm) double-crust pie	
½ cup	granulated sugar	125 mL
½ cup	all-purpose flour	125 mL
1 tsp	ground cinnamon	5 mL
¼ tsp	ground nutmeg	1 mL
4	medium peaches, cut in thin slices	4
3 cups	strawberries, hulled and sliced	750 mL
3 tbsp	lemon juice	45 mL
1	egg	1
1 tbsp	water	15 mL

NOTE: Delicious when served warm with a scoop of vanilla ice cream.

Preheat oven to 425°F (220°C)
9-inch (23 cm) pie plate and baking sheet

1. In a small bowl, combine sugar, flour, cinnamon and nutmeg. Mix to blend.
2. In a large bowl, combine peach and strawberry slices. Add dry mixture to the fruit mixture. Toss to combine. Add lemon juice and stir to blend well.
3. On a lightly floured surface, roll out half of pastry and fit into pie plate. Beat egg and water and brush some of it inside bottom pie crust. Spoon fruit mixture into pastry shell.
4. Roll out remaining pastry to fit over filling and cut into ten ½-inch (1 cm) wide strips to form a lattice crust (see tip, page 131). Brush lattice top with remaining egg glaze. Place pie plate on a baking sheet to catch any overflowing juice.
5. Bake in preheated oven for 10 minutes. Reduce oven temperature to 350°F (180°C) and bake for another 45 to 50 minutes, until bubbly and crust is golden brown. Cool on wire rack.

TIP: The rule of thumb for baking a good fruit pie is to begin baking in a 425°F (220°C) oven, with the pie or tarts on the bottom rack, for about 10 minutes to make the crust firmer. Then reduce oven temperature to 350°F (180°C) for the remainder of the baking time.

Glazed Strawberry Pear Pie

	9-inch (23 cm) single-crust pie shell, baked and cooled	
2	cans (each 14 oz/ 398 mL) pear halves	2
1	package (10 oz/300 g) frozen strawberries, thawed	1
2 tbsp	cornstarch	25 mL
¼ cup	currant jelly	50 mL
	Whipped cream (optional)	
	Fresh strawberries (optional)	

9-inch (23 cm) pie plate

1. Drain pears and strawberries and reserve the juices for glaze.
2. Slice pears and arrange with the strawberries in prepared pie crust.
3. Pour reserved pear juice and strawberry juice into a measuring cup to equal 1 cup (250 mL) of liquid. Pour into a saucepan, and add cornstarch and jelly. Cook over low heat, stirring constantly, until mixture bubbles and becomes thick. Spoon over fruit in crust. Cool to set, and serve garnished with whipped cream and fresh strawberries, if desired.

Glazed Strawberry Tart

Serves 6 to 8		

CRUST

1 cup	sifted all-purpose flour	250 mL
3 tbsp	granulated sugar	45 mL
1/4 tsp	salt	1 mL
6 tbsp	butter or margarine, chilled	90 mL
1 tsp	grated lemon zest (optional)	5 mL
1	egg white	1

FILLING

1/4 cup	granulated sugar	50 mL
3 tbsp	all-purpose flour	45 mL
Pinch	salt	Pinch
3/4 cup	light (5%) cream	175 mL
4	egg yolks, beaten	4
1/3 cup	whipping (35%) cream, whipped	75 mL
2 tbsp	orange liqueur	25 mL
2 cups	whole fresh strawberries	500 mL

GLAZE

1/2 cup	currant jelly	125 mL
1 tbsp	orange liqueur	15 mL

8-inch (20 cm) round metal cake pan, lined with foil, or tart pan with removable bottom

1. *Prepare crust:* In a bowl, combine flour, sugar and salt. Cut in butter with a pastry blender or two knives until mixture resembles coarse crumbs. Stir in lemon zest, if using, and egg white, mixing until a dough forms and leaves bowl clean.

2. Set aside 1/3 of the dough and press the remaining dough into bottom of prepared pan. Press the reserved 1/3 dough around the sides to make a rim about 1 1/4 inches (3 cm) high. Prick crust with a fork and freeze for 1 1/2 hours.

3. Preheat oven to 375°F (190°C). Bake crust for 25 to 30 minutes, or until golden brown. Cool in pan on a wire rack, and when cooled, remove to a serving plate, using foil to lift out of pan. Discard foil.

4. *Prepare filling:* In a medium saucepan, combine sugar, flour and salt. Stir in cream and cook over medium heat, stirring constantly, until mixture has boiled for about 1 minute and has thickened. Stir half of this hot mixture into the bowl of beaten egg yolks, and then stir this mixture back into saucepan. Cook, stirring, for another 1 to 2 minutes, until mixture becomes thick again. Chill in refrigerator.

5. Fold whipping cream and liqueur into chilled filling. Spread evenly into bottom of crust on plate. Arrange the strawberries, standing upright, on top of filling.

6. *Prepare glaze:* In a small saucepan, melt the currant jelly and stir in the liqueur. Cool to room temperature, about 10 to 15 minutes, and then brush over berries. Chill tart in refrigerator for at least 30 minutes, or until ready to serve.

> **TIP:** In any recipe that calls for separated eggs, remember this rule: eggs separate more easily when they are very cold, but whipped egg whites gain more volume if they are at room temperature.

Quick 'n' Easy Lemon Pie

Serves 6 to 8

	9-inch (23 cm) single-crust pie shell, baked and cooled	
2¼ cups	water, divided	550 mL
1	envelope (¼ oz/7 g) unflavored gelatin	1
1	package (7 oz/212 g) lemon pie filling and pudding mix	1
½ cup	granulated sugar	125 mL
⅔ cup	evaporated milk	150 mL
2 tbsp	lemon juice	25 mL

8-inch (20 cm) round metal cake pan

1. In a large saucepan, combine ½ cup (125 mL) of the water and gelatin to soften. Stir in pudding mix, sugar and the remaining water. Cook over medium heat, stirring, until mixture comes to a boil and thickens. Transfer to a bowl and chill until mixture mounds from a spoon.

2. Pour the milk into the cake pan and chill in freezer until soft ice crystals form around the edges, about 10 to 15 minutes. Transfer to a small mixer bowl and whip until stiff. Add lemon juice and beat until very stiff. Fold into cooled pudding. If necessary, beat until mixture is smooth.

3. Spoon into prepared pie crust and chill for about 2 hours, or until firm and set.

Lemon Ice Cream Pie

Serves 6 to 8

	9-inch (23 cm) single-crust pie shell, baked and cooled	
6 tbsp	butter or margarine	90 mL
1¼ cups	granulated sugar, divided	300 mL
1 tsp	grated lemon zest	5 mL
⅓ cup	freshly squeezed lemon juice	75 mL
Pinch	salt	Pinch
2	eggs	2
2	egg yolks	2
2 cups	vanilla ice cream, softened	500 mL
2	egg whites	2

9-inch (23 cm) pie plate

1. In a medium saucepan, over low heat, melt butter and stir in 1 cup (250 mL) of the sugar, lemon juice and a pinch of salt.

2. In a small bowl, whisk eggs and egg yolks, then stir into the butter mixture. Stir until mixture is boiling, then remove from heat and chill for at least 30 minutes.

3. Spread the ice cream into the pastry shell and top with the chilled lemon mixture. Freeze until firm.

4. Preheat oven to 500°F (260°C). In a small mixer bowl, on high speed, beat egg whites and a pinch of salt until soft peaks form. Gradually add the remaining sugar, by spoonfuls, and beat until stiff peaks form. Fold in lemon zest and spread over frozen pie, sealing edges.

5. Bake in preheated oven for 3 minutes, or until top becomes lightly browned. For best results, serve immediately.

TIP: Before squeezing a lemon, lime or orange for juice, grate the peel and freeze it for use in later recipes.

Perfect Lemon Meringue Pie

	Pastry for a 9-inch (23 cm) single-crust pie	
1¾ cups	granulated sugar	425 mL
¼ cup	cornstarch	50 mL
3 tbsp	all-purpose flour	45 mL
¼ tsp	salt	1 mL
2 cups	water	500 mL
4	egg yolks, lightly beaten	4
1 tbsp	grated lemon zest	15 mL
½ cup	freshly squeezed lemon juice (about 1½ lemons)	125 mL
1 tbsp	butter	15 mL

MERINGUE

4	egg whites	4
¼ tsp	cream of tartar	1 mL
½ cup	granulated sugar	125 mL

Preheat oven to 450°F (230°C)

9-inch (23 cm) pie plate

1. On a lightly floured surface, roll out pastry and fit into pie plate. Prick bottom of crust with a fork and bake in preheated oven for 8 to 10 minutes, or until golden brown. Cool on wire rack. Reduce oven temperature to 400°F (200°C).

2. In a medium saucepan, combine sugar, cornstarch, flour and salt, mixing well to blend. Add the water gradually, and stir until mixture is smooth. Bring to a boil over medium heat, stirring constantly, and boil for 1 minute, until mixture is shiny and clear.

3. Quickly stir some of the hot mixture into the beaten egg yolks and then pour back into the remaining hot mixture. Return to heat, stir and cook over low heat for 5 minutes, until thick.

4. Remove from heat and add lemon zest, lemon juice and butter, stirring until well blended. Pour into baked pie shell.

5. *Prepare meringue:* In a mixer bowl, on medium speed, beat egg whites and cream of tartar until foamy. Gradually beat in the sugar, 2 tbsp (25 mL) at a time. Then beat on high until stiff peaks form. Spread meringue over hot filling, carefully sealing to the edge of the crust and swirling the top decoratively with a spatula.

6. Bake for 7 to 9 minutes, or until meringue is golden brown. Cool completely on a wire rack for 3 hours.

VARIATION

Lime Meringue Pie: Substitute lime zest and juice for the lemon, and add a few drops of green food coloring to the filling just before pouring it into the pie shell.

TIP: If you sprinkle a little granulated sugar over your meringue before browning, it will produce a topping that will cut more easily.

Lemon Cream Cheese Pie

Pastry for a 9-inch
(23 cm) deep-dish
single-crust pie

CHEESE LAYER

¼ cup	granulated sugar	50 mL
8 oz	cream cheese, softened	250 g
1	egg	1

LEMON LAYER

2	eggs	2
2 tsp	grated lemon zest	10 mL
⅓ cup	lemon juice	75 mL
½ cup	corn syrup	125 mL
2 tbsp	butter or margarine, melted	25 mL
1 tbsp	cornstarch	15 mL
	Whipped topping (optional)	
	Lemon zest (optional)	

Preheat oven to 350°F (180°C)

9-inch (23 cm) deep-dish pie plate

1. On a lightly floured surface, roll out pastry and fit into pie plate.
2. *Prepare Cheese Layer:* In a mixer bowl, cream sugar and cream cheese until smooth. Add the egg and blend well. Spread over prepared pie shell.
3. *Prepare Lemon Layer:* In a mixer bowl, beat eggs until frothy. Add lemon zest, lemon juice, corn syrup, butter and cornstarch, beating until well blended. Pour over cheese layer.
4. Bake in preheated oven for 50 to 55 minutes, or until set and golden brown. Cool on wire rack. Decorate with whipped topping and a strip of lemon zest, if desired.

TIP: When baking a pie with a very wet filling, brush the pie crust with a beaten egg before baking. The egg will help seal the crust during baking and keep it from getting soggy.

Lemon Pear Pie

Serves 6 to 8

	Pastry for 9-inch (23 cm) double-crust pie	
1	egg, lightly beaten	1
1 cup	granulated sugar	250 mL
1 tbsp	butter or margarine	15 mL
1 tsp	grated lemon zest	5 mL
¼ cup	lemon juice	50 mL
2	cans (each 14 oz/ 398 mL) pear halves, drained and diced	2

Preheat oven to 400°F (200°C)

9-inch (23 cm) pie plate

1. In a small saucepan, over low heat, combine egg, sugar, butter, lemon zest and lemon juice. Cook, stirring constantly, until mixture bubbles and is thick. Remove from heat.
2. On a lightly floured surface, roll out half of pastry and fit into pie plate. Arrange diced pears in bottom of pie crust. Top with the lemon mixture.
3. Roll out remaining pastry to fit over filling. Make several slits in top crust, near the center, and place over filling. Trim overhang, turn edges under, flush with rim, and flute or crimp edge.
4. Bake in preheated oven for 30 to 35 minutes, or until top crust is golden brown. Cool on wire rack.

TIP: For a flaky top for your pies, brush the top crust with a little water.

Classic Key Lime Pie

Serves 6 to 8

	Coconut Crumb Crust (see recipe, page 122) or Graham Cracker Crust (see recipe, page 123), baked and cooled	
3	eggs, separated	3
1	can (10 oz/284 mL) sweetened condensed milk	1
1 tsp	grated key lime zest	5 mL
½ cup	freshly squeezed key lime juice (about 4 key limes)	125 mL
¼ tsp	cream of tartar	1 mL
	Graham wafer crumbs (optional)	
	Whipped cream (optional)	
	Toasted, flaked coconut (sweetened or unsweetened, optional)	
	Key lime slices or extra zest	

Preheat oven to 350°F (180°C)

9-inch (23 cm) pie plate

1. In a large mixer bowl, combine egg yolks, milk, lime zest and lime juice, beating until blended.
2. In a small mixer bowl with clean beaters, on high speed, beat egg whites and cream of tartar until stiff, but not dry, peaks form. Fold gently into egg yolk mixture and spoon into prepared pie crust. Sprinkle wafer crumbs over top, if desired.
3. Bake in preheated oven for about 25 minutes, or until center is set. Cool on wire rack. Garnish with whipped cream or coconut, if desired, and lime slices or zest.

Fluffy Whipped-Lime Pie

Serves 6 to 8

	Graham Cracker Crust (see recipe, page 123), baked and cooled	
1 cup	sour cream	250 mL
1	can (10 oz/284 mL) sweetened condensed milk	1
2 tbsp	freshly squeezed lime juice	25 mL
	Green food coloring (optional)	
2 cups	frozen whipped topping, thawed	500 mL

8-inch (20 cm) or 9-inch (23 cm) pie plate

1. In a large bowl, combine sour cream, milk, lime juice, and if desired, about 5 drops of food coloring. Gently fold in whipped topping until well combined.
2. Spoon into prepared pie crust. Chill in refrigerator for 12 hours, or overnight, before serving.

Old-fashioned Fresh Peach Pie

Serves 6 to 8

	Pastry for a 9-inch (23 cm) double-crust pie	
1 cup	granulated sugar	250 mL
1/4 cup	all-purpose flour	50 mL
1/2 tsp	ground cinnamon	2 mL
Pinch	ground nutmeg	Pinch
9	medium fresh peaches, sliced (about 9 cups/2.25 L)	9
1 tsp	lemon juice	5 mL
2 tbsp	butter or margarine, softened	25 mL

Preheat oven to 425°F (220°C)

9-inch (23 cm) pie plate

1. On a lightly floured surface, roll out half of pastry and fit into pie plate.
2. In a small bowl, combine sugar, flour, cinnamon and nutmeg. Mix to blend. In a large bowl, mix peaches and lemon juice. Add dry mixture to peaches. Spoon into bottom crust. Dot with butter.
3. Roll out remaining pastry to fit over filling. Cut into 10 strips, about 1/2 inch (1 cm) wide. Moisten rim of bottom crust with water and place strips to form a lattice top (see tip on page 131). Pinch to make a stand-up edge and then flute.
4. Bake in preheated oven for 40 to 45 minutes, or until filling is bubbly and crust is golden brown. Cool on wire rack.

TIP: If you want your pie to have a sugary top, remove the pie from the oven 5 minutes before it is done, sprinkle with granulated sugar, and return it to the oven.

Peaches 'n' Cream Pie

Serves 6 to 8

9-inch (23 cm)
single-crust pie shell,
baked and cooled

8 oz	cream cheese, softened	250 g
2 tbsp	milk	25 mL
2 tbsp	granulated sugar	25 mL
1/4 tsp	almond extract	1 mL
2	packages (each 10 oz/300 g) frozen sliced peaches, drained (reserve juice)	2

GLAZE

1/4 cup	granulated sugar	50 mL
1 tbsp	cornstarch	15 mL
2/3 cup	reserved peach juice	150 mL
1 tbsp	lemon juice	15 mL
1 tbsp	butter or margarine	15 mL

9-inch (23 cm) pie plate

1. In a medium bowl, combine cream cheese and milk. Mix well until smooth and blended. Add sugar and almond extract, and mix until well blended. Spoon onto prepared pie crust. Chill in refrigerator for at least 30 minutes.

2. Arrange peach slices on top of cream cheese mixture.

3. *Prepare glaze:* In a saucepan, combine sugar, cornstarch, reserved juice and lemon juice. Cook over medium heat, stirring until mixture is clear and thick. Stir in butter until dissolved, about 2 to 3 minutes. Set aside to cool to room temperature, about 10 to 15 minutes.

4. When glaze has cooled, pour over peach slices.

Peach Custard Pie

Serves 6 to 8

9-inch (23 cm)
single-crust pie shell,
baked and cooled

1	can (19 oz/540 mL) peach pie filling	1
1 cup	drained crushed canned pineapple	250 mL
8 oz	cream cheese, softened	250 g
1 cup	sour cream	250 mL
2	eggs, lightly beaten	2
1/3 cup	granulated sugar	75 mL
	Ground nutmeg (optional)	

Preheat oven to 375°F (190°C)

9-inch (23 cm) pie plate

1. In a bowl, mix together pie filling and pineapple. Spoon into prepared pie crust.

2. In a mixer bowl, combine cream cheese and sour cream, beating until smooth. Add eggs and sugar and continue beating until blended and smooth. Spoon over peach mixture. Sprinkle some nutmeg over top, if desired.

3. Bake in preheated oven for 30 to 35 minutes, or until top is golden brown. Cool on wire rack.

Peach Melba Pie

Serves 6 to 8		
Graham Cracker Crust (see recipe, page 123), baked and cooled		
⅔ cup	boiling water	150 mL
1	package (3 oz/90 g) peach-flavored gelatin	1
2 cups	ice cubes	500 mL
2 cups	frozen whipped topping, thawed	500 mL
1 cup	fresh peaches, sliced and dipped in lemon juice (about 2)	250 mL
3 tbsp	raspberry jam	45 mL

9-inch (23 cm) pie plate

1. In a bowl, dissolve the gelatin in the boiling water, stirring until completely dissolved. Add ice cubes and stir constantly until mixture starts to thicken, about 3 minutes. Remove any unmelted ice.

2. Immediately fold whipped topping into gelatin mixture and beat until well blended.

3. Arrange peach slices on prepared baked crust. Spoon gelatin mixture over top of peaches.

4. In a small bowl, stir jam to soften and then drizzle over pie. Use a knife or spatula to make swirls or a marbling effect. Chill in refrigerator for several hours, until firm.

Peach Streusel Pie

Serves 6 to 8		
Crunchy Oatmeal Crust (see recipe, page 124)		
1	can (19 oz/540 mL) peach pie filling	1
½ cup	raisins	125 mL
½ tsp	ground cinnamon	2 mL
STREUSEL TOPPING		
⅓ cup	quick-cooking rolled oats	75 mL
¼ cup	all-purpose flour	50 mL
¼ cup	firmly packed brown sugar	50 mL
3 tbsp	butter or margarine, softened	45 mL

NOTE: Excellent when served warm with ice cream, whipped cream or yogurt.

Preheat oven to 375°F (190°C)

9-inch (23 cm) pie plate

1. In a medium bowl, combine pie filling, raisins and cinnamon. Mix together to blend. Spoon into prepared pie crust.

2. *Prepare Streusel Topping:* Combine oats, flour and brown sugar, mixing to blend. Cut in butter with a fork until mixture resembles coarse crumbs. Sprinkle over top of peach mixture.

3. Bake in preheated oven for 25 to 30 minutes, or until topping is golden brown.

Plum and Peach Galette

CRUST

1¼ cups	all-purpose flour	300 mL
2 tbsp	granulated sugar	25 mL
¼ tsp	salt	1 mL
½ cup	unsalted butter, chilled	125 mL
3 tbsp	ice water	45 mL

FILLING

1 cup	granulated sugar	250 mL
2 tbsp	quick-cooking tapioca	25 mL
¼ tsp	salt	1 mL
1 tsp	ground cinnamon	5 mL
1 tsp	grated lemon zest	5 mL
4 cups	peeled, sliced fresh red or purple plums (about 6)	1 L
4 cups	peeled, sliced fresh peaches (about 5)	1 L
2 tsp	lemon juice	10 mL
1 tsp	ground mace (optional)	5 mL
1	egg	1
	Granulated sugar	

Preheat oven to 400°F (200°C)
Baking sheet

1. *Prepare crust:* In a large bowl, combine flour, sugar and salt, and mix to blend. Cut in butter with a pastry blender or two knives until mixture resembles coarse crumbs. Add ice water, 1 tbsp (15 mL) at a time, until dough is of right consistency. Then shape into a round disk, wrap in plastic wrap and chill in refrigerator for at least 1 hour.

2. *Prepare filling:* In a large bowl, combine sugar, tapioca, salt, cinnamon, lemon zest, plums, peaches, lemon juice and mace, if using. Mix together well and let stand for about 20 minutes.

3. On a lightly floured surface, roll out dough to form a circle, about 14 inches (35 cm) in diameter. Place on baking sheet. Place fruit mixture in center and spread over dough, leaving a border of 2 inches (5 cm). Fold the border in toward the center of the fruit filling, leaving the filling exposed in the center. Make an egg wash by lightly beating egg in a small bowl. Brush egg wash over folded border and sprinkle granulated sugar over top.

4. Bake in preheated oven for about 45 to 50 minutes, or until crust is golden brown and fruit is tender. Cool tart on the baking sheet for 1 to 2 hours, and then place onto a serving plate. Best when served warm.

Pumpkin Purée

Having a good recipe for pumpkin purée can make a real difference to many pumpkin recipes. To make 2 cups (500 mL) of purée, use a 3-lb (1.5 kg) ripe pumpkin. Wash the pumpkin well and cut in half. Scoop out seeds and fibers and then cut into quarters. Place pieces into a baking dish. Set dish in a pan of hot water and bake at 350°F (180°C) for 45 minutes, or until tender. Scrape the pulp from the pumpkin rind. Place pulp in a blender, or food processor, and purée.

Old-fashioned Pumpkin Pie

Serves 6 to 8

	Pastry for a 9-inch (23 cm) single-crust pie	
¾ cup	granulated sugar or packed brown sugar	175 mL
2 cups	Pumpkin Purée (see recipe, above) or canned (not pie filling)	500 mL
1	can (13.5 oz/385 mL) evaporated milk	1
2	eggs, slightly beaten	2
1 tsp	ground cinnamon	5 mL
½ tsp	ground nutmeg	2 mL
½ tsp	ground ginger	2 mL
½ tsp	salt	2 mL
¼ tsp	ground cloves	1 mL
	Whipped cream or topping (optional)	

NOTE: I always love pumpkin pie with whipped cream or ice cream! In place of the spices, you can also use 2 tsp (10 mL) of pumpkin pie spice.

Preheat oven to 425°F (220°C)
9-inch (23 cm) pie plate

1. On a lightly floured surface, roll out pastry and fit into pie plate.
2. In a large bowl, combine sugar, pumpkin, milk and eggs. Mix together until well combined. Add cinnamon, nutmeg, ginger, salt and cloves, and mix well. Spoon into prepared pastry shell, spreading evenly.
3. Bake in preheated oven for 15 minutes. Reduce oven temperature to 350°F (180°C) and bake for another 45 to 50 minutes, or until a knife inserted in the center comes out clean and dry. Cool on wire rack. Decorate with whipped cream or topping, or as desired.

TIP: If your pumpkin filling contains milk or cream, warm it slightly so that the filling sets more quickly, and bake your pie as soon as you have added the filling to the crust. Too much time standing before baking allows the filling to soak into the pastry, causing a soggy crust.

Caramel Pecan Pumpkin Pie

Serves 8 to 10

	Pastry for a 9-inch (23 cm) single-crust pie	
¾ cup	granulated sugar	175 mL
1 tbsp	all-purpose flour	15 mL
1 tsp	finely grated lemon zest	5 mL
½ tsp	ground cinnamon	2 mL
¼ tsp	ground nutmeg	1 mL
¼ tsp	salt	1 mL
Pinch	ground allspice	Pinch
½ tsp	vanilla	2 mL
2 cups	Pumpkin Purée (see recipe, page 151) or canned (not pie filling)	500 mL
2	eggs, lightly beaten	2
¼ cup	milk	50 mL

TOPPING

2 tbsp	butter or margarine, softened	25 mL
½ cup	firmly packed brown sugar	125 mL
½ cup	chopped pecans	125 mL

Preheat oven to 375°F (190°C)

9-inch (23 cm) pie plate

1. On a lightly floured surface, roll out pastry and fit into pie plate.

2. In a small bowl, combine sugar, flour, zest, cinnamon, nutmeg, salt, allspice and vanilla.

3. In a large bowl, combine pumpkin, eggs and milk. Mix well to blend. Add dry mixture to pumpkin mixture. Stir until mixture is well combined and spoon into pie crust.

4. Bake in preheated oven for 25 minutes. If edges seem to be browning too quickly, cover the edge with a strip of tin foil.

5. *Prepare topping:* In a small bowl, combine butter, brown sugar and pecans. Mix well. Sprinkle evenly over top of pie and bake for another 20 to 25 minutes, or until golden brown and bubbly and a knife inserted in the center comes out clean and dry. Cool on wire rack until cool to the touch. Chill in refrigerator for at least 30 minutes, or until ready to serve.

TIP: To prevent the crust of a pumpkin pie from becoming soggy, use only enough water to allow the dough to clump into a ball. Too much moisture can contribute to a soggy crust.

Crustless Pumpkin Pie

Serves 6 to 8		
½ cup	prepared biscuit mix	125 mL
¾ cup	granulated sugar	175 mL
2½ tsp	pumpkin pie spice	12 mL
1	can (13.5 oz/385 mL) evaporated milk	1
2	eggs	2
2 cups	Pumpkin Purée (see recipe, page 151) or canned (not pie filling)	500 mL
2 tbsp	butter or margarine, softened	25 mL
2 tsp	vanilla	10 mL

Preheat oven to 350°F (180°C)
9-inch (23 cm) pie plate, greased

1. In a large mixer bowl, mix together biscuit mix, sugar and spice, until blended.

2. Add milk, eggs, pumpkin, butter and vanilla. Beat on medium speed until blended. Then beat on high speed for 2 minutes, until thoroughly blended. Spoon into prepared pie plate.

3. Bake in preheated oven for 50 to 55 minutes, or until knife inserted in the center comes out clean and dry. Cool on wire rack.

TIP: To prepare your own pumpkin pie spice, mix together 1 tsp (5 mL) ground cinnamon, ¼ tsp (1 mL) ground nutmeg, ¼ tsp (1 mL) ground ginger and a dash of ground cloves. Store in an airtight container.

Lite Pumpkin Pie with Phyllo Crust

Serves 6 to 8

PHYLLO CRUST

4	sheets phyllo pastry	4
	Non-stick cooking spray	

FILLING

½ cup	firmly packed brown sugar	125 mL
1 tbsp	cornstarch	15 mL
1 tsp	ground cinnamon	5 mL
1 tsp	ground ginger	5 mL
¼ tsp	ground cloves	1 mL
Pinch	salt	Pinch
1½ cups	Pumpkin Purée (see recipe, page 151) or canned (not pie filling)	375 mL
1	can (13 oz/385 mL) fat-free evaporated milk	1
½ cup	liquid egg substitute	125 mL
1 tsp	vanilla	5 mL

Preheat oven to 350°F (180°C)

9-inch (23 cm) pie plate, lightly coated with non-stick cooking spray

1. *Prepare Phyllo Crust:* Cut each sheet of phyllo pastry in half across the short side, to make 8 sheets. Place one sheet on work surface with a short side facing you. Spray lightly with cooking spray. Starting at the left edge of the first sheet, place another sheet in the same direction, overlapping 1 inch (2.5 cm) to the right of the left edge, and spray lightly with cooking spray. Repeat with remaining sheets, placing each 1 inch (2.5 cm) to the right of the left edge of the previous sheet and spraying lightly. This will form a large rectangle.

2. Carefully fit rectangle of pastry into prepared pie plate, pressing to the bottom gently. Starting at one corner, roll edges down and around, to form a ridge around the plate. Bake in preheated oven for 8 to 10 minutes, or until golden brown. If bottom starts to puff up halfway through baking, press it down gently with a wooden spoon. Cool completely on a wire rack.

3. *Prepare filling:* In a large bowl, combine brown sugar, cornstarch, cinnamon, ginger, cloves and salt. Mix together to blend. In another bowl, combine pumpkin purée, milk, egg substitute and vanilla. Beat until thoroughly combined. Add the pumpkin mixture to the brown sugar mixture and beat until well blended.

4. Spoon into cooled phyllo crust and bake for 50 to 60 minutes, or until knife inserted in the center comes out clean and dry. Cool completely on wire rack. Garnish as desired.

> **TIP:** Fruit pies will slice more attractively if you add 1 to 2 tbsp (15 to 25 mL) of cornstarch into the dry filling ingredients. It gives the filling more body and, therefore, it slices much better.

Double-Creamy Pumpkin Pie

Serves 8 to 10

Graham Cracker Crust
(see recipe, page 123),
baked and cooled

CREAM FILLING

4 oz	cream cheese, softened	125 g
1 tbsp	granulated sugar	15 mL
1 tbsp	milk	15 mL
1½ cups	frozen whipped topping, thawed	375 mL

PUMPKIN FILLING

1 cup	cold milk	250 mL
2 cups	Pumpkin Purée (see recipe, page 151) or canned (not pie filling)	500 mL
2	packages (each a 4-serving size) vanilla instant pudding	2
1 tsp	ground cinnamon	5 mL
½ tsp	ground ginger	2 mL
¼ tsp	ground cloves	1 mL
	Whipped topping (optional)	
	Nutmeg (optional)	
	Nuts (optional)	

9-inch (23 cm) pie plate

1. *Prepare Cream Filling*: In a large mixer bowl, on low speed, combine cream cheese and sugar. Add milk and beat until smooth and blended. Slowly fold in whipped topping, and blend well. Spoon into crust in pie plate, spreading evenly.

2. *Prepare Pumpkin Filling*: In a large bowl, whisk milk, pumpkin, pudding mix, cinnamon, ginger and cloves, until mixture is thick. Spread over cream cheese layer.

3. Chill in refrigerator for 4 to 5 hours, or until set. Garnish with a dollop of whipped topping sprinkled with cinnamon or nutmeg, or nuts, if desired.

> **TIP:** If you have a large amount of leftover pumpkin pie spice, especially at holiday time, sprinkle on sweet potatoes or carrots.

Mile-High Apricot Meringue Pie

Serves 6 to 8

	9-inch (23 cm) single-crust pie shell, baked and cooled	
2 cups	granulated sugar	500 mL
3 tbsp	cornstarch	45 mL
¼ tsp	salt	1 mL
1½ cups	water	375 mL
1½ cups	chopped dried apricots (about 12 oz/375 g)	375 mL
4	egg yolks, lightly beaten	4
2 tbsp	butter or margarine, softened	25 mL

MERINGUE TOPPING

4	egg whites	4
¼ tsp	cream of tartar	1 mL
½ cup	granulated sugar	125 mL

Preheat oven to 325°F (160°C)

9-inch (23 cm) pie plate

1. In a medium bowl, mix together the sugar, cornstarch and salt.

2. In a medium saucepan, over medium heat, bring water and apricots to a boil. Reduce heat to low, and simmer for about 10 to 12 minutes, or until apricots are softened.

3. Add the sugar mixture to the apricot mixture and, stirring, bring to a boil. Reduce heat and cook for 1 to 2 minutes, until mixture is thickened. Remove from heat, add a small amount into the egg yolks and then pour back into saucepan. Bring to a gentle boil, stirring constantly, for about 1 to 2 minutes, or until mixture is glossy and clear. Remove from heat and stir in the butter until it dissolves.

4. *Prepare Meringue Topping:* In a small mixer bowl, beat egg whites and cream of tartar until soft peaks form. Gradually add sugar, by spoonfuls, and beat on high speed until stiff peaks form.

5. Spoon hot filling into prepared pie crust. Spoon meringue over top, spreading evenly, and sealing the edges of the crust.

6. Bake in preheated oven for 30 minutes, or until meringue is golden brown. Cool for 10 minutes on a wire rack and then chill in refrigerator for several hours.

Old-fashioned Banana Cream Pie

Serves 6 to 8

	9-inch (23 cm) single-crust pie shell, baked and cooled	
4	medium, firm ripe bananas (not green)	4
1 cup	whipping (35%) cream	250 mL
½ to 1 tsp	granulated sugar (optional)	2 to 5 mL

NOTE: This seems almost too easy, but I remember when my Mom used to make this pie. With real whipped cream, not frozen whipped topping, this pie seems to melt in your mouth.

9-inch (23 cm) pie plate

1. Slice bananas and pile into prepared, cooled, pie crust. Fill pie crust as full as you like.

2. In a small mixer bowl, beat whipping cream until stiff peaks form. If desired, add granulated sugar while beating.

3. Spoon scoops of whipped cream over top of bananas, piling as high as you like. Keep in refrigerator until ready to serve.

Banana Split Pie

Serves 6 to 8		
	9-inch (23 cm) single-crust pie shell, baked and cooled	
3	medium, firm ripe bananas	3
1 tbsp	lemon juice	15 mL
2 cups	strawberry ice cream, slightly softened	500 mL
1 cup	frozen whipped topping, thawed	250 mL
	Maraschino cherries, whole or halved	
2 tbsp	finely chopped walnuts	25 mL

CHOCOLATE SAUCE

1 cup	semi-sweet chocolate pieces	250 mL
2/3 cup	evaporated milk	150 mL
1/2	jar (1 cup/250 mL) marshmallow crème	1/2

9-inch (23 cm) pie plate

1. Slice bananas into thin slices and place in a bowl. Sprinkle lemon juice over top. Arrange as desired on bottom of prepared pie crust.

2. In a bowl, stir ice cream to soften sufficiently and to make smooth. Spread over top of banana slices. Freeze until firm.

3. Spread whipped topping over the ice cream. Top with maraschino cherries, either whole or halved. Sprinkle nuts over top. Place in freezer until firm. When ready to serve, leave at room temperature for 30 minutes.

4. *Prepare Chocolate Sauce:* In a saucepan, over low heat, combine chocolate and milk. Cook, stirring, until well blended. Whisk in half the jar of marshmallow crème, beating until mixture is thoroughly combined. Drizzle over each slice of pie.

Black Forest Cherry Pie

Serves 6 to 8		
	9-inch (23 cm) single-crust pie shell, baked and cooled	
2/3 cup	granulated sugar	150 mL
3 tbsp	cornstarch	45 mL
1/4 tsp	salt	1 mL
2 cups	milk	500 mL
2	eggs, lightly beaten	2
2 tbsp	butter or margarine	25 mL
1 tsp	vanilla	5 mL
2 oz	semi-sweet chocolate, melted	60 g
2 cups	drained canned dark sweet cherries, halved	500 mL
1/2 cup	whipping (35%) cream	125 mL

9-inch (23 cm) pie plate

1. In a medium saucepan, combine sugar, cornstarch and salt. Gradually stir in milk and cook, over low heat, until mixture is bubbly, then cook for 2 minutes more. Stir a small amount of this mixture into the eggs and then return to saucepan and cook for 2 minutes more.

2. Remove from heat and stir in the butter and vanilla, mixing until blended. Stir 1/2 cup (125 mL) of the egg mixture into melted chocolate. Spread evenly onto bottom of prepared crust.

3. Cover the hot egg mixture with plastic wrap or waxed paper. Cool for 25 to 30 minutes.

4. Place cherry halves, cut side down, onto layer of chocolate in crust, setting aside 8 halves. When egg mixture is cooled, spread it on top of the cherries. Chill in refrigerator until firm.

5. In a small mixer bowl, on high speed, beat whipping cream until stiff peaks form. Spoon on top of pie and use the reserved cherry halves to decorate.

Supreme Lattice Cherry Pie

Serves 6 to 8		
	Pastry for a 9-inch (23 cm) double-crust pie	
4 cups	frozen pitted tart red cherries, thawed, juice reserved	1 L
¾ cup	granulated sugar	175 mL
2½ tbsp	cornstarch	32 mL
Pinch	salt	Pinch
¼ cup	butter or margarine, melted	50 mL
6	drops of almond extract	6

Preheat oven to 425°F (220°C)

9-inch (23 cm) pie plate

1. On lightly floured surface, roll out half of pastry and fit into pie plate.

2. Drain the cherries, reserving 1 cup (250 mL) of the juice.

3. In a medium saucepan, over low heat, combine sugar, cornstarch and salt. Slowly stir in cherry juice and cook until smooth. Keep stirring until mixture becomes thick and clear. Remove from heat and add butter and almond extract, and stir until smooth and well blended. Cool to room temperature, about 10 or 15 minutes.

4. Add cherries to cooled cornstarch mixture, mix well, and pour into bottom of your prepared crust.

5. Roll out remaining pastry to fit over filling. Cut into 10 strips, ½ inch (1 cm) wide. Top with lattice crust (see tip, page 131) and crimp edges high. To keep top from browning too quickly, place a strip of foil loosely around edge of pie.

6. Bake in preheated oven for 35 to 40 minutes, or until top is golden brown. Remove the foil about 10 minutes before the end of baking time. Cool on wire rack.

TIP: Use a pizza cutter when cutting strips of dough for a lattice crust.

Concord Grape Pie

Serves 6 to 8

	Pastry for a 9-inch (23 cm) single-crust pie	
4 cups	Concord grapes (about 1½ lbs/750 g)	1 L
¾ cup	granulated sugar	175 mL
⅓ cup	all-purpose flour	75 mL
¼ tsp	salt	1 mL
2 tbsp	butter or margarine, melted	25 mL
1 tbsp	lemon juice	15 mL

TOPPING

½ cup	granulated sugar	125 mL
½ cup	all-purpose flour	125 mL
¼ cup	butter or margarine, softened	50 mL

Preheat oven to 375°F (190°C)

9-inch (23 cm) pie plate

1. In a large bowl, combine sugar, flour and salt.

2. Slip skins from grapes by pressing grape between your fingers, gently. Skins should slip off easily. Set skins aside.

3. In a large saucepan, bring skinned grapes to a boil. Reduce heat and simmer, uncovered, for about 5 minutes. Place this pulp into a sieve to remove the seeds. Add the reserved grape skins to this pulp. Cool to room temperature, about 10 to 15 minutes. Stir grape mixture, melted butter and lemon juice into the dry mixture. Mix well until thoroughly blended.

4. On a lightly floured surface, roll out pastry and fit into pie plate. Spoon filling into crust.

5. Bake in preheated oven for 20 minutes.

6. *Prepare topping:* In a bowl, combine sugar and flour. Add butter and stir with a fork until mixture resembles coarse crumbs. Sprinkle evenly over pie and bake for another 20 to 25 minutes, or until topping is golden brown. Cool on wire rack.

Nectarine Pie

Serves 6 to 8

	Pastry for a 9-inch (23 cm) double-crust pie	
4 cups	peeled, sliced fresh nectarines	1 L
½ cup	granulated sugar	125 mL
¼ cup	all-purpose flour	50 mL
¼ cup	firmly packed brown sugar	50 mL
1 tsp	grated lemon zest	5 mL
1 tsp	lemon juice	5 mL
½ tsp	ground cinnamon	2 mL
Pinch	salt	Pinch
2 tbsp	butter or margarine	25 mL
1 tbsp	milk or cream (half-and-half (10%) or table (18%))	15 mL
	Whipped topping (optional)	

Preheat oven to 425°F (220°C)
9-inch (23 cm) pie plate

1. On a lightly floured surface, roll out half of pastry and fit into pie plate.
2. Place fruit in a large bowl. Sprinkle over top with granulated sugar, flour, brown sugar, lemon zest, lemon juice, cinnamon and salt. Toss together lightly to combine. Spoon into bottom crust and dot with butter.
3. Roll out remaining pastry to fit over filling. Make several slits near the center of the top crust and place over top of filling. Trim overhang, turn edges under flush with rim and flute or crimp edge all around. Brush top with milk.
4. Bake in preheated oven for 45 to 50 minutes, or until juices are bubbly and top crust is golden brown. Serve with whipped topping, if desired.

TIP: To avoid leakage from fruit pies, sprinkle fine dry bread crumbs on the bottom crust before adding filling.

Mandarin Orange Cream Pie

Serves 6 to 8

	Graham Cracker Crust (see recipe, page 123), baked and cooled	
1	can (10 oz/284 mL) mandarin orange segments	1
8 oz	cream cheese, softened	250 g
	Water	
1	package (3 oz/90 g) orange-flavored gelatin	1
8 oz	frozen whipped topping, thawed	250 g

9-inch (23 cm) pie plate

1. Drain the orange segments and reserve the juice. Place about half of the orange segments and the cream cheese in a bowl. Mix well to combine.
2. Put the reserved juice in a measuring cup and add enough water to make 1 cup (250 mL). Pour into a small saucepan and bring to a boil. Add the gelatin, and stir until completely dissolved.
3. Add gelatin mixture to the cream cheese mixture and chill in refrigerator until almost set. Fold in whipped topping, gently, until well blended. Spoon into prepared pie crust and arrange remaining orange segments over top. Chill in refrigerator until completely set.

Lemon Tarts with Raspberry Glaze *(page 168)* ➤

Pear Crumble Pie

Serves 6 to 8

	Pastry for a 9-inch (23 cm) single-crust pie	
½ cup	granulated sugar	125 mL
2 tbsp	quick-cooking tapioca	25 mL
1 tsp	ground cinnamon	5 mL
¼ tsp	ground nutmeg	1 mL
¼ tsp	salt	1 mL
6	medium, firm ripe pears, peeled and sliced (about 6 cups/1.5 L)	6
1 tbsp	fresh lemon juice	15 mL

TOPPING

½ cup	all-purpose flour	125 mL
⅓ cup	granulated sugar	75 mL
¼ cup	old-fashioned rolled oats	50 mL
1 tsp	ground cinnamon	5 mL
3 tbsp	butter or margarine, softened	45 mL

CARAMEL PECAN SAUCE (OPTIONAL)

10	soft vanilla caramels	10
3 tbsp	milk	45 mL
¼ cup	chopped pecans	50 mL

Preheat oven to 400°F (200°C)

9-inch (23 cm) pie plate

1. On a lightly floured surface, roll out pastry and fit into pie plate.

2. In a bowl, combine sugar, tapioca, cinnamon, nutmeg and salt. Place pears in a large bowl and sprinkle with the lemon juice. Add dry mix to pears and mix, gently, just to blend. Let stand for 15 to 20 minutes, then spoon into prepared pastry crust.

3. *Prepare topping:* In a small bowl, combine flour, sugar, oats, cinnamon, and butter. Mix with a fork until mixture resembles coarse crumbs. Sprinkle evenly over top of pear filling.

4. Bake in preheated oven for 45 to 50 minutes, or until golden brown.

5. *If desired, prepare Caramel Pecan Sauce:* Melt caramels into milk in a saucepan over low heat. Stir in chopped pecans. Drizzle over pie and continue baking for 10 minutes, or until lightly browned. Cool on a wire rack. Best when served warm.

Pear Apple Crunch Pie

Preheat oven to 400°F (200°C)
9-inch (23 cm) pie plate

Serves 6 to 8		
	Pastry for a 9-inch (23 cm) single-crust pie	
⅓ cup	granulated sugar	75 mL
2 tbsp	all-purpose flour	25 mL
1 tsp	ground cinnamon	5 mL
¼ tsp	salt	1 mL
1	can (14 oz/398 mL) pear halves, drained and sliced	1
3	Granny Smith apples, peeled and sliced	3
½ tsp	grated lemon zest	2 mL
1 tbsp	lemon juice	15 mL
½ cup	raisins	125 mL

NUT TOPPING

½ cup	firmly packed brown sugar	125 mL
¼ cup	all-purpose flour	50 mL
½ tsp	salt	2 mL
¼ cup	butter or margarine, softened	50 mL
½ cup	chopped walnuts (or other nuts)	125 mL

1. On a lightly floured surface, roll out pastry and fit into pie plate.

2. In a large bowl, combine sugar, flour, cinnamon and salt. Mix to blend. Add pear and apple slices and toss to blend. Stir in lemon zest, lemon juice and raisins, and mix thoroughly. Spoon mixture into prepared pastry pie shell.

3. *Prepare Nut Topping:* In a bowl, combine brown sugar, flour and salt. Cut in the butter with a fork until mixture resembles coarse crumbs. Stir in chopped walnuts. Sprinkle over top of filling.

4. Bake in preheated oven for 15 minutes. Cover with foil and continue baking for 25 to 30 minutes more, or until apples are tender and top is golden brown. Cool on wire rack.

Coconut Pineapple Cream Pie

	Serves 6 to 8	
	Coconut Crumb Crust (see recipe, page 122), baked and cooled	
1	package (3 oz/90 g) vanilla tapioca pudding mix	1
1	package (3 oz/90 g) lemon-flavored gelatin	1
1¼ cups	milk	300 mL
⅓ cup	frozen unsweetened pineapple juice concentrate, thawed	75 mL
1	package (2 oz/60 g) dessert topping mix	1
¾ cup	well-drained canned crushed pineapple (14 oz/398 mL)	175 mL

9-inch (23 cm) pie plate

1. In a medium saucepan, mix pudding mix and gelatin. Stir in milk and cook, over medium heat, until mixture boils. Remove from heat and stir in pineapple juice concentrate. Chill in refrigerator until partially set.

2. Prepare the dessert topping mix according to package instructions. Fold into the pudding mixture. Fold in pineapple, gently, until mixture is thoroughly combined.

3. Spoon into coconut crust and chill in refrigerator for 5 to 6 hours, or overnight.

Spicy Tart Plum Pie

	Serves 6 to 8	
	Pastry for a 9-inch (23 cm) double-crust pie	
1¾ cups	granulated sugar	425 mL
½ cup	all-purpose flour	125 mL
1 tsp	grated lemon zest	5 mL
½ tsp	ground cinnamon	2 mL
¼ tsp	ground nutmeg	1 mL
Pinch	salt	Pinch
4 cups	pitted, quartered red or purple plums (about 6)	1 L
2 tbsp	butter or margarine	25 mL

Preheat oven to 425°F (220°C)
9-inch (23 cm) pie plate

1. On a lightly floured surface, roll out half of pastry and fit into pie plate.

2. In a small bowl, combine sugar, flour, lemon zest, cinnamon, nutmeg and salt. Mix well to blend thoroughly. Sprinkle 2 tbsp (25 mL) of this mixture over bottom of prepared crust.

3. Arrange about ¼ of the plums over the sugar mixture in bottom crust. Sprinkle about ½ cup (125 mL) of the sugar mixture over plums. Repeat with the remaining plums and sugar mixture to make 3 more layers of each. Dot with the butter.

4. Roll out remaining pastry to fit over filling. Cut several slits near the center of top crust. Cover top of pie and trim, seal and flute or crimp edges.

5. Bake in preheated oven for 10 minutes. Reduce oven temperature to 350°F (180°C) and bake for another 40 to 45 minutes, or until juices bubble up and the top is golden brown. Cool on wire rack.

Old-fashioned Rhubarb Custard Pie

<table>
<tr><td colspan="3">Serves 6 to 8</td></tr>
<tr><td colspan="3">Pastry for a 9-inch (23 cm) single-crust pie</td></tr>
<tr><td>2</td><td>eggs, lightly beaten</td><td>2</td></tr>
<tr><td>¾ cup</td><td>granulated sugar</td><td>175 mL</td></tr>
<tr><td>3 tbsp</td><td>all-purpose flour</td><td>45 mL</td></tr>
<tr><td>1 tsp</td><td>ground cinnamon</td><td>5 mL</td></tr>
<tr><td>4 cups</td><td>chopped fresh rhubarb</td><td>1 L</td></tr>
</table>

Preheat oven to 400°F (200°C)

9-inch (23 cm) pie plate

1. On a lightly floured surface, roll out pastry and fit into pie plate. Brush pastry with a tiny bit of the beaten eggs, just enough to coat the bottom.
2. In a mixer bowl, combine eggs, sugar, flour and cinnamon. Beat on high speed until mixture becomes thick.
3. Place rhubarb in the pie shell, and pour egg mixture over the rhubarb, spreading evenly to the edges.
4. Bake in preheated oven for 30 to 35 minutes, or until top is lightly browned. Cool on wire rack.

Sour Cream Rhubarb Pie

<table>
<tr><td colspan="3">Serves 6 to 8</td></tr>
<tr><td colspan="3">Pastry for a 9-inch (23 cm) single-crust pie</td></tr>
<tr><td>1 cup</td><td>granulated sugar</td><td>250 mL</td></tr>
<tr><td>⅓ cup</td><td>all-purpose flour</td><td>75 mL</td></tr>
<tr><td>¾ cup</td><td>sour cream</td><td>175 mL</td></tr>
<tr><td>4 cups</td><td>chopped fresh rhubarb</td><td>1 L</td></tr>
<tr><td colspan="3">TOPPING</td></tr>
<tr><td>½ cup</td><td>packed brown sugar</td><td>125 mL</td></tr>
<tr><td>½ cup</td><td>all-purpose flour</td><td>125 mL</td></tr>
<tr><td>¼ cup</td><td>butter or margarine, softened</td><td>50 mL</td></tr>
</table>

Preheat oven to 450°F (230°C)

9-inch (23 cm) pie plate

1. On a lightly floured surface, roll out pastry and fit into pie plate.
2. In a large bowl, combine granulated sugar, flour and sour cream. Add rhubarb and toss until well combined and coated. Spoon into prepared pie crust.
3. *Prepare topping:* In a small bowl, combine brown sugar and flour. Cut in butter with a fork, mixing until mixture is crumbly. Sprinkle over top of pie filling.
4. Bake in preheated oven for 15 minutes. Reduce heat to 350°F (180°C) and continue baking for another 35 to 40 minutes, or until fruit is tender and top is lightly browned. Cool on wire rack for about 20 to 25 minutes before serving.

Tarts

Blueberry Tarts

	Makes 24 tarts	
24	2½- by 1-inch (6 by 2.5 cm) tart shells (see recipe, page 127), unbaked	24
⅓ cup	packed brown sugar	75 mL
1 tbsp	all-purpose flour	15 mL
½ cup	corn syrup	125 mL
1 tsp	vanilla	5 mL
1 tsp	lemon juice	5 mL
1	egg, lightly beaten	1
3 tbsp	butter or margarine, melted	45 mL
1½ cups	fresh blueberries	375 mL

Preheat oven to 375°F (190°C)
Baking sheet, if necessary

1. In a small bowl, mix together brown sugar and flour.

2. In a large bowl, combine corn syrup, vanilla, lemon juice and egg. Beat just until blended. Add dry mixture to corn syrup mixture. Add melted butter and mix well until thoroughly combined. Spoon berries into prepared tart shells equally. Spoon in egg mixture and fill each shell to the top. If you are using individual tart tins, place them on a baking sheet.

3. Bake in preheated oven for 15 minutes, or until filling is bubbly and crust is lightly browned. Cool completely in pan on a wire rack. The filling will become firm as tarts cool.

Classic Butter Tarts

	Makes 24 tarts	
24	2½- by 1-inch (6 by 2.5 cm) tart shells (see recipe, page 127), unbaked	24
¾ cup	packed brown sugar	175 mL
¼ cup	butter or margarine, softened	50 mL
¼ cup	corn syrup	50 mL
1 tbsp	lemon juice	15 mL
1 tsp	vanilla	5 mL
2	eggs	2
¾ cup	raisins	175 mL

Preheat oven to 425°F (220°C)
Baking sheet, if necessary

1. In a large mixer bowl, cream brown sugar and butter until smooth. Add corn syrup, lemon juice and vanilla, beating to blend. Beat in eggs, one at a time, beating after each addition just until combined.

2. Sprinkle raisins equally onto the bottom of each tart shell. Spoon batter over raisins. If you are using individual tart tins, place them on a baking sheet.

3. Bake in preheated oven for 5 minutes. Then reduce oven temperature to 350°F (180°C) and bake for another 8 minutes, or until filling is set and pastry is golden brown. Cool in pans on a wire rack for 10 minutes. Carefully loosen around edges with a knife and remove from pans. Cool tarts completely on wire rack.

TIP: To make tarts using muffin pans, use twelve 3- by 1½-inch (7.5 by 4 cm) tart shells. Increase baking time at 350°F (180°C) to about 15 minutes. Cool in pans for 15 minutes before removing tarts.

Chocolate Butter Tarts

	Makes 24 tarts	
24	2½- by 1-inch (6 by 2.5 cm) tart shells (see recipe, page 127), unbaked	24
¾ cup	packed brown sugar	175 mL
¼ cup	corn syrup	50 mL
2 tbsp	butter or margarine, softened	25 mL
1 tsp	vinegar	5 mL
1 tsp	vanilla	5 mL
1	egg	1
3 oz	bittersweet chocolate, chopped	90 g
1 oz	bittersweet chocolate, melted	30 g

Preheat oven to 450°F (230°C)

Baking sheet, if necessary

1. In a large mixer bowl, combine brown sugar, corn syrup, butter, vinegar, vanilla and egg. Beat until blended.

2. Sprinkle equal amounts of chopped chocolate into the bottom of each tart shell. Spoon filling over chocolate until shells are about ¾ full. If you are using individual tart tins, place them on a baking sheet.

3. Bake in preheated oven for 5 minutes, then reduce oven temperature to 350°F (180°C) and bake for another 12 to 15 minutes, until filling is bubbly and pastry is lightly browned. Cool in pans on a wire rack for 10 minutes. Carefully loosen around edges with a knife and remove from pans. Cool tarts completely on wire rack. Drizzle melted chocolate over tops.

Old England Chess Tarts

	Makes 24 tarts	
24	2½- by 1-inch (6 by 2.5 cm) tart shells (see recipe, page 127), with fluted edges, unbaked	24
1 cup	firmly packed brown sugar	250 mL
½ cup	butter or margarine, softened	125 mL
2	eggs	2
¾ cup	chopped dates	175 mL
¾ cup	chopped walnuts	175 mL
½ cup	raisins	125 mL
1 tsp	grated lemon zest	5 mL
½ cup	sour cream	125 mL
	Walnut halves (optional)	
	Sour cream (optional)	

Preheat oven to 450°F (230°C)

Baking sheet, if necessary

1. In a large mixer bowl, cream brown sugar and butter until softened and smooth. Beat in eggs, one at a time, beating after each addition. Stir in dates, chopped walnuts, raisins, lemon zest and the ½ cup (125 mL) sour cream.

2. Spoon into prepared tart shells, dividing evenly. If you are using individual tart tins, place them on a baking sheet.

3. Bake in preheated oven for 5 minutes. Reduce oven temperature to 350°F (180°C) and continue baking for 12 to 15 minutes longer, or until filling is firm and shells are lightly browned. Cool in pans on a wire rack for 10 minutes. Carefully loosen around edges with a knife and remove from pans. Cool tarts completely on wire rack.

4. Garnish with a dollop of sour cream and a walnut half, if desired.

> **TIP:** To remove baked tarts easily when you're using individual tart tins, press up from the bottom of the foil cup.

Lemon Tarts with Raspberry Glaze

	Makes 24 tarts	
24	2½- by 1-inch (6 by 2.5 cm) tart shells (see recipe, page 127), unbaked	24
1	can (19 oz/540 mL) lemon pie filling	1
1 cup	sour cream	250 mL
1	package (10 oz/ 300 g) frozen raspberries, thawed	1
RASPBERRY GLAZE		
2 tbsp	granulated sugar	25 mL
1 tbsp	cornstarch	15 mL

1. In a small bowl, mix pie filling and sour cream. Chill in refrigerator, for at least 30 minutes.
2. Drain raspberries and reserve ⅔ cup (150 mL) of the liquid.
3. *Prepare Raspberry Glaze:* In a small saucepan, mix sugar and cornstarch. Gradually add the reserved raspberry liquid and cook over medium heat, stirring constantly, until mixture thickens and boils. Transfer to a bowl, cover, and chill in refrigerator.
4. Fill prepared tart shells with lemon mixture and top with a few raspberries. Spoon about 1 tbsp (15 mL) of the raspberry glaze over top of each.

Neapolitan Ice Cream Tarts

	Makes 12 3-inch (7.5 cm) tarts	
2 cups	all-purpose flour	500 mL
1 cup	unsweetened cocoa powder, sifted	250 mL
2 tbsp	packed brown sugar	25 mL
½ tsp	salt	2 mL
1 cup	butter or margarine, softened	250 mL
2	eggs, slightly beaten	2
	Neapolitan ice cream	
	Raspberries or blueberries (optional)	

Two tart or muffin pans and baking sheet

1. In a large mixer bowl, mix together flour, cocoa powder, brown sugar and salt. Add butter and mix well, until mixture resembles coarse crumbs. Add eggs and mix well, until blended and mixture forms a dough. Roll into a ball and wrap in plastic wrap. Chill in refrigerator for about 1 hour, until firm.
2. Preheat oven to 450°F (230°C). Place ball of dough onto a floured surface and roll out into a thin sheet. Using a round cookie cutter, or the top of a glass, cut into circles about 3.5 inches (9 cm) in diameter. Turn muffin tin(s) upside down. Fit circles over the backs of cups, making pleats so the dough will fit closely. Prick with a fork, thoroughly, to prevent puffing of dough. Place tins upside down on a baking sheet.
3. Bake in preheated oven for 8 to 10 minutes, or until lightly browned. Cool completely on muffin pans, on baking sheet, on a wire rack.
4. Just before serving, place a scoop of Neapolitan ice cream in each tart. Top with a handful of berries, if desired.

Chocolate Pies

Chocolate Chip Cookies 'n' Cream Pie

Serves 6 to 8		
6 oz	unsweetened chocolate, chopped	175 g
2 tbsp	water	25 mL
8 oz	slice-and-bake chocolate chip cookie dough (½ roll)	250 g
2 cups	vanilla ice cream, slightly softened	500 mL

Preheat oven to 375°F (190°C)

9-inch (23 cm) pie plate, greased and lightly sugared

1. In a small saucepan, melt chocolate and water. Set aside to cool to room temperature, about 10 to 15 minutes.
2. Slice the cookie dough into ⅛-inch-thick (0.25 cm) slices. Line bottom and sides of prepared pie plate by slightly overlapping each slice of cookie dough.
3. Bake in preheated oven for 8 to 10 minutes, or until lightly browned. Cool completely in plate on a wire rack.
4. Arrange scoops of ice cream over bottom of pie crust, then drizzle over top with the melted chocolate mixture. Serve immediately, or wrap and freeze for up to 6 months. If frozen, leave at room temperature for 20 minutes before serving.

Chocolate Ice Cream Pie

Serves 8 to 10		
	Chocolate Crumb Crust (see recipe, page 122), baked and cooled	
4 cups	vanilla ice cream, slightly softened	1 L
4 cups	chocolate ice cream, slightly softened	1 L
	Chocolate shavings or curls	

9-inch (23 cm) pie plate

1. Place vanilla ice cream in a bowl and mix lightly until softened and smooth. Using an ice cream scoop, place a row of scoops around the edge of pie shell.
2. Place chocolate ice cream in a bowl and mix lightly until softened and smooth. Arrange two rows of scoops of chocolate ice cream inside the row of vanilla scoops.
3. Use remaining vanilla ice cream to fill up the center of pie.
4. Freeze until firm, about 4 to 5 hours. Sprinkle chocolate shavings or curls over top of pie.

Chocolate Cream Pie

Serves 8

	9-inch (23 cm) single-crust pie shell, baked and cooled	
1 cup	granulated sugar	250 mL
¼ cup	cornstarch	50 mL
¼ tsp	salt	1 mL
2¾ cups	milk	675 mL
3	egg yolks	3
1 tbsp	butter or margarine, softened	15 mL
1 tsp	vanilla	5 mL
3 oz	unsweetened chocolate, coarsely chopped	90 g
	Whipped topping	
	Chocolate shavings or curls (optional)	

This was my first introduction to pies, and is still #1 on my list!

9-inch (23 cm) pie plate

1. In a medium saucepan, combine sugar, cornstarch and salt and mix to blend. Over medium heat, whisk in milk until mixture is smooth, and, stirring constantly, bring to a boil. Boil for 1 to 2 minutes, stirring gently until slightly thickened. Remove from heat.

2. In a small bowl, beat egg yolks and slowly whisk in about ½ to 1 cup (125 to 250 mL) of the hot milk mixture and pour that back into the saucepan. Whisk constantly and return to a boil. Boil for 1 to 2 minutes more until thick.

3. Remove from heat and whisk in butter and vanilla, then the chocolate, and whisk until mixture is blended and completely smooth.

4. Pour into baked pastry crust and cool for 15 to 20 minutes on a wire rack. Cover the filling with a piece of plastic wrap or foil and chill in refrigerator for 5 hours, or overnight. When ready to serve, spread whipped topping either around the edge of pie, or over the complete pie. Garnish with chocolate shavings, if desired.

VARIATION

Black Forest Pie: Take 1 can (19 oz/540 mL) of cherry pie filling and divide in half. Before spooning chocolate filling into pie crust, fold in half of the cherry pie filling and then refrigerate as above. Just before serving, top with the remaining half of cherry pie filling. Garnish with whipped topping, if desired.

Chocolate Mint Pie

	Chocolate Crumb Crust (see recipe, page 122)	
1½ cups	sweetened condensed milk	375 mL
1½ tsp	peppermint extract	7 mL
	Green food coloring (optional)	
2 cups	whipped topping or whipping (35%) cream, whipped	500 mL
	Chocolate curls or chocolate mints, crumbled (optional)	

9-inch (23 cm) pie plate

1. In a large bowl, combine condensed milk, peppermint extract and, if desired, 5 to 10 drops of food coloring (according to your taste).

2. Fold in whipped topping, gently, until well combined. Spoon into prepared pie crust, cover, and freeze for several hours, until firm. Decorate with chocolate curls or chocolate mints, if desired.

Chocolate Orange Pie

	Chocolate Crumb Crust (see recipe, page 122), baked and cooled	
6 oz	white chocolate, finely chopped	175 g
¼ cup	butter or margarine	50 mL
¼ cup	whipping (35%) cream	50 mL
2 tbsp	grated orange zest	25 mL
1 tbsp	orange liqueur or orange juice	15 mL
6	chocolate cookies or wafers	6
TOPPING		
8 oz	bittersweet chocolate, finely chopped	250 g
½ cup	whipping (35%) cream	125 mL
¼ cup	butter or margarine	50 mL
¼ cup	almonds, toasted and chopped	50 mL
	Whipped cream or topping	
	Orange segments	
	Grated orange zest (optional)	

9-inch (23 cm) pie plate

1. In a double boiler, over hot but not boiling water, melt the white chocolate, butter and whipping cream. Stir until smooth. Remove from heat, fold in orange zest and liqueur and mix to blend. Spoon into prepared pie crust.

2. Break the 6 chocolate wafers, by hand, into coarse chunks and sprinkle over top of filling. Chill in refrigerator until firm.

3. *Prepare topping:* In the double boiler, over hot but not boiling water, melt the bittersweet chocolate, whipping cream and butter. Remove from heat and fold in the nuts. Spoon over chilled white chocolate layer. Chill in refrigerator until firm. Garnish with whipped cream and orange segments, and orange zest, if desired.

Chocolate Pecan Pie

	Serves 6 to 8	
	9-inch (23 cm) single-crust pie shell, baked and cooled	
½ cup	granulated sugar	125 mL
⅔ cup	corn syrup	150 mL
2 oz	unsweetened chocolate, chopped	60 g
2 tbsp	butter or margarine, softened	25 mL
2	eggs	2
½ tsp	vanilla	2 mL
Pinch	salt	Pinch
½ cup	coarsely chopped pecans	125 mL
¾ cup	pecan halves	175 mL

Preheat oven to 350°F (180°C)
9-inch (23 cm) pie plate

1. In a small saucepan, combine sugar and corn syrup, and cook over medium heat until dissolved. Remove from heat and add chocolate and butter, stirring until melted. Cool slightly.

2. In a small bowl, whisk eggs, vanilla and salt. Add to sugar mixture and mix until well blended.

3. Sprinkle the chopped pecans evenly over the bottom of prepared crust. Spoon in filling, spreading evenly. Arrange pecan halves over top.

4. Bake in preheated oven for 25 minutes, or until filling is set when pie is jiggled slightly. Cool completely on wire rack.

TIP: To determine whether an egg is fresh, immerse it in a pan of cool, salted water. If it sinks, it is fresh. If it rises to the surface, throw it away.

Triple-Layer Chocolate Graham Pie

	Serves 6 to 8	
	Graham Cracker Crust (see recipe, page 123), baked and cooled	
2	packages (each a 4-serving size) instant chocolate pudding	2
2 cups	cold milk	500 mL
8 oz	frozen whipped topping, thawed	250 g
	Chocolate curls (optional)	

9-inch (23 cm) pie shell

1. In a large bowl, mix the packages of instant pudding to blend. Add milk and whisk for 1 to 2 minutes, until well blended.

2. Spoon 1½ cups (375 mL) of this mixture into prepared pie crust, spreading evenly.

3. Into the remaining pudding mixture, add half of the whipped topping and mix to blend. Spoon this mixture over the first layer. Top with the remaining whipped topping.

4. Chill in refrigerator for 5 hours, or until set. Garnish with chocolate curls, if desired.

Fudge Brownie Pie à la Mode

Preheat oven to 350°F (180°C)
8-inch pie plate, lightly greased

Serves 6 to 8

	8-inch (20 cm) single-crust pie shell, baked and cooled	
½ cup	all-purpose flour	125 mL
⅓ cup	unsweetened cocoa powder, sifted	75 mL
¼ tsp	salt	1 mL
2	eggs, beaten	2
1 cup	granulated sugar	250 mL
½ cup	butter or margarine, melted	125 mL
½ cup	chopped nuts	125 mL
1 tsp	vanilla	5 mL
	Vanilla ice cream	

FUDGE SAUCE

¾ cup	granulated sugar	175 mL
½ cup	unsweetened cocoa powder	125 mL
½ cup	evaporated milk	125 mL
⅓ cup	light corn syrup	75 mL
⅓ cup	butter or margarine	75 mL
1 tsp	vanilla	5 mL

1. In a small bowl, mix together flour, cocoa powder and salt to blend.

2. In a mixer bowl, combine eggs, sugar and melted butter. Add flour mixture to egg mixture and beat on low speed until combined. Add nuts and vanilla and mix well to thoroughly combine. Spoon into prepared pie crust.

3. Bake in preheated oven for 25 to 30 minutes, or until filling is almost set when pie is jiggled slightly. Cool completely on wire rack.

4. *Prepare Fudge Sauce:* In a small saucepan, mix together sugar and cocoa powder. Stir in milk and corn syrup. Bring to a boil over medium heat, stirring constantly, and boil for 1 to 2 minutes. Remove from heat and stir in butter and vanilla. Keep warm.

5. Serve each wedge of pie topped with a scoop of vanilla ice cream and with hot fudge sauce drizzled over top.

Other Pies

Coconut Meringue Pie

Serves 6 to 8

	9-inch (23 cm) single-crust pie shell, baked and cooled	
²⁄₃ cup	granulated sugar	150 mL
¼ cup	cornstarch	50 mL
¼ tsp	salt	1 mL
2 cups	milk	500 mL
3	egg yolks, lightly beaten	3
1 cup	flaked coconut (sweetened or unsweetened)	250 mL
2 tbsp	butter or margarine	25 mL
½ tsp	vanilla	2 mL

MERINGUE TOPPING

3	egg whites	3
¼ tsp	cream of tartar	1 mL
⅓ cup	granulated sugar	75 mL
½ cup	toasted, flaked coconut (sweetened or unsweetened)	125 mL

Preheat oven to 350°F (180°C)

9-inch (23 cm) pie plate

1. In a medium saucepan, combine sugar, cornstarch and salt. Cook over low heat. Add milk gradually and bring to a boil on medium heat. Stirring constantly, cook for 2 minutes, or until mixture is thickened.

2. Place egg yolks in a small bowl. Stir in about 1 cup (250 mL) of the hot mixture and pour this mixture back into the saucepan. Bring to a boil, stirring constantly, and boil gently for 2 to 3 minutes, until thick. Remove from heat.

3. Stir in coconut, butter and vanilla, and mix until all of the butter is melted. Spoon into prepared pie crust.

4. *Prepare Meringue Topping:* In a small, clean mixer bowl, on high speed, beat egg whites and cream of tartar until frothy. Gradually beat in sugar, one spoonful at a time, until stiff peaks form. Spread over filling, sealing edges to crust.

5. Bake in preheated oven for 15 minutes, or until top is lightly browned. Cool completely on a wire rack and then chill in refrigerator until serving. Top with toasted coconut.

> **TIP:** If you want to bake a meringue pie ahead of time, the pie will freeze, but the meringue doesn't. It is best to freeze the pie without the meringue, then put a meringue on the pie and bake it the day you will serve it.

Lazy Day Grasshopper Pie

Serves 6 to 8		
25 to 30	chocolate wafer cookies (about 6 oz/175 g)	25 to 30
1	jar (2 cups/500 mL) marshmallow crème	1
¼ cup	milk	50 mL
4 drops	peppermint extract	4 drops
	Green food coloring	
1 cup	whipping (35%) cream, whipped, or frozen whipped topping, thawed	250 mL

9-inch (23 cm) pie plate

1. Line the bottom of pie plate with the cookies, filling in spaces with pieces of cookie. Then line the sides with half cookies, close together or overlapping.

2. In a mixer bowl, combine marshmallow crème, peppermint extract and 5 or 6 drops (or more, if you like) of food coloring. Beat on medium speed until fluffy.

3. Fold in the whipped cream, slowly but thoroughly. Spoon into cookie crust and place in freezer for 8 hours, or preferably overnight. Garnish with more whipped cream, or crumble a few cookie wafers and sprinkle over top. Decorate with stand-up pieces of cookie.

Maple Sugar Pie

Serves 6 to 8		
	9-inch (23 cm) single-crust pie shell, baked and cooled	
⅔ cup	firmly packed brown sugar	150 mL
⅔ cup	pure maple syrup	150 mL
2 tbsp	unsalted butter	45 mL
3	eggs	3
¼ tsp	vanilla	1 mL
	Pinch of salt	
	Whipped cream or ice cream (optional)	

Preheat oven to 375°F (190°C)
9-inch (23 cm) pie plate

1. In the top of a double boiler, over simmering water, combine brown sugar, maple syrup and butter. Cook until melted. Remove from heat. Cool slightly.

2. Add eggs, beating in one at a time. Then add vanilla and salt and mix until well blended. Spoon into prepared pie crust.

3. Bake in preheated oven for 25 to 30 minutes, until browned. Cool completely on wire rack. Serve with whipped cream or ice cream, or as desired.

Passover Cheese Pie

Serves 8 to 10

CRUST

3 tbsp	granulated sugar	45 mL
½ tsp	salt	2 mL
½ cup	shortening, softened	125 mL
1½ cups	matzo meal	375 mL
1 tbsp	water	15 mL

FILLING

1 cup	cottage cheese (creamed or dry)	250 mL
8 oz	cream cheese, softened	250 g
3	eggs, separated	3
¾ cup	granulated sugar	175 mL
1 cup	sour cream	250 mL
1 tbsp	potato starch	15 mL
1 tsp	grated lemon zest	5 mL

Preheat oven to 350°F (180°C)

9-inch (23 cm) or 10-inch (25 cm) deep dish pie plate

1. *Prepare crust:* In a medium bowl, cream sugar, salt and shortening until smooth. Add the matzo meal and mix well to blend thoroughly. Stir in water gradually. Spoon into prepared pie plate and pat down.

2. *Prepare filling:* In a large mixer bowl, beat cottage and cream cheeses until smooth and fluffy. Add egg yolks and sugar and beat until smooth and blended. Stir in sour cream, potato starch and lemon zest. Mix well.

3. In a small, clean mixer bowl with clean beaters, on high speed, beat egg whites until stiff peaks form, but whites are not dry. Fold into cheese mixture, slowly but thoroughly. Spoon into pie plate.

4. Bake in preheated oven for 1 hour, or until a knife inserted in the middle comes out clean and dry. Cool completely on wire rack.

Eggnog Pie

Serves 6 to 8

	9-inch (23 cm) single-crust pie shell, baked and cooled	
1	envelope (¼ oz/7 g) unflavored gelatin	1
1	package (3 oz/90 g) no-bake custard mix	1
¼ tsp	ground nutmeg	1 mL
2¼ cups	milk	550 mL
2 tbsp	rum or 1 tsp (5 mL) rum flavoring	25 mL
4 oz	frozen whipped topping, 125 g thawed	
	Peaches or other fruit (optional)	

9-inch (23 cm) pie plate

1. In a medium saucepan, combine gelatin, custard mix and nutmeg. Add milk and, stirring constantly, bring to a boil over medium heat. Remove from heat.

2. Stir in rum and mix to blend. Transfer to a bowl and place plastic wrap directly on the surface. Chill in refrigerator until partially set.

3. Fold in whipped topping and chill again, if necessary, until mixture mounds.

4. Spoon into prepared pie crust and chill in refrigerator for 4 to 5 hours, or until firm. Garnish with peach slices or other fruit, or sprinkle a bit of nutmeg over top.

TIP: To transport a pie, place an empty pie plate on top as a cover. This works great with any pie, and especially with meringue pies.

Southern Pecan Pie

	Serves 8 to 10	
	Pastry for a 9-inch (23 cm) single-crust pie	
1 cup	firmly packed dark brown sugar	250 mL
3	eggs, slightly beaten	3
1 cup	light corn syrup	250 mL
1/3 cup	butter or margarine, melted	75 mL
1 tsp	vanilla	5 mL
1/2 tsp	salt	2 mL
1 1/4 cups	pecan halves	300 mL
	Whipped topping (optional)	

Preheat oven to 350°F (180°C)

9-inch (23 cm) pie plate

1. On a lightly floured surface, roll out pastry and fit into pie plate.

2. In a large bowl, whisk together brown sugar, eggs, corn syrup, butter, vanilla and salt until well blended. Spoon into pie crust, spreading evenly. Sprinkle with the pecan halves over top.

3. Bake in preheated oven for 45 to 50 minutes, or until a toothpick inserted in the center of the pie comes out clean and dry. Cool completely on wire rack. Decorate with whipped topping, or as desired.

Shoo-Fly Pie

	Serves 6 to 8	
	Pastry for a 9-inch (23 cm) single-crust pie	
1 1/2 cups	all-purpose flour	375 mL
1/2 cup	granulated sugar	125 mL
1/2 tsp	baking soda, divided	2 mL
1/4 cup	butter or margarine	50 mL
1/2 cup	fancy molasses	125 mL
1/2 cup	hot water	125 mL

This pie was first baked because it was sticky and sweet; it was meant to lure flies away from other foods

Preheat oven to 375°F (190°C)

9-inch (23 cm) pie plate

1. On a lightly floured surface, roll out pastry and fit into pie plate.

2. In a large bowl, combine flour, sugar and 1/4 tsp (1 mL) of the baking soda. Cut in the butter by hand, or mixing with a fork, until mixture resembles coarse crumbs.

3. In another bowl, combine molasses, hot water and the remaining 1/4 tsp (1 mL) of baking soda. Mix well. Spoon 1/3 of the molasses mixture into pie crust. Sprinkle with 1/3 of the flour mixture. Repeat layers, ending with the flour mixture.

4. Bake in preheated oven for 40 to 45 minutes, or until lightly browned. Cool completely on wire rack.

Sour Cream Raisin Pie

Serves 8 to 10		
	9-inch (23 cm) single-crust pie shell, baked and cooled	
1½ cups	dark raisins	375 mL
¾ cup	granulated sugar	175 mL
¼ cup	cornstarch	50 mL
½ tsp	ground cinnamon	2 mL
¼ tsp	ground nutmeg	1 mL
¼ tsp	salt	1 mL
2 cups	milk	500 mL
3	egg yolks, lightly beaten	3
1 cup	sour cream	250 mL
1 tbsp	lemon juice	15 mL
	Whipped cream (optional)	

9-inch (23 cm) pie plate

1. In a large saucepan, over medium heat, combine raisins, sugar, cornstarch, cinnamon, nutmeg and salt. Add milk and stir until mixture is well blended and smooth. Cook, stirring constantly, until mixture boils. Boil for 1 minute, then remove from heat.

2. Spoon a small amount of the hot mixture into the egg yolks, and then add egg yolks to saucepan. Stir in sour cream and mix well. Cook, stirring, until mixture starts to bubble and is thick. Remove from heat. Stir in lemon juice. Set aside to cool for 10 to 15 minutes.

3. Spoon into prepared pie shell. Chill in refrigerator for 3 hours, or until set. If desired, garnish with some whipped cream.

Esther's Favorite Pies

Esther's Mock Apple Pie

Serves 6 to 8

	Pastry for a 9-inch (23 cm) single-crust pie	
1 cup	granulated sugar	250 mL
2 tsp	cream of tartar	10 mL
2 cups	water	500 mL
30	whole Ritz crackers	30
1 tbsp	lemon juice	15 mL
½ tsp	ground cinnamon	2 mL

CRUMB TOPPING

30	Ritz crackers, finely rolled into crumbs	30
½ cup	lightly packed brown sugar	125 mL
⅓ cup	butter or margarine, melted	75 mL

Preheat oven to 400°F (200°C)

9-inch (23 cm) pie plate

1. On a lightly floured surface, roll out pastry and fit into pie plate.

2. In a medium saucepan, combine sugar, cream of tartar and water. Bring to a boil over medium heat. Add the crackers and keep boiling for 5 to 6 minutes. Spoon into pie crust and sprinkle over top with lemon juice and cinnamon.

3. *Prepare Crumb Topping:* In a bowl, mix together cracker crumbs, brown sugar and melted butter until well blended. Sprinkle over top.

4. Bake in preheated oven for 15 minutes, then reduce heat to 350°F (180°C) and continue baking for another 15 to 20 minutes, or until topping is browned. Best when served warm.

Mildred's Streusel-Topped Apple Pie

Serves 6 to 8

	Frozen or homemade 9-inch (23 cm) deep-dish pie shell, baked and cooled	

FILLING

5	apples, peeled and sliced	5
⅓ cup	firmly packed brown sugar	75 mL
1 tbsp	cornstarch	15 mL
½ tsp	ground cinnamon	2 mL

STREUSEL TOPPING

1 cup	all-purpose flour	250 mL
½ cup	granulated sugar	125 mL
½ cup	butter or margarine, softened	125 mL

Preheat oven to 450°F (230°C)

9-inch (23 cm) pie plate

1. *Prepare filling:* In a large bowl, toss together apples, brown sugar, cornstarch and cinnamon. Mix well and spoon into pie shell.

2. *Prepare Streusel Topping:* In another bowl, combine flour and sugar. Cut in butter until mixture resembles coarse crumbs. Sprinkle over the apple mixture.

3. Bake in preheated oven for 10 minutes. Reduce oven temperature to 350°F (180°C) and continue baking for about 40 to 45 minutes, or until apples are tender. Serve warm.

Bernice's Apricot Parfait Pie

Serves 6 to 8		
	Graham Cracker Crust (see recipe, page 123)	
1	can (13 oz/370 g) apricot nectar	1
1	package (3 oz/90 g) orange-flavored gelatin	1
2 cups	vanilla ice cream	500 mL
1	medium-sized milk chocolate bar	1
	Whipping (35%) cream, whipped	
	Chocolate curls	

NOTE: You could line pan with peach slices, tangerine or orange slices before filling.

9-inch (23 cm) pie plate

1. In a small saucepan, bring apricot nectar to a boil. Remove from heat and stir in the orange gelatin.
2. Cut ice cream into chunks and add to gelatin until all of the ice cream melts. Chill in refrigerator until mixture mounds slightly when dropped from a spoon.
3. Pour into prepared crust and chill until set. Top with whipped cream and chocolate curls. Serve cold.

Poffy's Rhubarb Strawberry Pie

Serves 6 to 8		
	Pastry for a 9-inch (23 cm) double-crust pie	
3	soda crackers, crushed	3
1	egg	1
1 cup	granulated sugar	250 mL
3 cups	chopped rhubarb	750 mL
2 cups	chopped fresh strawberries	500 mL
	Granulated sugar	

Preheat oven to 400°F (200°C)

9-inch (23 cm) pie plate

1. On a lightly floured surface, roll out half of pastry and fit into pie plate. Spread crushed soda cracker crumbs evenly onto bottom pie crust.
2. In a large bowl, whisk egg. Add sugar and whisk to blend. Stir in rhubarb and strawberries and mix well. Spoon into pie crust.
3. Roll out remaining pastry to fit over filling. Cut several slits in top crust, near the center to allow steam to escape, and place over fruit filling. Trim, seal and flute edges or press with a fork all around. Sprinkle a little granulated sugar over the top.
4. Bake in preheated oven for 20 minutes, then reduce oven temperature to 350°F (180°C) and continue baking for 1 hour. Cool completely on a wire rack.

Esther's Strawberry Swirl Pie

Serves 12 to 16

CRUST

2¼ cups	graham wafer crumbs (about 30 whole wafers)	550 mL
½ cup	butter or margarine, melted	125 mL

FILLING

6 cups	miniature white marshmallows (about 10 oz/300 g)	1.5 L
½ cup	milk	125 mL
1	package (6 oz/175 g) strawberry-flavored gelatin	1
1⅓ cups	boiling water	325 mL
2	packages (each 10 oz/300 g) frozen strawberries, thawed, including juice	2
1 cup	whipping (35%) cream, whipped	250 mL
	Graham wafer crumbs (optional)	

Preheat oven to 350°F (180°C)

13- by 9-inch (3 L) glass baking dish, ungreased

1. *Prepare crust:* In a small bowl, mix together wafer crumbs and melted butter. Press firmly onto bottom of prepared baking dish. Bake in preheated oven for 10 minutes. Cool.

2. In the top of a double boiler, over hot water, melt the marshmallows with the milk, stirring until cold, refreshing water as necessary to keep cool, and stirring marshmallow mixture often.

3. *Prepare filling:* In a large bowl, combine the strawberry gelatin with the boiling water. Mix well. Add the thawed strawberries. Stir until blended and cool in refrigerator until partially jelled, about 20 minutes, stirring occasionally.

4. When gelatin mixture is almost set, fold whipped cream into marshmallow mixture. Spread half of the marshmallow mixture over crust and top with half of the strawberry mixture. Repeat layers with remaining filling, swirling with a spatula to make a marble effect. Sprinkle lightly with additional wafer crumbs, if desired. Chill in refrigerator for at least 1 hour, or until set.

TIP: If your whipping cream won't whip, chill the bowl, beaters and cream. You can also set the bowl into a larger bowl of ice while you whip. If that doesn't work, gradually whip in 3 or 4 drops of lemon juice.

National Library of Canada Cataloguing in Publication

Brody, Esther
    250 best cakes and pies / Esther Brody.

Includes index.
ISBN 0-7788-0077-6

1. Cake. 2. Pies.
I. Title. II. Title: Two hundred fifty best cakes and pies.

TX771.B763 2003   641.8'652   C2003-901455-X

Index